California

CRIMINAL
PROCEDURE

Fourth Edition

Devallis Rutledge, J.D.

WADSWORTH
CENGAGE Learning™

Australia • Brazil • Japan • Korea • Mexico • Singapore • Spain • United Kingdom • United States

WADSWORTH
CENGAGE Learning

California Criminal Procedure, Fourth Edition

Devallis Rutledge

Photo credit: Mark C. Ide

For product information and
technology assistance, contact us at **Cengage Learning Customer & Sales Support, 1-800-354-9706**

For permission to use material from this text or product, submit all requests online at **www.cengage.com/permissions**
Further permissions questions can be emailed to
permissionrequest@cengage.com

Library of Congress Control Number: 90-83953

ISBN-13: 978-0-942728-97-2

ISBN-10: 0-942728-97-1

Wadsworth
20 Davis Drive
Belmont, CA 94002
USA

Cengage Learning is a leading provider of customized learning solutions with office locations around the globe, including Singapore, the United Kingdom, Australia, Mexico, Brazil, and Japan. Locate your local office at **www.cengage.com/global**

Cengage Learning products are represented in Canada by Nelson Education, Ltd.

To learn more about Wadsworth, visit
www.cengage.com/wadsworth

Purchase any of our products at your local college store or at our preferred online store **www.CengageBrain.com**

Printed in the United States of America
8 9 10 11 12   15 14 13 12 11

FD250

TABLE OF CONTENTS

CHAPTER 8

ALTERNATIVES TO TRIAL 171

CHAPTER 9

PREPARATION FOR TRIAL 189

CHAPTER 10

TRIAL PROCEDURE 207

INTRODUCTION

California has roughly 10 percent of the nation's population. It also has approximately 10 percent of America's crime and 10 percent of its law enforcement personnel. Uniquely, California also has a highly-refined set of procedural rules and systems, based on state law, for the administration of criminal justice.

Unlike the large number of states that have essentially adopted the Federal Rules of Criminal Procedure, California has developed an *independent body* of statutory, regulatory and decisional law governing the pretrial, trial, and post-trial phases of the criminal adjudication (court decision) process.

For years, criminal justice educators and students in California have had to adjust to criminal procedure texts designed to be sufficiently generic for use in any state. Such books are necessarily unspecific as to the practical details of criminal procedure in any one state. And, they require constant qualification by instructors who seek to provide their students with a more useful, more relevant preparation for participation in California's criminal justice system — whether as peace officers, attorneys, paralegals, or other key personnel.

One major disadvantage of this non-specific study is that it subjects the graduate, after embarking on his or her professional career, to an uncomfortably long period of "on-the-job training" to learn the "nuts and bolts" of practical criminal procedure in California. The finer points and critical distinctions between classroom theory and actual procedure as it is applied day-to-day in the California system take even longer to master.

California Criminal Procedure was specifically written to help prepare students in all of the law-related disciplines for their roles in the criminal justice system in California. This book, therefore, covers not only the general concepts, constitutional principles, and universal procedures applicable throughout the American system, but also the *particular* aspects of applied procedure in California. For example, while the generic text treatment of a pretrial suppression hearing is usually limited to a general explanation of *Mapp v. Ohio*, this text takes the student directly to California's implementation of *Mapp* in Penal Code section 1538.5 and Welfare & Institutions Code section 700.1. *California Criminal Procedure* goes beyond the generic mention of "due process" and "speedy trial" guidelines and explains their particular application in such cases as *Rost, Serna, Hitch, Aranda, Ramey* and *Wheeler*, etcetera.

What are the rules in California on retention of a police officer's rough notes of an interview with a suspect? What is a "645/*Kellet*" bar to prosecution? What are the grounds in California for granting a motion for new trial? How does a PC 1000 drug "diversion" work? What is a *Tahl* form? What is a *Dennis H.* hearing? These are the kinds of everyday questions criminal justice personnel confront in the real world. They are the kinds of questions generic texts cannot address. They are the kind of questions specifically answered for the student in this book.

For ease of both teaching and learning, the material is presented in a straightforward manner, with frequent citation to statutes, case law, or other sources, and direct quotations where appropriate. Each chapter includes discussion of applicable federal and state guidelines, covering those procedural topics identified as POST (Peace Officer Standards and Training Commission), CAAJE (California Association of Administration of Justice Educators), CAPTO (California Association of Police Training Officers), CADA (California Academy Director's

Association), and other training authorities. Each chapter includes information aimed at familiarizing students with the most common concepts and terms encountered in the system. The format features learning goals, textual discussion, summary points, and suggested issues for essay test items or classroom discussion.

As criminal procedure evolves, knowledge and understanding of its purposes and principles are the keys to intelligent use and revision. As an author who is or has been involved in the criminal justice system as a police officer, a prosecutor, and instructor, I regularly see and appreciate the critical role of the criminal justice educator and the dedication to professionalism among our students. I hope that instructor and student alike will find *California Criminal Procedure* helpful to greater knowledge and understanding of our state's criminal process.

Devallis Rutledge

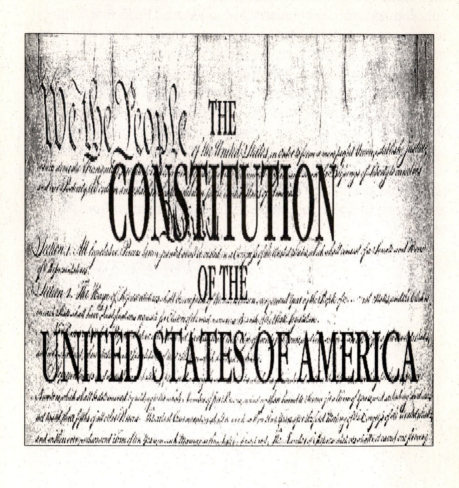

CHAPTER

1

SOURCES OF
CRIMINAL PROCEDURE

Learning Goals: After studying this chapter, you will be able to correctly answer the following questions:

√   Why do we have criminal laws?

√   What is the "social contract" theory?

√   What are the various sources of laws and procedural rules?

√   What are the relation and effect of the "supremacy clause," the "due process clause," and "independent state grounds"?

√   Where is the law found? How is it authenticated?

CRIMINAL PROCEDURE

Criminal procedure is the process we use to enforce the substantive law. For example, a substantive law might prohibit the theft of another's personal property. But how do we determine when someone has violated this law? How do we identify and accuse the perpetrator? How do we determine his guilt? How do we impose and carry out his punishment?

The mechanism for enforcing the substantive criminal law is a detailed set of uniform rules that comprise our criminal procedure. Adherence to the proper procedure is deemed so important in providing the "equal protection of the law" mandated by the Fourteenth Amendment that a mistake in procedure can sometimes mean than even an apparently-guilty party may be permitted to go unpunished.

Failing to follow proper procedures may also create civil liability for governmental officers and their employing entities. These potential consequences make it vital that criminal justice personnel be aware of and comply with *procedural* requirements as they process *substantive* violations.

Examination and understanding of criminal procedure begin by looking at its derivation.

THE SOCIAL CONTRACT

Where do laws come from? The answer depends on the nature of the government. In a dictatorship, the dictator simply decrees the law; in a centralized state, a central committee establishes the law; in a representative democracy, such as we enjoy in the United States, laws are promulgated by selected representatives "with the consent of the governed."

Collective self-government has always presented the problem of balancing the conflicting goals of *freedom* and *security*. By nature, human beings want the liberty to live at will to go where we please, to do as we please, to say what we please, and to pursue our personal happiness as we see fit. At the same time, we have an innate yearning for a sense of security, we want protection of ourselves, our families and our possessions against adverse forces and circumstances.

Put in more concrete terms, we want to be free to walk down the street without being stopped by police, and yet we want the police to accost others on the street who may intend some aggression toward us. We cherish our freedom of speech, but we jealously protect our children against speech by others that we perceive as obscene and indecent. We do not want our car stopped by the highway patrol except when a thief is driving it. We want maximum freedom for ourselves, but we want (and need) protection against the possibility that someone else's exercise of his freedoms might infringe on our security.

How should society balance these competing needs? In the absence of any social controls on behavior, the situation would obviously be one of survival of the fittest, or "might makes right." The most clever, most powerful and most ruthless would enjoy the greatest freedom and security, while the slow, the weak and the meek would enjoy very little of either. Because everyone is at risk, to a greater or lesser degree, in an arrangement based exclusively on individual strength, self-governing civilizations have generally adopted the "social contract" approach.

Under the social contract theory, no one has either absolute freedom or absolute security. Instead, society agrees among itself to guarantee a certain degree of security by surrendering the corresponding degree of freedom; conversely, the social contract guarantees a certain degree of freedom at the expense of greater security.

It is the particular balance struck between these two ideals that characterizes any particular democratic society: those governments providing a relatively high atmosphere of security must necessarily sacrifice personal liberties accordingly, just as those "permissive" societies affording greater personal freedoms inevitably forfeit higher levels of security.

In the United States, the balance was struck in *general* terms by the Constitution. Within constitutional guidelines, the precise balance in a given state or local community frequently varies from place to place, and from time to time. Thus, we provide the greatest security as against traffic accidents by imposing 15 mph speed zones near schools, while we allow the greatest freedom of movement on 65 mph highways, with a consequent reduction of security. One city may restrict freedom of juveniles with a 10:00 p.m. curfew, thereby providing greater security against youthful offenses at night, while a neighboring city sacrifices its security interests by imposing no curfew on its juveniles' freedom.

The balancing point moves, within constitutional limits, as the public perceives that one objective or the other has been advanced too far, at the expense of the other. (Historically, in the 1960s and 1970s, both the US and California governments moved the balance point in the direction of greater freedom. In reaction to the resulting loss of security, both levels of government began adjusting the balance point in the opposite direction in the 1980s and 1990s.)

COMMON LAW HERITAGE

Long before the social contract was reduced to written constitutions, statutes and court decisions, our English forebears had settled informally on many basic notions of right and wrong and fairness. These principles, collectively referred to as the "English common law," were largely incorporated into both the US and California Constitutions, and many were codified in our statutes.

Although some states have retained a "common law" tradition of enforcing unwritten laws, California has not done so. Those common-law features we chose to adopt have been included in our written laws; others are simply not enforceable in this state (e.g., California does not recognize common-law marriages or common-law crimes) (See, e.g., Penal Code section 6).

Nevertheless, English common law provided the model for our criminal procedure system. Parallels are easily drawn between the King's court and our own, between "his majesty" and "his honor," and between the accusatorial system that evolved in England after Magna Carta and our present-day adversarial system. In fact, many of our leading Supreme Court decisions directly quote, or are traceable to, recorded decisions of the King's bench. Although modern criminal procedure is far more technical (and arguably less efficient), it is essentially an extension of the English common law.

SEPARATION OF POWERS

Every school child learns in elementary government classes that the drafters of the Constitution intentionally divided governmental power into the three separate branches (legislative, executive and judicial) as a guarantee of checks and balances against excessive centralized power. This same division is incorporated into California's Constitution, giving lawmaking duties to the state assembly and state senate, regulatory and enforcement powers to the governor and executive departments, and adjudication duties to the courts. This scheme would suggest that criminal procedure would be established by laws enacted by the state legislature; however, each branch of government sometimes exercises a rule-making function, with the result that some provisions of criminal procedure come from all three sources.

Legislative law is basically of two varieties: (1) state statutes and (2) local ordinances. California statutes are enacted as "bills" originating either in the assembly, e.g., AB (Assembly Bill) 301, or in the senate (SB 103), and are then approved by the governor or an overriding legislative majority. Final laws are "chaptered" into one of the twenty-eight topical codes. For example:

→ The *Civil Code* contains laws defining civil obligations and rights, such as landlord-tenant relations, contracts, property law, and family matters.

→ The *Code of Civil Procedure* establishes rules to be followed in civil lawsuits.

→ The *Evidence Code* contains rules of evidence applicable to court proceedings, such as admissibility rules, examination of witnesses, and testimonial immunities.

→ The *Business & Professions Code* concerns advertising and sales laws, professional services, and the control of alcoholic beverages.

- The *Health & Safety Code* covers issues of public health, including control of dangerous drugs and narcotics.

- The *Vehicle Code* governs automobiles and driving rules.

- The *Welfare & Institutions Code* includes laws affecting juveniles and deranged persons.

- The *Penal Code* defines many of the substantive crimes, and sets forth most of the rules of criminal procedure.

- The *Government Code* defines the duties and immunities of public officers.

Local *ordinances* are made at both the city level and the county level. They may not govern conduct already "pre-empted" (covered) by state or federal law, but generally relate to the conduct of local business, and control such behavior as loitering at schools, drinking in public places, performing lewd acts in local establishments, and disposing of hazardous materials.

Most parking offenses are governed by local ordinance, as are curfews and the possession and use of fireworks and discharge of firearms.

Administrative law is promulgated by agencies falling under the executive branch of government. Technically, administrative law is not actual law in the same sense as legislative law. It is regulatory, and governs the conduct of administrative officers and administrative hearings. For example, the rules of the Alcoholic Beverage Control Board on the operation of drinking establishments are regulatory, administrative law, followed in the absence of legislation or judicial decision invalidating them.

As chief law enforcement officer of the state, the California Attorney General (an executive official) issues published, numbered decisions on issues that have not been directly addressed by either the legislature or the courts. These advisory opinions, while not themselves law, are another source of procedural guidance until either of the other branches of government passes on the issue.

For instance, in 1985 an attorney-general's opinion concluded that mechanical "butterfly knives" violated Penal Code section 653k (68 Ops. Cal. Atty. Gen. 332); three years later, the Court of Appeal adopted this opinion in holding such knives illegal under Penal Code 653k [*People v. Quattrone* (1989) 211 CA3d 1389].

Judicial law, also referred to as "case" law or "decisional" law, is contained in the published, written opinions of reviewing courts. Again, it is not law in the sense that it creates crimes or imposes duties on the citizenry, as does legislative law, but under their "inherent powers" to carry out their duties, the courts exercise considerable power in interpreting the official acts of the other two branches of government, and in decreeing procedural rules for the adjudication of cases brought before them. Case law thus is a significant source of criminal procedure in California.

Determining the status of case law is not always easy. Unlike statutes and regulations, which are conveniently collected together and arranged by topic, court decisions are necessarily issued on a case-by-case basis. Thus, the case law on a particular issue might include a number of decisions written over a period of several decades and contained in widely-separated volumes of published opinions.

Moreover, a single case decision might discuss any number of unrelated issues, and might emanate from any one of several levels of reviewing courts. The study and application of decisional law thus requires a knowledge of the *hierarchy* (levels) of appellate decisions, and an awareness of the difference between the *holding* of a decision, and its *dicta*.

By virtue of the "supremacy clause" in Article VI of the Constitution, decisions of the US Supreme Court interpreting the Constitution are binding on the states. Likewise, California Supreme Court decisions are binding throughout the state on matters of California law. Next in the decisional hierarchy are published opinions of the Court of Appeal, and below these are the occasional published opinions of the appellate department of a superior court.

Published opinions of the US Circuit Court of Appeals are of "persuasive" authority in California (meaning they should be considered but need not be followed by state courts), whereas US Supreme Court decisions are "mandatory" authority. Where two or more decisions of different districts of the California Court of Appeal contradict each other, a lower court is free to follow either decision, and is not necessarily bound to adopt the decision of its own district court. *People v. Stamper* (1987) 195 CA3d 1608.

In reading and analyzing a particular court decision, it is important to distinguish the *holding* which is binding on subordinate courts from the *dictum* which has no particular authority as precedent. Essentially, the *holding* of a case is the resolution of a question of law that is necessary to support the decision; any further, gratuitous discussion by the author of the opinion that is merely elaboration on a point (such as what might be termed "collateral" or "off on a tangent") is *dictum* (plural: "*dicta*").

The necessity to differentiate between holding and dicta is especially critical in the adversary system when the adversary, finding no published holding to support her client's position, refers the judge to language in an opinion amounting to dicta; the judge can be urged to disregard such unauthoritative material.

As an example, if a case on appeal presented the issue of whether a prosecutor could properly inform the jury of a defendant's prior *felony* conviction to impeach his testimony, the holding of the court that such conduct was permissible might be necessary to affirm the defendant's conviction. If the appellate decision also discussed the propriety or impropriety of using prior *misdemeanor* convictions to impeach, such discussion would be nonbinding dicta, since this issue need not have been resolved in this case.

Although the California Supreme Court is not always in agreement with the holdings reached in all published opinions of the six district Courts of Appeal, the state high court hardly has the time to grant review in all such cases and issue a modified opinion. The court has addressed this dilemma by a process known as *depublication*.

If an appellate decision is certified by the Court of Appeal for publication and the state Supreme Court does not wish for the opinion to become citable authority, it simply directs the reporter of official opinions not to publish the appellate decision. This procedure means that newly-issued opinions of the Court of Appeal must be "tracked" for about sixty days to see if they become published case law, or are ordered depublished.

In addition to published court decisions, the courts also provide procedural guides in the *rules of court*. The superior courts have issued a broad set of rules, and each local court district usually adopts other specific rules on filing requirements, law and motion, and other matters. The rules of court are usually maintained in loose-leaf binders in local law libraries.

From time to time, the California electorate take a hand in defining their own laws. By the constitutional amendment *initiative* process, voters can act directly to change laws whenever they feel the legislature and the judiciary are not responsive to the public will. For example, in 1990 the voters overwhelmingly passed a ballot measure known as "Proposition 115," which abrogated (voided) a number of court decisions and legislative acts seen as too restrictive on law enforcement and too protective of criminal defendants. Such ballot initiative measures are a further source of criminal procedure in California.

CONSTITUTIONAL DUE PROCESS

For many years, the criminal procedure provisions of the US Constitution such as those in the Fourth, Fifth, Sixth and Eighth Amendments were considered to be applicable only to the federal government and, therefore, only to trials in federal court. However, the Fourteenth Amendment, adopted during the aftermath of the Civil War in 1868, included the following command on the state governments:

> No State shall make or enforce any law which shall abridge the privileges or immunities of citizens of the United States; nor shall any State deprive any person of life, liberty, or property, without due process of law....
>
> *US Constitution, Amendment XIV.*

On the theory that they are components of "due process," the various criminal procedure provisions of the "bill of rights" have been held applicable to the states by several Supreme Court decisions; see *Mapp v. Ohio* (1961) 367 US 643 (Fourth Amendment); *Malloy v. Hogan* (1964) 378 US 1 (Fifth Amendment); *Powell v. Alabama* (1932) 287 US 45 (Sixth Amendment); and *Robinson v. California* (1962) 370 US 660 (Eighth Amendment).

By operation of the supremacy clause and the due process clause, therefore, all US Supreme Court decisions defining criminal procedures under the Constitution are binding in state-court proceedings, as minimum standards.

INDEPENDENT STATE GROUNDS

The US Supreme Court has frequently observed that "a state is free as a matter of its own law to impose greater restrictions on police activity" than the federal Constitution requires. *Oregon v. Hass* (1975) 420 US 714, 719. This means that the states may provide greater protection for accused persons than they are entitled to under the Constitution, but not less. However, because US Supreme Court decisions construing the Constitution are "supreme," and binding on the states exactly as written, a state court could not purport to base a differing procedural standard on *federal* constitutional law (thus, there can be no such thing as different "*Miranda* rights" in California, for example).

A state court wishing to impose greater restrictions on police and prosecutors and thereby to afford greater protection to criminal suspects and defendants can lawfully do so by basing its decisions on its own *state* constitution and laws, without incorporating federal organic law. This is known as the doctrine of "independent state grounds," and became quite popular with the California Supreme Court in the 1960s and 1970s. Even though a provision of the California Constitution might be a verbatim or near-verbatim duplication of a corresponding provision in the US Constitution, the California Supreme Court could, and frequently did, interpret the state provision differently.

As noted above, California voters reacted to what was widely viewed as an abuse of the state high court's powers under independent state grounds by curbing the court's power to exclude relevant evidence that would be admissible under the US Constitution. As a result of the passage of Proposition 8, the California Supreme Court acknowledged, in *In re Lance W.* (1985) 37 C3d 873, its duty to apply federal standards in the litigation of search-and-seizure issues. And in *People v. May* (1988) 44 C3d 309, the state Supreme Court held that independent state grounds could no longer be used to exclude a suspect's incriminating statements, if the statements would be admissible under US Supreme Court rulings.

Note that Proposition 8 did not eliminate the use of independent state grounds in other areas of the law, but only as a basis for court-created exclusionary rules affecting evidence that would be admissible under prevailing US Supreme Court decisions.

FINDING THE LAW

Law libraries are found in major cities and counties, at the courthouse, at law schools, and in larger police departments and academies. CD-rom and Internet services, such as Westlaw, Lexis, Law Desk and others, are available for computerized research. If you have access to a law library, how do you go about locating the law on a particular issue?

A good starting point is the *annotated codes*. Both West's and Deering's annotated codes are commonly available. These are multi-volume sets of all California codes, with topical indexes (either in the first or last volume of each code) to help you find the code sections related to your issue. At that section, the publishers list cross-references to other research sources and related code sections. This information is then followed by a summary of leading court decisions interpreting and applying the particular section. Scan these annotations to find a case on point.

To look up a published court decision, identify the *report*, the *series*, the *volume*, and the *page number* where the written opinion is found. For example, suppose you want to find out whether a trial judge is legally required to answer the jury's questions about the law, after their deliberations have begun. You look in the annotated Penal Code, find the index, and look under "Jury Additional Instructions," where you are referred to section 1138. At that location, you find citations to several cases; the brief summaries indicate that the answer may be found and explained in *People v. Kageler* (1973) 32 CA3d 738, at 746, and *People v. House* (1970) 12 CA3d 756, at 765.

Finding the law requires only a basic knowledge of research methods.

If you want to read the cited cases, how do you find them? California has basically two levels of published case law: decisions of the state Supreme Court are reported in *California Reports* (abbreviated *Cal.* or *C*); the decisions of the Court of Appeal are in the *California Appellate Reports* (abbreviated *Cal. App.* or *CA*).

Each of the official reports is divided into four series, according to the year of publication, as follows:

(1) Cal., or C, and Cal. App., or CA... before 1934

(2) Cal.2d, or C2d, and Cal. App. 2d, or CA2d... 1934-1969

(3) Cal.3d, or C3d, and Cal. App. 3d, or CA3d... 1969-1991

(4) Cal.4th, or C4th, and Cal. App. 4th, or CA4th... after 1991

Although the official citation is to Cal. or Cal. App., it is increasingly common to see C, or CA, etc. For brevity, this text uses the abbreviations C, C2d, C3d, C4th, CA, CA2d, CA3d, and CA4th.

Each series of reports is made up of numerous *volumes*, and each volume usually contains up to 1000 pages, or so. When a court decision is cited, therefore, it is necessary to designate the *page*, of the *volume*, of the *series*, of the *report* where the written opinion can be found. The official citation also includes the *name* of the action, and the *year* of decision. Thus, a citation to *People v. Kageler* (1973) 32 CA3d 738, means that the decision of the Court of Appeal issued in a criminal case ("*People versus*") in 1973 is found in volume 32 of the third series, beginning at page 738.

Any particular opinion may run to many pages, and cover many issues. To pinpoint the location, within an opinion, of a specific point of discussion, the citation may include the page number(s) where the reader or researcher should look. For example, *People v. Kageler* (1973) 32 CA3d 738, 746, indicates that the point for which the case is being cited is specifically discussed on page 746 of a decision beginning on page 738.

In addition to the two primary *state* reports, there are two *federal* reports: decisions of the US Supreme Court are reported in *United States Reports* (abbreviated *US*), and are also available in unofficial reports called *Supreme Court Reporter (S. Ct.)*, and *Lawyers Edition (L.Ed., or L.Ed.2d)*.

Opinions of the US Court of Appeals are in *Federal Reports (Fed., or Fed. 2d*; also abbreviated *F, or F2d)*.

Thus, a citation to *Robinson v. California* (1962) 370 US 660, tells you that you will find the Supreme Court's 1962 opinion, starting on page 660, of volume 370, of the US Reports.

From time to time, newer case decisions may modify or overrule the holdings of prior decisions, or a higher court may overrule a lower court's published decision. Before it is safe to cite or rely on a particular opinion, therefore, it is always necessary to check the subsequent history to determine the present status of the case.

Publications and computer services are available to the legal researcher for this purpose (the leading service, called "Shepard's Citations," is available in one or more formats in most law libraries; when someone speaks of "Shepardizing" a case, she means checking in Shepard's system to see if the opinion is still good law).

Although the intricacies of legal research are outside the scope of this text, it is important for the criminal procedure student to be aware that published opinions are subject to change or disapproval, and must be authenticated. Otherwise, there is a risk of continued reliance on a case after it has been nullified.

For example, the infamous decision of the US Supreme Court in *Escobedo v. Illinois* (1964) 378 US 478, was later acknowledged by the Court to have been wrongfully decided, and "the Court has limited the holding of *Escobedo* to its own facts." *Kirby v. Illinois* (1972) 406 US 682, 689; see also *Johnson v. New Jersey* (1966) 384 US 719, 729; *Moran v. Burbine* (1986) 475 US 412, 430.

Limiting a decision to its own facts is legally tantamount to declaring that the case should not be cited as authority, unless a new case presents exactly the same factual scenario (which is practically impossible). In other words, *Escobedo* cannot properly be cited for any general rule of law. Instead, it is the law only as between Danny Escobedo and the State of Illinois, and only in the one case that was settled in 1966. It has no broad application to present or future cases.

In addition to the annotated codes, other starting points for finding the law include such digests and commentaries as *Cal Jur* (*2d* and *3d*), West's *California Digest 2d*, and Witkin's *California Criminal Procedure*.

SUMMARY

√ Criminal procedure is the established process used to identify violations, accuse offenders, determine guilt or innocence, and carry out punishment. It is the means of enforcing substantive criminal law.

√ The "social contract" is organized society's method of balancing the competing objectives of liberty and security.

√ The English common law was the model for both American and California statutory law.

√ Under the "separation of powers" structure, California has legislative law, administrative law, and judicial law.

√ By operation of the "supremacy clause" and the Fourteenth Amendment "due process clause" of the US Constitution, certain minimum standards of criminal procedure defined by the US Supreme Court are binding on California authorities in processing state criminal cases.

√ Published opinions of the US Supreme Court, California Supreme Court, and California Court of Appeal are binding "case law," subject to later modification or overruling.

ISSUES FOR DISCUSSION

1. What are some examples of the "social contract" theory we observe in everyday life?

2. Can you identify some principles of English common law carried over into modern-day California criminal procedure? What are some principles we devised that were not part of the common law?

3. List some examples of legislative laws, administrative regulations, and case law.

4. The US Supreme Court's holding in *Miranda v. Arizona* (1966) 384 US 436, interpreted the Fifth Amendment of the US Constitution. Could California apply *Miranda* differently than the US Supreme Court, based on independent state grounds? Why? Why not?

5. How would you write the citation to an opinion of the California Supreme Court, issued in 1969, in a prosecution against a defendant named "Bradley," beginning on page 80 of volume 1 of the third series of California Reports?

6. Is the citizens' ability to modify criminal procedures by ballot initiative, whenever they disagree with the legislative, executive, or judicial views of the law, a good thing or a bad thing? How does it fit within the social contract?

CHAPTER 2

CRIMINAL PROCEDURE CONCEPTS

Learning Goals: After studying this chapter, you will be able to correctly answer the following questions:

√   What are the benefits of an accusatorial, adversary system of justice?

√   What are the three essential elements of a criminal prosecution?

√   Why do we have a "*corpus delicti*" rule? What is its effect?

√   What are the principles of *ex post facto* and retroactivity?

√   What is the effect of the presumption of innocence?

√   What are the various burdens of proof in a criminal case, and where do they apply?

√   What are the principles of *stare decisis*, collateral estoppel, *res judicata*, and law of the case?

√   What is proof? What are its forms?

THE ADVERSARY SYSTEM

History is full of examples of approaches to identifying guilty suspects that seem by modern standards to have been irrational, if not barbaric. Variations on the concept of "trial by ordeal" set tasks for the suspected party that would usually kill him as they demonstrated his guilt or innocence. For instance, requiring the suspect to slay a wild animal with his hands, to remain afloat in the river while weighted down, to walk across burning coals, or to endure the bite of a venomous snake to prove that he was under divine protection—and therefore innocent —often proved a painful or fatal way of clearing himself.

Equally uncivilized and untrustworthy as a truth-finding device was the medieval practice of "trial by torture," in which a suspect was stretched on a rack, or beaten, or otherwise physically abused until he confessed his guilt, for which he was then punished.

"Trial by inquisition" relied on the unsworn, untested statements of appointed informers to identify offenders, and a tribunal of inquisitors to demand confirming self-incrimination from the suspect, who never was confronted by his informers.

These and other procedures used throughout history (and in some places even today) have the obvious disadvantage of producing a high proportion of untrue, unjust findings of guilt. If the truth is that no crime has in fact occurred, it is an injustice to find someone guilty. If a crime has occurred but the truth is that the suspected party did not commit it, it is a double injustice to find him guilty: an innocent person will have been wrongly punished, and the truly guilty party will have gone unpunished.

Given these logical conclusions, members of a self-governing society based on the social contract, seeking both the freedom to avoid unjust punishment of themselves and the security of protection from guilty others, had to devise a criminal procedure that would tend to serve both of these purposes. And since the administration of justice depends on first determining the *truth*, a primary feature of the criminal procedure had to be its tendency to promote accurate fact-finding.

The accusatorial, adversarial system that has evolved with civilization over the past several centuries has generally filled the bill. Because it forces the government to formally accuse a particular suspect of a specific crime, it prevents the practice of "rounding up all the usual suspects" (Inspector Renault, in "Casablanca"), and subjecting guilty and innocent alike to the inquisition. And because it pits the state against the accused in a contest to see which of them can convince a neutral fact-finder that their version of events is the truth, it gives each adversary a strong incentive to expose the other's inconsistencies, prevarications and evidentiary shortcomings. Just as an athletic contest is an ideal means of identifying the best athlete or team, or as marketplace competition is a dependable way to select the superior product, a courtroom contest between the state's proof and the accused's proof is a reliable method by which the trier of fact can determine the truth of a criminal charge.

PRESUMPTION OF INNOCENCE

To insure that any competitive, adversarial system does its job of selection or differentiation, both adversaries must generally start even, and have equal access to the competition. For example, track runners start in a staggered line that takes curvature of the track into account; football teams start at a score of zero, and both play by the same rules. If one adversary begins with an advantage over the other, the result may not be a conclusive indication of their relative worthiness.

Since the same principle holds true for the contest of proof, adversaries in the criminal justice process are required to start even in their attempts to prove their "truth" to judge or jury. So although the fact that an accused person has been arrested by police, charged by a prosecutor and arraigned by a magistrate prior to trial might suggest that there must be good reason to believe him guilty — and therefore that he is *not* starting even — the trier of fact is required to disregard this appearance of guilt and presume the accused innocent. "A defendant in a criminal action is presumed to be innocent until the contrary is proved...." *Penal Code* § 1096.

Contrary to popular misconception, there is no presumption-of-innocence language in the Constitution itself. The Supreme Court has held, however, that such a principle is implied in the concept of due process of law. See, e.g., *Morisette v. US* (1951) 342 US 246, 275.

In practical terms, what is the effect of the defendant's presumption of innocence? "...the effect of this presumption is only to place upon the state the burden of proving him guilty beyond a reasonable doubt." Penal Code § 1096.

BURDENS OF PROOF

When two adversaries are competing to establish a conclusive result, which one goes first? What if the contest ends in a draw? Who wins?

In the criminal justice system, the *state* has made the accusation, the *defendant* is presumed innocent, and therefore only the *state* has any need to prove anything. In view of the presumption of innocence, the defendant could hardly proceed first, for there would be no proof for him to defend against. Likewise, since he is presumed innocent "until the contrary is proved," he would be entitled to an acquittal in case of a "draw."

The presumption of innocence thus puts the burdens of "going first" and of demonstrating guilt decisively on the state. These are two *separate* burdens: the first is called the "burden of going forward," and the second is the "burden of proof."

A "burden of going forward" is a procedural assignment, recognizing that the adversary seeking to invoke the court's power to provide some relief or sanction should come forward with justification to support the request. In filing a criminal accusation against a defendant, it is the state that seeks to obtain a court judgment that the defendant is guilty and should be punished. Thus, the state has the initial burden of going forward with its justification.

The "burden of proof" is the duty to produce evidence that proves the matter in controversy. When the controversy is whether or not the accused committed the charged crime, the state bears the burden of proof. How much proof is sufficient to sustain the burden? By statute (PC § 1096), this burden is set at *proof beyond a reasonable doubt*, which was defined as follows:

> It is not a mere possible doubt; because everything relating to human affairs is open to some possible or imaginary doubt. It is that state of the case, which, after the entire comparison and consideration of all the evidence, leaves the minds of jurors in that condition that they cannot say they feel an abiding conviction of the truth of the charge.
>
> Penal Code § 1096

Although *guilt* must be proven beyond a reasonable doubt, not all matters in controversy need be so conclusively established. Other issues can be decided on the basis of lesser standards of proof.

For example, the standard of *clear and convincing evidence* (which means enough evidence, of sufficient quality, to indicate a *high probability*) applies to the determination of whether a juvenile under the age of 14 knew the wrongfulness of his act. This standard of proof is something less than proof beyond a reasonable doubt. *In re Manuel L. (1994) 7 C4th 229.*

A still lower standard of proof is a *preponderance of evidence* (that is, enough to show a *probability*, or at least a 51 percent likelihood). This is the only burden that need be met to prevail in a civil lawsuit, for example, or to establish that a criminal suspect's confession was voluntarily made. *People v. Markham* (1989) 49 C3d 63.

Prima facie proof, which is only a slight showing of circumstances that appear, on their face, to warrant drawing a particular conclusion, is the standard of proof that applies to such procedural steps as the preliminary hearing, or the establishment of a *corpus delicti* at trial (see below). *People v. Alcala* (1984) 36 C3d 604, 624-625.

JURISDICTION, ELEMENTS AND IDENTIFICATION

The state's burden of going forward with evidence that proves guilt beyond a reasonable doubt requires establishing that the court has *jurisdiction* over the offense, that each *element* of the crime is satisfied, and the accused can be *identified* as the perpetrator. If any one of these three matters is not proven beyond a reasonable doubt, the state will not have met its burden of proof, and the defendant must be acquitted.

Jurisdiction of the offense includes proof of both the *time* and *place* of the crime. To prevent stale prosecutions of offenses that may have occurred so long ago that society has lost its interest in enforcement, and the accused has lost his ability to assemble evidence for his defense, the law imposes a *statute of limitations* on most prosecutions. Unless the suspect is accused within this statutory period by the filing of formal charges or the issuance of an arrest warrant, the court loses jurisdiction to try him.

The statute of limitations as to most misdemeanors is *one year* (PC § 801); most alternative misdemeanor/felony crimes (called "wobblers") and most felonies have a *three-year* statute of limitations, except certain sex crimes which have *six-year* limits (PC §§ 800, 801(b)); and such crimes as murder, embezzlement of public money, falsifying public records and kidnaping for ransom have *no* statute of limitations (PC § 799). Any period of time while the suspect was outside the state is excluded in computing expiration date of the SOL (PC § 802).

In addition to proving that the charged crime occurred within the applicable time limit, the state must also prove that it was planned or perpetrated within the court's jurisdictional territory (usually, the county where the court is located, or a judicial district within the county). See, generally, Penal Code §§ 777-796.

To establish both parts of the jurisdictional requirement, the prosecutor will normally ask her first witness a question such as, "Mr. Lewis, on October 12, 1989, did you park your car in the 400 block of South Main Street, Santa Ana, Orange County, California?" If the witness answers, "Yes," both the time and place of an auto theft can be quickly established, and the court's jurisdiction satisfied.

Elements of the charged offense must *each* be proven beyond a reasonable doubt. Every crime consists of two or more elements, sometimes with a specified intent or guilty knowledge or other conditions, that must occur together to constitute the offense. If any essential element is missing (or not proved), there can be no conviction.

Consider, for example, *Vehicle Code § 27* (Impersonation of Patrol Member): "Any person who without authority impersonates, or wears the badge of, a member of the California Highway Patrol with intent to deceive anyone is guilty of a misdemeanor." This offense has *three* elements:

1. Either impersonating a CHP officer, or wearing a CHP badge

2. Without authority

3. With intent to deceive

Thus, an actor who wears a CHP badge, without official authority, for dramatic purposes but without any intent to deceive anyone, would not be guilty of violating this section.

Occasionally, the concept of *elements* of a crime is confused with another concept, discussed below, known as the *corpus delicti* of a crime. The two are not necessarily identical. It is sufficient to note for now that neither of these terms is a synonym for the other, they cannot correctly be used interchangeably, and they do not refer to the same thing.

Identification of the person who committed each proven element of the crime falling within the court's jurisdiction is the remaining component of the prosecution that must be shown beyond a reasonable doubt. ID of the accused as the perpetrator can be established by his confession, by physical evidence linking him to the crime, or through the testimony of eyewitnesses.

THE CORPUS DELICTI RULE

Hollywood always gets this one wrong. According to the movie version of the *corpus delicti* rule, a prosecution for a murder could not succeed unless a body were found.

In fact, there are numerous instances of murder convictions where no body is ever located, but where other evidence proves beyond a reasonable doubt that a murder occurred. This is possible because the term "*corpus delicti*" does not refer to a "corpse" of a human being, but to the *body of a crime*. Notice, this is not a case-specific reference to the body of *the crime* charged, but a generic reference to the body of *a crime*. Therefore, no matter what specific violation of law is charged, the *corpus delicti* is defined the same way:

The *corpus delicti* of a crime includes (1) the fact of the injury, loss, or harm, and (2) the existence of a criminal agency as its cause. *People v. Wright* (1989) 48 C3d 168, 200.

In other words, no matter what the *elements* of a category of crimes may be, the *corpus delicti* remains generally the same. For example, compare the elements of the two crimes of *murder* (PC § 187) and *voluntary manslaughter* (PC § 192):

Murder defined:

1. Unlawful killing

2. Of a fetus or human being

3. With malice aforethought.

Voluntary Manslaughter defined:

1. Unlawful killing

2. Of a human being

3. Without malice

4. On sudden quarrel or heat of passion

Clearly, the *elements* are different. For example, malice afore-thought is an element of murder, but not of manslaughter. However, the *corpus delicti* of any homicide is generally stated as "the death of the victim by criminal agency," which would apply to either murder or manslaughter. *Ureta v. Superior Court* (1962) 199 CA2d 672, 676.

The *corpus delicti* is not intended to include every element of a statutory offense, or every other fact necessary to prove guilt. It is intended only to constitute the "bare bones" of a crime, so as to serve one specific purpose — *to insure that no person is convicted, from his own mouth, of a nonexistent crime.* To protect against the self-destructive habits of the compulsive confessor, and to guard against the possibility that a defenseless individual might be pressured into con-fessing to a crime that never occurred, the prosecution is required to prove the *corpus delicti* of an offense independently from the state-ments of an accused. *People v. Towler* (1982) 31 C3d 105, 115. This is the *corpus delicti* rule.

In operation, the *corpus delicti* rule means that a death under circumstances giving no independent indication of foul play cannot become the subject of a homicide prosecution solely on the basis of the statements of a self-confessed killer. Even if a distraught stepfather tells police he intentionally held a young child under water during the bath, no murder prosecution can succeed unless an independent witness or some physical evidence shows a *prima facie* case of death by criminal agency (as opposed to accident or misfortune).

The *corpus delicti* rule applies to all criminal prosecutions, regardless of the charge. In a case of arson, the prosecution must have *slight proof* of a corpus — loss or injury (the burning of a structure), by human agency (rather than by lightning, accident or spontaneous combustion) — before the arsonist's confession to setting the fire can be used to convict him. Or, if a traffic officer arrests an intoxicated person found passed out behind the steering wheel of a car pulled off the side of the road, the prosecutor must establish that the car was driven by someone under the influence, before the defendant's state-ments will be competent evidence to convict him of driving under the influence.

Once the corpus has been established by slight proof, the defendant's admissions can be used to prove all of the following matters, since none of them is a part of the corpus: *degree* of the crime [*People v. Scofield* (1983) 149 CA3d 368, 371]; *motive* [*People v. Cullen* (1951) 37 C2d 614, 624]; *identity* of the perpetrator [*In re Robert P.* (1981) 121 CA3d 36, 38]; *location* where the crime occurred [*People v. Garcia* (1970) 4 CA3d 904, 911]; *date* of the offense [*People v. Walsh* (1987) 194 CA3d 40, 49]; perpetrator's *state of mind* [*People v. McGlothen* (1987) 190 CA3d 1005, 1014].

EX POST FACTO AND RETROACTIVITY

The US Constitution, in Article I, sections 9 and 10, and the California Constitution, in Article I, section 9, both prohibit laws that are ex post facto meaning "after the fact." It was the collective sense that it is unfair to pass a new law penalizing conduct that has already occurred. Criminal laws can take effect, therefore, only *prospectively* (in the future), beginning on their effective date. In California, a law becomes effective when signed by the governor (if designated as an "urgency" measure), or on January 1st of the next year following enactment (the majority of new laws).

When a statute is amended to increase the prescribed punishment, this new, greater punishment can only be imposed on persons who commit the specified crime after the effective date of the new law. Defendants who had already committed the crime but were not yet convicted or sentenced would have to be punished under the sentencing scheme in effect when their crime occurred; otherwise, the law would amount to a prohibited *ex post facto* penalty.

Although it might seem, logically, that the reverse would also hold true—that is, that when conduct is decriminalized or the punishment lowered, or a new procedural protection for defendants imposed, it would not benefit those defendants who had already committed their crimes—the general rule is to the contrary: if a change in the law or interpretations would extend a new benefit to a defendant whose case is not final, it is applied to his case retroactively. *Griffith v. Kentucky* (1987) 479 US 314, 378.

PREDICTABILITY AND CONSISTENCY

Just as the prohibition of ex post facto laws is intended to insure that everyone is given advance notice of what the law requires and forbids, certain principles of judicial case law are aimed at making interpretation of the law predictable, and its application consistent. Since the Fourteenth Amendment prohibits the states from denying its inhabitants "equal protection of the laws," it is necessary to try to apply case law uniformly, from one case to the next, and from place to place throughout the state. Also, to prevent the endless relitigation of issues that have been fairly decided, it is necessary to regard prior decisions with some degree of finality. Several principles of case law exist toward these ends.

Stare decisis refers to the rule that case law becomes binding precedent for future cases, and except for changes in the law or distinguishing factual circumstances, new cases should apply the settled holdings of earlier cases. Thus, if a US Supreme Court decision held that *Miranda* warnings need not precede custodial interrogation designed to neutralize an immediate threat to the public safety [as it held in *New York v. Quarles* (1984) 467 US 649], subsequent federal and state cases involving the same issue would be bound to apply the same rule [as, for example, in *People v. Cole* (1985) 165 CA3d 41, and *People v. Gilliard* (1987) 189 CA3d 285].

Res judicata (thing decided) is the principle that insures that except for retrial after appellate reversal or a mistrial, a particular case will only be tried once; after this particular matter has once been adjudicated, it cannot be brought back before the court in controversy. *People v. Gephart* (1979) 93 CA3d 989, 997. *Res judicata* thus gives conclusive effect to the prior decision of the court in the same case, and prevents a party from bringing the same criminal prosecution (or civil lawsuit) repeatedly, just to harass the defendant.

Res judicata is not necessarily the same thing as *double jeopardy* (discussed under defenses, in Chapter 6). Even in instances where a defense of double jeopardy would not apply (such as dismissal of a case during a pretrial hearing, long before jeopardy has even attached), the doctrine of *res judicata* is still available to prevent repetitious litigation of the same issues. If a court held a hearing, for example, on a defendant's motion to dismiss for lack of speedy trial and ruled, after a fair presentation by both parties, that the defendant's right to speedy trial had been irreparably violated, a dismissal of the case on that basis would be a *res judicata* bar to further prosecution for the same offense.

Collateral estoppel, closely related to the doctrine of *res judicata*, prevents the relitigation of an *issue* (point in dispute) within a particular case, when that same issue was previously litigated and decided under circumstances that make it fair to bind the present parties to the prior order. Such circumstances must include an identity of parties (or other parties "in privity" with the present parties), identity of issues, and an adequate opportunity to present evidence in the prior proceeding.

For example, in *Lockwood v. Superior Court* (1984) 160 CA3d 667, the parents of an abused child first appeared in juvenile court to litigate a dependency case under Welfare and Institutions Code section 300; the state was represented by counsel; and the issue of the parents' alleged mistreatment of their child was adjudicated (judged); the juvenile court ruled that the evidence did not establish parental abuse of the child. When the district attorney later sought to prosecute the Lockwoods for a violation of Penal Code section 273a(1) (child abuse), the defendants invoked the doctrine of collateral estoppel. The court ruled that since the issue of whether or not the defendants had abused their child had been fully litigated in a collateral proceeding on a collateral case involving parties in privity, the state was estopped from relitigating the issue, and thus could not proceed with a criminal prosecution.

Collateral estoppel issues frequently arise where a related proceeding (DMV hearing, juvenile court hearing, ABC hearing, or other administrative or judicial trial or hearing) has already taken place before the criminal prosecution gets under way. If the defendant prevailed on a particular issue at the previous hearing, he will generally argue that the prosecutor is collaterally estopped from relitigating that issue in the criminal courts. In any such case, the court deciding this motion must consider the factors of identity, privity and finality in reaching a ruling as to whether or not the issue can be relitigated. [Compare *People v. Sims* (1982) 32 C3d 468 administrative welfare hearing collaterally estops (stops) criminal case with *Lofthouse v. DMV* (1981) 124 CA3d 730 no collateral estoppel from DMV hearing.]

Another related principle is the *law of the case*. This means that an issue fully litigated to decision in a particular case (not in a collateral proceeding) is binding on the court and the parties for all future proceedings in that same case. For example, if a defendant appeals his conviction on the ground that an erroneous jury instruction was given, an appellate court's ruling that the instruction should not have been given will become law of the case for any retrial of the matter. When the appeal court reverses the conviction and remands for a new trial, the appellate rulings are law of the case, and must be followed by the trial court during any subsequent trial.

Together, the principles of (1) *stare decisis*, (2) *res judicata*, (3) collateral estoppel and (4) law of the case contribute to predictability as to what rules of law and procedure will be applied in any given case. Also, they tend to reduce excessive litigation and relitigation of issues and cases.

METHODS OF PROOF

In order to meet his burden of proof, a party may rely on both evidence and procedural devices to establish what happened. Evidence is either direct, or circumstantial; available procedural devices include judicial notice, statutory presumptions, and stipulations.

Direct evidence (which may be either physical evidence or the testimony of witnesses) is evidence which, if believed by the trier of fact, conclusively proves any fact. For example, if a crime victim testifies that a man forced her to engage in an act of sexual intercourse against her will by use of force and threats, and if she identifies the accused in court as that man, her testimony, if believed by the jury, is sufficient proof of the defendant's guilt of rape, and need not be corroborated. Her testimony is said to directly prove the facts to which she credibly testifies.

Circumstantial evidence is evidence which proves a fact indirectly, in conjunction with other proved facts, by logical inference. In the previous example, if the rape victim's testimony established the fact of the crime but not the identity of the rapist, ID could be proved circumstantially by other evidence. For instance, if the victim testified that the rapist wore a ski mask and threatened her with a switch-blade knife, testimony from the arresting officer that the defendant was apprehended in the vicinity of the crime, a short time later, in possession of both a ski mask and a switch-blade, would be strong circumstantial evidence of his guilt.

Perhaps combined with such additional circumstantial evidence as a DNA comparison matching the defendant's blood specimen with DNA from the rapist's semen, and a pubic hair found on the defendant matching the victim's, these proved circumstances would convince a jury of defendant's guilt beyond a reasonable doubt.

Although the public is regularly bombarded with entertainment vehicles that characterize circumstantial evidence as inferior and unreliable, the law in California (as elsewhere) is that circumstantial evidence is just as competent as direct evidence in court:

It is not necessary that facts be proved by direct evidence. They may be proved also by circumstantial evidence or by a combination of direct evidence and circumstantial evidence. Both direct evidence and circumstantial evidence are acceptable as a means of proof. Neither is entitled to any greater weight than the other. *CALJIC 2.00*

Judicial notice is simply an acknowledgment by the court of a particular fact, so that it does not have to be proved by evidence. The procedure for requesting that the court take judicial notice is set forth in Evidence Code sections 450 through 460. Generally, these sections provide that judicial notice is *mandatory* with respect to the contents of statutory laws, and facts of universal knowledge. Thus, a court would be required to take judicial notice of the laws of physics, or facts of world geography. Since it is universally known that Baja California is a part of Mexico, a prosecutor could request the court to take judicial notice of this fact in a prosecution for abduction and removal from the country.

Judicial notice is *permissive* (depending on timely request and furnishing necessary citations, authorities, maps, etc.) as to case law, official records, and facts that are commonly-known in the local area. On request, a court can take judicial notice that Barstow is in San Bernardino County, or that the defendant is on probation from a prior conviction in a neighboring court, etc.

The effect of judicial notice is to relieve the party of any further need to produce evidence to prove the noticed fact. This saves needless time and effort attempting to prove facts that may be necessary to establish jurisdiction or some part of the case, but are not really in serious dispute. If a fact has been judicially noticed by the court, the jury must be instructed to accept the fact as true. Evidence Code § 457.

Statutory presumptions are matters presumed by law to be true (again relieving the party of the need to produce courtroom proof). Presumptions are considered conclusive if the law does not permit them to be contested. Pursuant to Evidence Code section 622, for example, the law conclusively presumes that the facts stated in a written agreement are true, as between the parties making the agreement. [There can be no conclusive presumptions in a criminal case that would operate to relieve the state of its burden of proving every element of its case beyond a reasonable doubt. *Carella v. California* (1989) 105 L. Ed. 2d 218.]

Presumptions are *rebuttable* if they establish a fact only until rebutted with contrary credible evidence. For example, under Evidence Code section 664, it is presumed that official duty has been properly performed. If it is established by testimony that a property custodian had the official duty to properly label all items of evidence booked into the police property room, then it is presumed that he did so. This presumption shifts the burden to the opposing party to offer evidence in rebuttal, if he can, to the effect that an item was not properly marked.

Stipulations are simply agreements between the parties to some fact that is not in issue. In a trial for driving under the influence, a defendant might agree to stipulate that he was in fact under the influence when arrested by a police officer (particularly if a proper test revealed a relatively-high blood alcohol content). He would be likely to do this, however, only where he was pleading some legal defense (such as entrapment or necessity), or where he was contesting the issue of whether or not he had been driving the vehicle. If the prosecutor and defense attorney (or defendant if representing himself) have stipulated to any facts in the trial of a case, the jury is instructed by the judge to regard the stipulated facts as proven. (See CALJIC 1.02.)

SUMMARY

√ The adversary system has the advantage of creating a competition in which both sides offer their most convincing case, while exposing the shortcomings of the other, with the result that the search for the truth by a neutral fact-finder is enhanced to the greatest possible degree.

√ Our accusatorial system starts with a presumption that the accused is innocent. The effect of this presumption is to place the burden of proving the defendant's guilt on the state.

√ The state's burden of proof in a criminal case is to produce evidence that convinces the fact-finder of the defendant's guilt beyond a reasonable doubt. Certain issues can be decided on the basis of lower standards of proof, such as clear and convincing evidence (a high probability), preponderance of evidence (more likely than not), and prima facie evidence (slight evidence to make a facial showing).

√ Three matters required to be established in every criminal prosecution are jurisdiction, elements of the charged offense, and ID of the accused as the perpetrator.

√ The *corpus delicti* rule requires the prosecution to show by independent evidence the existence of a loss or injury, caused by criminal agency, before relying on the accused's own confession to support a conviction.

√ Criminal laws may not be applied, ex post facto, to penalize conduct that was lawful when committed, nor to increase the severity of the punishment after the fact. Changes in the law that would benefit a defendant whose case is not yet final are generally extended to him retroactively.

√ To promote predictability and consistency, the courts follow the principles of stare decisis (new cases follow the precedent of earlier cases), res judicata (a fully-litigated case cannot be relitigated), collateral estoppel (issues decided in a collateral proceeding may not be relitigated in later, related actions), and law of the case (issues finally resolved in a case remain binding throughout proceedings on that case).

√ A party may discharge her burden of proof by use of direct and circumstantial evidence, judicial notice, statutory presumptions and stipulations.

ISSUES FOR DISCUSSION

1. Is the adversary system the best conceivable method of determining guilt or innocence? What are the alternatives?

2. Some societies commence criminal trials on a presumption of guilt. Is this fair? Is it less likely to produce reliable results?

3. Are the various designated burdens of proof really just legal fictions? Can jurors really tell when they are clearly convinced, but not beyond a reasonable doubt?

4. Should the *corpus delicti* rule be modified to permit a conviction on the defendant's confession where there is corroborative evidence of his crime, even though it might be insufficient to establish corpus?

5. Should a trial judge be collaterally estopped from adjudicating an issue wrongly decided in an administrative hearing by a non-attorney hearing officer?

CHAPTER 3

JUSTICE SYSTEM COMPONENTS

Learning Goals: After studying this chapter, you will be able to correctly answer the following questions:

√   What are the roles of victims and witnesses in the criminal process? What about "victimless" crimes?

√   Who are the various officials involved in the investigation of crimes?

√   How do the prosecutorial components operate at the city, county, state and federal levels?

√   What is the role of the defense attorney? What are a defendant's rights to have the services of a lawyer?

√   How many kinds and levels of judicial and other adjudicative components are there? What are the roles of various courtroom personnel?

√   How are juries drawn? What are the constitutional requirements for jury composition?

√   What are the components of the corrections system, and the roles of each?

VICTIMS

In many cases, the criminal himself is the triggering mechanism of the criminal justice procedure. It is his action in violation of established law that prompts the reaction of the entire justice system, beginning, usually, with the victim.

Many criminal offenses are direct violations of the security rights of a specific individual—the "victim." For example, theft offenses violate the property rights of the owners, while assaultive offenses violate the personal security rights of the persons assaulted (molested, raped, murdered, etc.). Because many of our criminal statutes are designed to protect either property rights or personal security, the processing of criminal cases involving specific victims is easily, and often, divided into two categories: (1) *crimes against property*, and (2) *crimes against persons*.

In either of these categories of crimes, the victim whose property or personal rights are infringed is usually the first component of the justice system to react. On discovery of the crime, the victim (or relatives or friends of a deceased victim) makes a crime report to the proper investigative agency. From this point on, the victim may remain closely-involved in most phases of the criminal procedure—serving as a witness to aid police and prosecutors during the pretrial proceedings, giving testimony in court at the preliminary hearing and trial, providing input to the sentencing judge and probation officer after conviction, and even appearing at parole-revocation hearings many years after a felony offense was committed.

Depending on the nature and seriousness of the crime, a victim may become involved not only with the criminal justice system, but also with insurance companies, civil lawsuits, the press, community-action groups, counseling services, medical treatment, and more. The sheer prospect of the ordeal of being an official victim is often cited as the reason many crimes are never reported. It is generally felt that such crimes as rape, child molest, and domestic violence are especially under-reported (and thus under-prosecuted and -punished) because of the further trauma the victims of these crimes may suffer in their aftermath. Recent "victims rights" legislation has addressed this problem by giving more protection to victims against harassment, setting up victim assistance programs and restitution funds, and mandating "sensitivity training" for police and prosecutors in various kinds of cases.

An example of victims grouping together to work for changes in the system is the national organization called Mothers Against Drunk Driving ("MADD"). Officials within the justice system credit MADD with focusing local and national attention on the problem of driving under the influence, with helping to bring about a dramatic change in the public perception of the social acceptability of this offense, and with motivating state legislatures, prosecutors and judges to crack down on drinking drivers. Partly as a result of MADD initiative, the California legislature *lowered* the presumptive level of intoxication, in 1990, from .10 percent blood-alcohol concentration to .08 percent, and has steadily *increased* the fines, jail terms, and license suspensions for DUI convictions.

Other crime victims and their families and supporters have banded together to deal with such problems as missing and exploited children, spousal abuse, rape, murder, and even investment fraud. To combat burglaries and auto crimes, communities have formed "neighborhood watch" programs, and may participate in local self-patrol committees. A few California urban communities have chapters of the New York-based "Guardian Angels," a group of civilian volunteers who seek to deter street crime through their anti-crime presence at events or locations having acute crime problems.

Although some victim and volunteer groups are greeted with mixed feelings by law enforcement professionals, there is general support for most of them, and common agreement that they represent an important, effective and often-necessary component of the public response to increasing crime.

In addition to the crimes against property and person that involve a specific victim, there are offenses against public order and morals that do not affect any one "victim" in society more than anyone else. This category of so-called "victimless" crime includes such activity as gambling, prostitution, pornography, environmental pollution, unfair business practices, and narcotics offenses. These kinds of crimes are viewed as victimizing all of the people of the state in general, rather than a particular individual (although some such crimes may indeed victimize the individuals who are specifically exploited or made miserable by their perpetration).

Because of the absence of a particular victim to initiate action in the "victimless" crime cases, their discovery and investigation require greater initiative by enforcement officers. Often, such initiative will include surveillance, "sting" operations, use of informants, and under-cover work. Public reluctance to accept police "trickery" or secretive investigations has historically hampered enforcement of laws enacted to preserve public order and decency.

This same public attitude projected by jurors makes it more difficult for prosecutors to obtain convictions when the absence of an identified "victim" forces police to use surreptitious tactics in crime detection. (A notorious example of this problem was the acquittal, by a federal jury in Southern California, of alleged cocaine trafficker John DeLorean, despite graphic videotaped evidence of his apparent complicity in drug transactions with undercover agents.)

A persistent philosophical minority have espoused the viewpoint that "victimless" crimes should be eliminated, on the theory that society has no moral right to impose its collective will on individuals who may want access to such things as narcotics, pornography, gambling and prostitution. However, the laws forbidding such activities are rarely repealed or modified. This, in spite of the fact that juries and the public at large are grudging in their approval of investigative techniques inherently necessary in such cases. Moreover, to eliminate crimes lacking an individual victim would deprive society of the ability to punish such conduct as toxic pollution, false advertising, and the sale of dangerous firearms and explosive devices.

Thus, though the label "victimless crime" may raise an emotional suspicion on the part of a public that cherishes individual liberty, and while public support for the covert investigation of such crime may be more sparingly given, the electorate and their legislators have not chosen to decriminalize "victimless" activity, on that basis alone. Indeed, as the human suffering and social costs of so-called "victimless crimes" become staggeringly apparent, society's willingness to tolerate them decreases. This declining tolerance is reflected in the ever-increasing penalties for narcotic sales, for example, in the face of growing evidence that addict-babies (as many as one in five births, in some California hospitals) will constitute a generation of disabled dependents, each costing society as much as $2 million for a lifetime of special care and support.

WITNESSES

Essential to the success of the criminal justice system is the role of the *witness*. A person may be a witness because she saw the crime, or some part of it, occur, or because she saw and can identify the perpetrator. This kind of witness is often referred to as an "eyewitness" to the crime. Although a victim will usually also be a witness, a witness obviously need not necessarily be a victim (for example, the observant bystander at the bank robbery, or a motorist who sees a hit-and-run accident occur).

Law enforcement officers attempt to identify and interview all potential witnesses as promptly as possible after a crime. Statements are either tape recorded or summarized by the investigating officer in the written crime report (discussed further in Chapter 4). All persons, whether potentially prosecution or defense witnesses, are contacted and their material information preserved and reported for future use.

To become a witness at trial, a person need not have been the victim or an eyewitness to the crime. Any person with knowledge that would be useful to the trier of fact in determining a defendant's guilt or innocence might be called upon to be a witness in court. Often, such witnesses are surprised (and sometimes annoyed) to receive a subpena to testify. A typical reaction is to ask, "Why do I have to come to court? I didn't actually see the guy commit the crime." In fact, even the *victims* of such crimes as burglary and auto theft frequently ask the prosecutor, "Why do I have to testify? I didn't see him do it, and my insurance company has paid my claim. Why can't the police testify? Isn't that what they're paid for? I told them everything I know!"

Witnesses not schooled in the laws of evidence and criminal procedure may be understandably confused about the necessity of appearing personally in court, to be confronted and cross-examined by the defendant, and to give a firsthand account of their knowledge of material facts. This sort of confusion can be alleviated by information and advice from the investigating officer, the prosecutor (or defense attorney), and the victim-witness assistant.

INVESTIGATIVE COMPONENTS

When people think of law enforcement officers, they usually think "police." In fact, we use the word "police" almost generically, to describe various categories of law officers. Municipal police officers are the largest and most visible component of the investigative force, but are by no means alone in law enforcement.

California Penal Code Chapter 4.5, beginning with section 830, defines a broad category of officials who are "peace officers" in this state. This group include city and state police officers, constables, sheriffs and their deputies, marshals and their deputies, California Highway Patrol officers, district attorney investigators, and designated officers of such agencies as the Department of Justice, Fish and Game, Corrections, Parks and Recreation, Forestry, Alcoholic Beverage Control, Consumer Affairs, Medical Quality, Motor Vehicles, Insurance, Contractors Licensing, and university, harbor and airport police, arson investigators, and reserve officers, among others.

In order to exercise the powers given to peace officers, such as making arrests and carrying concealed firearms, qualifying officers must successfully complete certain basic training requirements. The training agenda is established by the state Commission on Peace Officer Standards and Training (POST). Officers who complete the required training receive a POST basic certificate, which is necessary to continue their employment as peace officers.

POST has also established a schedule of continuing training and update instruction for in-service personnel. To maintain POST certification, peace officers undergo continuous training at regular intervals throughout their law enforcement careers. POST-certified courses are provided by academies, the community colleges, other educational institutions, and specialized training consultants.

In addition to the training mandated by POST, most law enforcement officers pursue further education and professional enhancement on their own initiative in degree programs, special schools, professional publications, and individual studies. Many agencies encourage and reward such efforts with extra pay and promotional opportunities, and other forms of recognition.

The standards of competence and professionalism established by California peace officers and educators have been adopted as goals by other states, which often send officers to California to observe and to be trained on procedures and techniques.

Although the bulk of criminal investigation is carried on by peace officers and administrative investigators, there are other investigative components to the system. Government Code section 27491 places responsibility for the investigation of the cause and circumstances of deaths on the *coroner*.

The coroner is an elected county officeholder, who need not herself be a physician. In some counties, she may hold no other office, while in others, she may also serve as public administrator or sheriff. If the coroner is not a pathologist, she may appoint medical doctors to perform autopsies and related medical procedures to identify the cause of death. A pathologist who performs these duties is sometimes referred to as a "medical examiner." Note, therefore, that "coroner" and "medical examiner" are not necessarily interchangeable terms.

The coroner has a statutory duty to take charge of the body and effects of a deceased, under a long list of specified circumstances, until the cause-of-death investigation is complete. Basically, there is a requirement of autopsy whenever the decedent died without a physician in attendance, or under any suspicious circumstances (accident, drowning, gunshot, poisoning, homicide, suicide, or decedent unidentified).

Following the autopsy and laboratory analysis, the coroner may convene a jury of citizens to hold a "coroner's inquest" for the purpose of deciding the official circumstances and cause of death. The coroner's inquest does not attempt to fix individual blame, or to accuse suspected killers, or to initiate judicial charges in homicide cases. Its verdict may simply be stated as "death by accident or misfortune," or "death by self-inflicted means," or "death at the hands of another," for example. Local homicide investigators and prosecutors frequently observe the coroner's inquest in any homicide case they have under investigation, to help determine the direction of the case.

Another investigative component is the county *grand jury*. The California Constitution (Article I, Section 23) requires each county to draw and summon a grand jury once a year. This is a body of select citizens (11, 19 or 23, depending on population) who meet regularly throughout the year to conduct investigations into local crimes and the operation of county government. The grand jury has the power to charge suspected criminals by filing an *indictment* in court, containing allegations of criminal violations by named defendants. (See further discussion in Chapter 5.)

To conduct its investigations, the grand jury utilizes the advice and assistance of the district attorney and county counsel, and has the power to subpena witnesses, including the suspect himself. Grand jury proceedings are conducted in relative secrecy, and grand jurors are not permitted to disclose their deliberaitons. *Penal Code § 924.1.* Although a suspect has the right to refuse to answer incriminating questions during grand jury proceedings, he has no right to refuse to be called as a witness, or to answer other questions put to him.

Most of the grand jury's investigative authority is discretionary. But Penal Code § 919 *requires* the grand jury to investigate cases of official corruption and conditions and operation of any public prisons within the county.

PROSECUTORIAL COMPONENTS

The government's criminal lawsuit against an accused defendant is presented by a prosecuting attorney. Depending on the particular offense charged, the prosecutor may be a city attorney, a district (county) attorney, the state attorney-general, or a United States attorney:

The words "prosecuting attorney" include any attorney, whether designated as district attorney, city attorney, city prosecutor, prosecuting attorney, or by any other title, having by law the right or duty to prosecute, in behalf of the people, any charge of a public offense. *Penal Code § 691.5*

Generally, the city attorney or city prosecutor handles cases charging violations of the city's municipal code, such as parking offenses, curfew and nuisance violations, and violations of zoning laws and land-use restrictions. In some cities, the city attorney also prosecutes misdemeanor violations of state laws occurring within the city. Smaller communities may employ a single city attorney, or even contract with a local practicing attorney to serve part-time as city prosecutor. In larger cities, the city attorney often has a legal staff of deputy city attorneys to handle the larger volume of local prosecutions.

The remaining misdemeanor prosecutions and most felony cases are pressed by the district attorney as public prosecutor. Each county has an elected district attorney who serves a four-year term, and may be assisted by one or more *deputy* district attorneys. The most populous counties have dozens, and in a few cases hundreds, of deputy district attorneys to prosecute criminal cases. One or more *assistant* district attorneys may be designated in larger offices to help supervise the staff of deputies. Many district attorneys also have the services of district attorney *investigators*, who are peace officers employed to do prosecution-related criminal investigations (including trial preparation and investigation of charges against public officials, for example).

The California Attorney General, a statewide elected officer with a four-year term, is the head of the Department of Justice and the state's chief public prosecutor. A staff of assistant and deputy attorneys-general initiate prosecutions in cases of statewide concern (particularly in such areas as environmental pollution and consumer fraud), and handle much of the appellate work in criminal cases originally brought by local prosecutors. In the event the local prosecutor cannot or will not pursue a criminal case, the Attorney General has full authority anyplace within the state to assume the prosecution of the case. The Attorney General has supervisory authority over all district attorneys and sheriffs. (California Constitution, Article V, Section 13.)

In some instances, an Assistant United States Attorney or a former prosecutor who has been involved in the investigation or preparation of a case may be temporarily designated as a special prosecutor to represent the state in the case. If no prosecutor appears on behalf of the state on a felony trial in superior court, the judge has the power to appoint any attorney at law to perform the prosecutorial function (see Penal Code § 1130).

Although many attorneys serving as a deputy city attorney, district attorney, or attorney-general decide upon public service careers in those positions, many others serve a limited number of years, gaining valuable trial experience, and then withdraw to the private sector, where earning potential is usually much greater. To accommodate the ongoing training needs of career prosecutors and to provide training to new attorneys entering the prosecution field, the Office of Criminal Justice Planning partially funds the California District Attorneys Association ("CDAA"). The CDAA, through a series of seminars, publications and other media, serves the public interest not only in providing prosecutorial training, but also in advocating and supporting criminal justice legislation. Most of the state's prosecuting attorneys are members of the CDAA.

DEFENSE COMPONENTS

The premise of our adversarial system of justice is that where both sides to a legal controversy are able to zealously advocate their positions, we stand our best chance of seeing the truth made known. Since the state can only be represented through its lawyer (the prosecuting attorney), the optimum adversarial contest on which we depend to identify the truth requires that the accused also be represented by a lawyer. Thus, while the defendant has a right to represent himself if he is competent to do so [*Faretta v. California* (1975) 422 US 806], he also has a Sixth Amendment right "to have the Assistance of Counsel for his defence." This federal constitutional right is duplicated in Article I, § 15, of the California Constitution, and is repeated in Penal Code § 686.

Application of the constitutional right to counsel has evolved throughout our history. Originally, it was considered that a defendant had the right to be represented if he could make his own arrangements with an attorney of his choice. Then, in *Powell v. Alabama* (1932) 287 US 45, the US Supreme Court ruled that the due process clause required appointment of counsel for an indigent defendant charged with a *capital offense.*

This holding was extended to all *felony* cases, capital or otherwise, in *Gideon v. Wainwright* (1963) 372 US 335, a decision that declared the Sixth Amendment applicable to state prosecutions. Since *Gideon*, all states (including California) have been required to furnish a court-appointed attorney to indigent felony defendants.

It was unclear for several years after *Gideon* whether appointed attorneys were required for those facing only misdemeanor charges without affordable counsel. In *Mempa v. Rhay* (1967) 389 US 128, 134, the Court referred to *Gideon* as having established a right to counsel in "felony prosecutions." The uncertainty was resolved in *Argersinger v. Hamlin* (1972) 407 US 25, with the Supreme Court ruling that *Gideon* applied to both *felony and misdemeanor* prosecutions if the defendant was sentenced to any term of incarceration.

Where either a misdemeanor or infraction conviction is punishable only by fine and not by jail, the Sixth Amendment right to counsel does not apply. *Scott v. Illinois* (1977) 440 US 367. By statute and case law in California, however, all charged misdemeanants are entitled to counsel—whether or not jail can be imposed (See Penal Code § 686; *Tracy v. Municipal Court* (1978) 22 C3d 760; and *In re Kevin G.* (1985) 40 C3d 644). Persons charged with infractions have no right to appointed counsel (Penal Code § 19.6).

If a defendant chooses to be represented by counsel, he has no right to act as his own "co-counsel," but must leave the presentation of his defense to the attorney. *People v. Hamilton* (1989) 48 C3d 1142. On the other hand, if the defendant has waived his right to counsel and elected to represent himself (referred to as proceeding *in propria persona*, or "pro per," and *pro se*), the court retains the option of appointing "standby counsel" to advise the defendant on procedural matters and courtroom protocol. *McKaskle v. Wiggins* (1984) 465 US 168.

The right to have the assistance of counsel "attaches only at or after the time that adversary judicial proceedings have been initiated." *Kirby v. Illinois* (1972) 406 US 682. This means that before formal charging or arraignment in court, the Sixth Amendment right to counsel does not apply. *US v. Gouveia* (1984) 467 US 180.

Whether a defendant is represented by his own retained attorney or by court-appointed counsel, his constitutional right is to representation that is "effective." *Strickland v. Washington* (1984) 466 US 668. If a defendant's attorney fails to perform within the range of competence demanded of attorneys in criminal cases, or if the attorney's inadequacy turns the trial into a farce or mockery or otherwise deprives the defendant of a fundamentally fair trial, the defendant will have been deprived of his constitutional right to the *effective* assistance of counsel. Any resulting conviction may ultimately be overturned due to "ineffectiveness of counsel," which is often referred to as "Pope error." *People v. Pope* (1979) 23 C3d 412.

As a practical matter, many convicted defendants whose trial counsel performed very ably will retain (or be appointed) a new lawyer to handle appeals, so that the appellate attorney can argue ineffectiveness of trial counsel as a basis for reversal. This fairly routine scenario casts criminal defense attorneys into mutual opposition, and forces the anomaly of a prosecutor "defending" the trial attorney's competence, in order to sustain the conviction.

In order to maintain their competence, most attorneys practicing criminal law participate in continuing legal education programs sponsored by the state or local bar associations, by private providers, by the Criminal Trial Lawyers Association, and by the California Public Defenders Association. Those attorneys meeting prescribed standards of experience and knowledge may become state-bar "Certified Specialists in Criminal Law," and are entitled to advertise themselves as such to the public.

Criminal defense attorneys may be classified in three groups: retained attorneys, public defenders, and court-appointed "conflict" attorneys. Every taxpayer's preference would no doubt be that those accused of crimes hire and pay their own lawyers, as the financially-able usually do. Unfortunately, most criminal suspects lack either the means or the inclination to spend their own resources for legal counsel; as a result, publicly-funded attorneys handle the lion's share of criminal defense cases.

Larger counties have a designated public defender. This attorney is not elected, but is appointed by the board of supervisors or other local officials, and has a staff of deputy public defenders and investigators. When a court determines that a defendant is unable to afford private counsel, the public defender is appointed. (In smaller counties, the court may have a "contract" defense attorney to whom cases are referred in the absence of a full-time public defender.)

If the public defender is unable to represent a particular defendant—such as where a conflict of interest exists between two or more indigent codefendant—she will "declare a conflict" and ask the court to make other appointments. Private criminal defense attorneys are then appointed, and are reimbursed with public funds, usually at a pre-established rate that is higher than public defender's pay, but lower than the average for retained attorneys.

After criminal proceedings are complete, if the court determines that a defendant has the financial ability to reimburse the county either fully or partially for the services of the public defender or other appointed counsel, the court will order appropriate payment.

The defense counterpart to the attorney general is the State Public Defender. This position is appointed by the governor, with legislative consent. A staff of deputy state public defenders represent criminal defendants as appointed by the court, particularly at the appellate level.

Whether an attorney is retained or appointed, his or her duty is to provide the defendant with the best possible defense, within the bounds of the law (ABA Canon 7). This duty often presents the attorney with conflict— especially where the defendant seeks the lawyer's help in concealing evidence, or presenting fabricated evidence or perjurious testimony in court. For while the attorney is duty-bound not to betray a privileged communication or to compromise a legitimate defense, s/he is also duty bound not to become an accessory to the client's crime by concealing evidence, nor to perpetrate a fraud on the court:

> It is an abuse of a lawyer's professional responsibility knowingly to take possession of and secrete the fruits and instrumentalities of a crime. Such acts bear no reasonable relation to the privilege and duty to refuse to divulge a client's confidential communication. The attorney made himself an active participant in a criminal act, ostensibly wearing the mantle of the loyal advocate, but in reality serving as accessory after the fact.
>
> *In re Ryder* (CA4 1967) 381 F2d 713

California cases are in accord; see, e.g., *People v. Lee* (1970) 3 CA3d 514, 526, and *People v. Superior Court (Fairbank)* (1987) 192 CA3d, 39-40.

If the defendant informs his attorney that he intends to testify and will commit perjury, the attorney's first duty is to attempt to dissuade the defendant from testifying falsely [*Nix v. Whiteside* (1986) 475 US 157, 169]. If the defendant persists in his intentions, the attorney may privately advise the judge of the situation and, depending on the status and complexity of the case, may request to withdraw from the case. Where these measures are not sufficient to eliminate the problem, the attorney can call his client to the stand for whatever "statement" he may wish to make, but should not assist the defendant, such as by asking specific questions to draw out the perjured testimony. Nor should the attorney argue the defendant's perjurious version of events to the jury. *Nix v. Whiteside, supra.*

Where no ethical conflicts exist, the attorney's duty is to represent his client zealously, within the bounds of the law. This duty is no less, even though the defendant may be a particularly cruel and vile individual, morally guilty of an atrocious and heinous offense. Thus, while the defense attorney may find his client personally repugnant and the task of rising to the defense morally distasteful, the success of our adversary system of justice requires the most forceful and challenging defense of the state's case, and the best possible presentation of the defendant's position, to enhance reliability of the fact-finding process. It is this necessity, and vigilance for the constitutional precepts of due process and equal protection of the laws, that motivate the scrupulous attorney to do his or her duty, and not necessarily any personal belief in the defendant's factual innocence.

ADJUDICATIVE COMPONENTS

An adversarial system requires an impartial referee to insure that both adversaries follow the rules, to impose sanctions for infractions of the rules, to decide contested issues, and to declare the outcome. Our system of criminal justice has assigned various of these duties to the judge and jury.

California has five levels of courts for the adjudication of criminal (and civil) cases. Each variety of court has both a *subject-matter* jurisdiction and a *territorial* jurisdiction. For a court to be able to render an enforceable judgment in a case, it must have jurisdiction over the parties and the subject matter (as discussed in Chapter Two), and must be the proper court within which to bring the action, as defined in the state constitution and by statute. Article VI of the California Constitution provides generally for the creation and powers of the five kinds of state courts: justice court, municipal court, superior court, court of appeal, and supreme court.

In judicial districts with fewer than 40,000 residents, the Constitution provides for one or more *justice* courts. The justice court has essentially the same function as the municipal court. Originally, there was no requirement that a judge of the justice court be a lawyer. Although such a requirement is now in effect, non-lawyers who were serving as judges before the new requirement was imposed were allowed to remain in those positions.

Districts within a county containing more than 40,000 residents have one or more *municipal* courts. These courts have jurisdiction of the *infractions* and *misdemeanors* alleged to have occurred within the district. The judges of the municipal courts, sitting as magistrates (Penal Code § 808), also have the power to issue arrest and search warrants, and to conduct preliminary hearings and make preliminary orders in felony cases.

Judges of the municipal courts must have practiced law in California for at least *five* years before selection; they may be appointed to a vacant position by the governor, or may be elected by the voters. The term of office for a municipal court judge is six years. In counties which have approved court unification, municipal courts have been converted into *superior* courts, which have general trial jurisdiction over *both* misdemeanors and felonies and appelate juris- diction over misdemeanor cases. In the few counties which have not approved court unification, the municipal courts and superior courts continue to operate separately.

Each county has one or more *superior* courts, with countywide jurisdiction over the trial of *felony* cases, and appeals from the justice and municipal courts. (The juvenile court is also a superior court (see Chapter Fourteen.) Judges of the superior court may perform the functions of a magistrate (issuing warrants, setting bail, arraigning defendants, and conducting preliminary hearings), in addition to pre- siding over felony proceedings and misdemeanor appeals.

Judges of the superior courts must have been admitted to the practice of law in California (or serving on a municipal bench) for the *ten* years immediately preceding their selection. As with municipal court judges, they may initially be appointed or elected, and must stand for re-election every six years (if opposed).

California is geographically divided into six appellate districts, each containing one or more divisions of the *court of appeal*. These appellate courts hear appeals from the superior courts within their districts, sitting in three-judge panels (the opinion of two judges can constitute the appellate ruling).

Judges of the courts of appeal are referred to as "justices," indicating their primary role as interpreters of the law, rather than as finders of fact in trial. A justice of the court of appeal requires the same minimum qualifications as a superior court judge, but is appointed by the governor (if confirmed by the Commission on Judicial Appoint- ments) for a twelve-year term. At twelve-year intervals, the name of the justice is placed, unopposed, on the general-election ballot, and the voters are given the choice of voting for retention, or not. If the justice is not retained (a rare occurrence), the vacancy is filled by gubernatorial appointment.

The *California Supreme Court* is composed of seven justices; the concurrence of four or more constitutes the court's judgment. The Supreme Court has jurisdiction of criminal appeals allowed from the appellate courts (discretionary with the Supreme Court, if they decide to "grant review"). In cases where a judgment of death was pronounced by the superior court, the Supreme Court has automatic and direct appellate jurisdiction. (California Constitution, Article VI, §§ 11,12.) The Supreme Court also has authority to transfer cases from one appellate court to another, thereby conferring jurisdiction.

Justices of the Supreme Court are appointed by the governor (subject to confirmation by the Commission on Judicial Appointments) and, as with appellate justices, must ask for voter approval every twelve years. Experience of at least ten years as a California attorney or judge is required for eligibility for selection.

One of the seven Supreme Court justices is designated (by the governor's nomination) to be the "Chief Justice;" the remaining six justices are then referred to as "Associate Justice." Similarly, on the appellate court panels, the governor nominates one of their member to be "Presiding Justice" of the court of appeal; the others are associates. Both the superior courts and the municipal courts select one of their own (usually on the basis of an annual rotation) to be the presiding judge of the court. At all court levels, these presiding judges or justices exercise somewhat greater power than their associates, in that they make job assignments, control the court's calendar of cases, and decide who will author case decisions. As such, the chief and presiding positions are viewed within the legal profession as more prestigious than panel positions.

Because there rarely ever are adequate numbers of full-time judges to staff all of the court positions, a number of categories of other judicial officers exists to help adjudicate cases. Both the superior and municipal courts often utilize court *commissioners*. These are full time jurists who meet the same qualifications as judges, but who are appointed by, and serve at the pleasure of, the judges of the court. Commissioners are paid at 90% of the salary rate for the corresponding judges. They obtain the power to render enforceable judgments in criminal cases only where both the prosecutor and defendant stipulate (agree) to have the commissioner serve as the judge.

A similar description applies to *referees*. These positions are usually found at juvenile courts or other special-purpose courts. As with commissioners, referees serve by local appointment, and preside over cases by stipulation of the parties. Both commissioners and referees wear traditional judicial robes, and are properly addressed in their courtrooms with the same respect as judges. Due to their specialized focus on a single area of the law, commissioners and referees become highly proficient in handling their cases—a fact which may largely explain why experienced attorneys will usually stipulate quite readily to these jurists.

When a temporary shortage of judges exists, the presiding judge may notify the Judicial Council and request the assistance of "visiting" judges from other jurisdictions. For the less-crucial cases, such as traffic trials and minor misdemeanors, the presiding judge may appoint experienced practicing attorneys to be temporary judges "pro tem." Attorneys volunteer their time for these assignments, without pay, and they also require stipulations by both parties in order to adjudicate a case.

Early in their judicial careers, new judges attend "judges' college," to receive orientation and information about courtroom demeanor and control, calendar management, judicial ethics and other topics. Their continuing education includes periodic seminars, local training programs, and national "colleges" and conferences, as well as individual study.

To monitor performance and to investigate complaints against judges, there is the Commission on Judicial Performance. The Commission receives reports from the public and from attorneys regarding alleged judicial misconduct, conducts confidential investigations, and imposes or recommends appropriate discipline. The Commission itself may admonish a judge for improper conduct, or may recommend to the state Supreme Court that the judge be censured, suspended or even removed from the bench. Occasionally, such drastic discipline is imposed—particularly where the judge has failed to respond to previous discipline.

For example, a judge who tried to hold people in contempt for critical remarks made out of court, and tried to tell the district attorney what charges to file, and told sexually offensive jokes to female attorneys in chambers, and habitually worked only until about two o'clock each afternoon, was removed from the bench and suspended from the practice of law for misconduct. *Ryan v. Commission on Judicial Performance* (1988) 45 C3d 518.

To assist the judge in court, there is a court *clerk*. The clerk receives and processes papers filed with the court, sets up a court file for each pending matter, places cases on the court's calendar (or "docket"), annotates the docket sheet during court proceedings to document actions taken, keeps minutes of any oral orders issued by the judge ("minute orders"), marks evidentiary items and maintains custody of all exhibits received in evidence, and assists the judge with written orders, judgments, and numerous other matters.

In most courts, security and order are maintained by the court *bailiff*. This officer may be a deputy sheriff, marshal, constable or other assigned peace officer. The bailiff opens the court for the judge, controls any audience, moves prisoners into and out of court, and is responsible for protecting the confidentiality of jury deliberations. Once a jury has begun its deliberations, all further communications are directed through the bailiff, until the jury returns to the courtroom with its verdict. It is improper for the bailiff to discuss the case with the jury before verdict, or to overhear their discussions, or to permit anyone else to do so. A violation of these rules may result in the reversal of a criminal conviction. *People v. Hedgecock* (1988) 201 CA3d 174.

In courts conducting felony or appellate proceedings, a verbatim transcript of all court business conducted "on the record" is made by the court *reporter*. This person is usually a certified stenographer who uses a stenographic machine to take a form of shorthand of everything said aloud by the attorneys, witnesses, judge and jurors whenever court is officially in session. The reporter may also be required to record certain closed discussions in the judge's chambers ("in camera"). The reporter's notes are later interpreted by the reporter or by a programmed computer to produce a typewritten transcript that may be read by the parties. A typical transcript excerpt is as follows:

Cross-Examination

Q: (by Mr. Curran): Officer, this detention was part of an ongoing narcotics investigation?

A: Yes

Q: Initially you're at the Capri Motel looking for a particular person?

A: Yes

Q: Were you there surveilling the motel?

A: Yes

Q: You had a particular room number that you were watching?

A: Yes. Room 108.

The court *administrator* manages the business of operating the court (facilities, personnel, finances, supplies, etc.).

A court *interpreter* is used to give verbatim translations in court when either the defendant or a witness does not speak and understand English. If both the defendant and the witness need translation services, separate interpreters must be used, since the defendant is entitled to the full-time, undivided services of his own interpreter. *People v. Baez* (1987) 195 CA3d 1431.

To assist the courts with setting bail for booked arrestees and determining which individuals will be allowed OR release ("own recognizance," meaning that the defendant is released without bail, on his word that he will appear in court as directed), the courts use a *detention-and-release officer* ("DRO"). This individual is an officer of the court—not a peace officer—who carries out court policy on detention and release of booked prisoners, in liaison with the sheriff or other jailer.

In *Riverside County v. McLaughlin* (1991) 500 US 44, the Supreme Court ruled that states must provide procedures for review by a judicial officer, within 48 hours of warrantless arrest, of the officer's statement of probable cause. This judicial officer need not necessarily be a judge or magistrate. In some counties, the PC determinations made during regular court hours are handled by magistrates at arraignment, while night, weekend and holiday determinations are made by judicially-appointed hearing officers, on the basis of written reports.

THE JURY

All *legal* questions and issues arising in a criminal prosecution are ruled on by the judge; the *factual* issues of whether a crime occurred and whether the defendant has been proven guilty of committing it are decided by the jury. In California, the jury consists of twelve jurors mutually agreed on by the prosecution and defense (jury selection procedure is discussed in Chapter 10) to try the case.

Prospective jurors are summoned for jury duty by the *jury commissioner* or, in some counties, by the judges' secretary or county clerk. Eligible persons must be citizens, age eighteen or older, with no prior felony convictions, and be possessed of ordinary intelligence, sight and hearing, able to speak and understand English. Code of Civil Procedure, § 203. To find qualified jurors, the commissioner often uses lists of licensed drivers and state ID cardholders. Prospective jurors receive a summons to report for possible duty; if they are found qualified and are not excused, their names are placed in a pool from which panelists will be called for a definite period of time.

Law enforcement officers are exempt from being called for jury service (duty). Code of Civil Procedure, § 229. Eligible citizens in other occupations have no statutory exemption. Individuals may be granted a hardship exemption if such problems as infant care, serious illness or extreme financial burden would impair their ability to serve. Code of Civil Procedure, § 204(b).

Although jury service is considered to be a civic duty of all citizens, a nominal daily allowance of $5 is paid to jurors, with mileage of 15 cents per mile. CCP § 215. Some citizens, perhaps having watched too much television, come to jury duty with expectations that their meals will be provided during their term of service, or that they will be lodged in a hotel room every night during deliberations. In most cases, however, jurors are simply reminded by the judge of their duties before the lunch break and at the end of each day, and are left to their own arrangements for food and lodging. Only rarely, when the trial has been long and costly and publicity great, will the court authorize publicly-paid meals for a deliberating jury, or order "sequestering" in a hotel during deliberations. CCP § 217.

The ability of a jury to conduct its deliberations in confidence, free of extraneous influence, is considered so important that unlawful attempts to breach the jury's independence are variously punishable. See Penal Code §§ 92, 95, 95.1, 116 and 167.

Jury duty does not necessarily end with a single trial. Some jury panels are designated for call-up service for up to one year, and have weekly report-in duty for one to three months. Frequently, a juror may serve on several trials (both civil and criminal) during a single term of jury duty.

CORRECTIONS

If a defendant is acquitted at trial, the criminal justice system is through with him. If he is convicted, the next component of the system to deal with him is corrections.

Before a convicted person is sentenced, the judge refers him to the county *probation officer* ("PO") for an investigation and sentencing report (sometimes abbreviated a "P&S" report, for "probation and sentencing"), as described in Penal Code § 1203.10. Through interviews and investigations, the probation officer determines the defendant's family history, personal background, prior record and circumstances of the present offense. Based on this information, the probation officer makes a recommendation to the judge, within a written report, as to appropriate sentencing, and as to whether or not the defendant appears to be a suitable candidate for probation.

Before the sentencing hearing, the P&S report is furnished to the prosecutor and defense attorney (or to a self-represented defendant), who will have the opportunity to comment on the report and recommendations at sentencing.

If probation is granted, the defendant is released to the probation officer's care, under specified conditions and terms (which may include a period of local incarceration before release under supervision). Standard conditions include a waiver of Fourth Amendment protection as to searches and seizures, restrictions on the possession of weapons and controlled substances, drug testing (if appropriate), and school or work scheduling. Other typical conditions might include non-association with certain individuals or groups, regular meetings with the assigned probation case officer (derivation of the popular street slang, "He's on my case."), and counseling as appropriate to the criminal misconduct involved. If a victim suffered a monetary loss, a supervised restitution payment schedule is also imposed.

In more populous counties, the probation officer is assisted by deputy probation officers, staff counselors, psychologists, social work-

California Court System

SUPREME COURT
One Chief Justice
Six Associate Justices

COURTS OF APPEAL

1st District **San Francisco**	*2nd District* **Los Angeles** **Ventura**	*3rd District* **Sacramento**
4th District **San Diego** **San Bernardino** **Santa Ana**	*5th District* **Fresno**	*6th District* **San Jose**

Superior Courts
58 - one for each county
Death penalty automatically
appealed directly to the Supreme Court

Municipal Courts   *These courts are being phased-out*   **Justice Courts**

——— Line of Appeal   – – – Line of Discretionary Review

ers, and other specialists. Per Penal Code § 830.5, probation officers and their deputies have limited peace officer status. As with police, probation officers receive certification and ongoing training, as prescribed by the Commission on Standards and Training for Corrections.

If a convicted felon is not granted probation but is sentenced to prison, he will be remanded to the custody of the Director of the *Department of Corrections* for placement within the state's correctional system. Adult facilities include prisons, camps, vocational institutions, medical facilities and the drug rehabilitation center. These institutions are staffed by medical and correctional personnel, including *correctional officers* who are 830.5 peace officers. Each prison is supervised by a *warden*. Penal Code § 2901.

(Youthful offenders are usually lodged separately from adults, in facilities of the California Youth Authority. See Chapter 14.)

Prisoners who have served a specified portion of their commitments (usually, one-half the total sentence imposed), and who have maintained a record of good behavior and work or training, are subject to early release (parole) from correctional confinement. Decisions on parole eligibility are made by the *Board of Prison Terms*, as set forth in Penal Code § 3000.

Paroled prisoners are released into the community under the supervision of a *parole officer* (another "PO," also an 830.5 peace officer). Conditions of parole are similar to standard probation conditions, and special conditions may be tailored to the offender. A parolee remains on supervised parole for one year, in most cases, and is subject to reimprisonment for one year (not his unserved balance) if he violates the conditions of parole. See Penal Code § 3057.

SUMMARY

√   Crimes against the *person* and crimes against *property* are two categories of crimes victimizing identifiable individuals. So-called "victimless" crimes are viewed as victimizing the state.

√   Any person with relevant knowledge bearing on the defendant's guilt or innocence might be a trial witness, whether or not s/he was a victim or eyewitness.

√   California uses the generic term "peace officer," as defined in Penal Code § 830 et seq., to include police, sheriff, marshal, constable, Highway Patrol, and other officers. These officers are certified and trained under criteria established by the Commission on Peace Officer Standards and Training (POST).

√   Responsibility for investigation of the cause and circumstances of deaths is on the county *coroner*, who may convene a citizen jury, or a *coroner's inquest,* into the circumstances of a death.

√   Investigation of crime and of local government is conducted by the *grand jury*, which may charge a suspected criminal by *indictment*. Grand jury proceedings are strictly secret.

√   Prosecution may be pressed by the city attorney, district attorney or Attorney General, and their deputies and assistants.

√   The Sixth Amendment guarantees criminal defendants a right to the assistance of an attorney for their defense; indigent defendants are entitled to an appointed attorney under the Sixth Amendment only if a punishment of incarceration is imposed, but are allowed appointed counsel in California for any misdemeanor or felony charge.

√   A defendant has a right to represent himself, if he is competent to do so.

√   Assistance to counsel requires *effective* representation, to satisfy the Sixth Amendment.

√   A defense attorney has an ethical obligation not to conceal fruits or instrumentalities of the crime that come into his or her possession, nor to knowingly assist a defendant in presenting perjurious testimony in court.

√   Five kinds of state court in California are the justice court, municipal court, superior court, court of appeal, and supreme court.

√   Where existent, justice and municipal courts have jurisdiction of misdemeanor cases; elsewhere, superior courts have jurisdiction. In all counties, superior courts have felony trial jurisdiction.

√   To assist in adjudication of some cases, courts appoint commissioners, referees, judges pro tem, and judicial hearing officers.

√   Other judicial personnel may include the bailiff, clerk, reporter, interpreter, administrator and detention-release officer.

√   Jury panels are called by the jury commissioner. A person is not qualified to be a juror if s/he is not a citizen, does not speak English, has seriously impaired vision or hearing, or is a convicted felon.

√   Corrections personnel include the probation officer, correctional officers, and parole officers. Sentenced prisoners must serve at least one-half of their terms before receiving a one-year parole period, subject to a one-year reimprisonment (some exceptions). Paroles are set by the Board of Prison Terms.

ISSUES FOR DISCUSSION

1. Does the state really have any right to prohibit the kinds of activity referred to as "victimless crimes?" Why or why not? How does the "social contract" theory enter into this question?

2. In some countries, such as Australia, there is a national police force. This eliminates jurisdictional problems, duplication of efforts, and lack of uniformity. Would such a system work in the US? Why or why not?

3. Is too much discretion vested in the prosecutor to determine which cases get charged and which do not? Should victims have greater input? How could the latter work?

4. Does it make sense for the taxpayers to pay for both the attorney who is prosecuting the accused and the attorney who is defending him? Why?

5. Are juries, made up of citizens with no legal training and no demonstrated expertise at judging credibility or factual disputes, really the best means we have of resolving important criminal justice issues? What might be better? Should all jurors have to pass some sort of examination?

CHAPTER 4

INVESTIGATION AND ARREST PROCEDURE

Learning Goals: After studying this chapter, you will be able to correctly answer the following questions:

√   What is the typical organizational structure of a law enforcement agency?

√   What are the various sources of information used for the detection of crime?

√   What are the investigative guidelines on interrogation of criminal suspects?

√   What are the principles of collection and analysis of physical evidence?

√   How many procedures are there for obtaining an eyewitness identification of a suspect? What rules must officers follow in ID procedures?

√   What powers of arrest do police have?

√   What procedure is followed on completion of an investigation to initiate court proceedings?

POLICE DEPARTMENT ORGANIZATION

Law enforcement agencies, whether a police, sheriff, marshal, Highway Patrol or other specialized force (generically referred to as "police," for the sake of brevity), are generally organized according to their various missions, and according to size. In smaller agencies, all officers routinely perform all sorts of police functions, while in larger departments, assignments may be more specialized.

A basic structural subdivision includes command, patrol, traffic, investigation and support services. Depending, again, on size of the force of sworn peace officers, the command structure may be layered from chief through deputy chiefs, to captains, lieutenants, sergeants, corporals, and then to rank-and-file officers. The largest agencies include division commander, area commanders and assistant chiefs, while smaller agencies may simply consist of the sheriff and two deputies, or the chief and three officers, etc. If the agency is large enough to be subdivided, the breakdown is typically as follows.

The *command* officers will normally have been selected on the basis of experience, education, scoring on a written promotional exam, and performance on an "oral board" (an oral interview by a panel of seniors, sometimes conducted by an outside "assessment center," including officials from neighboring agencies—an attempt to eliminate subjective judgments or favoritism). Qualified candidates are numerically rated on a promotional list, and are promoted, in order, as vacancies occur. New lists may be established once a year (or more or less frequently), or after the old list is exhausted.

New command officers are usually sent to a leadership course or seminar appropriate to their command level. At such courses, management experts and veteran commanders teach such subjects as leadership, personnel matters, employee evaluations, discipline and control, team building, workload management, civil liability, administrative reports, and legal updates. Following the course, the new commander will typically serve a one-year probation in his or her new position. Newer commanders may get last choice of available assignments; thus, a detective who gets promoted to sergeant may find himself returning to uniformed patrol operations, supervising the midnight shift, until he establishes greater seniority in the sergeant ranks. (This prospect sometimes deters highly-qualified investigators from applying for promotion.)

In most municipal operations, the *patrol* division will be the largest component of the force. Patrol officers are uniformed men and women who are assigned to a given district (or "beat"), patrolling in marked police vehicles. These are the officers who have most of the public contact, take most of the initial crime reports, make most of the arrests based on observation, and answer calls for assistance from citizens. To insure round-the-clock police service, patrol is divided into three or more overlapping shifts, with variable days off for shift personnel.

Officers will typically spend several years on patrol assignment before qualifying for specialized assignments in other divisions. However, some officers choose to become career patrol officers, preferring the spontaneity, the variety, the close public contact and the "action" of patrol to "desk" work, or other assignments.

The *investigation* bureau is composed of experienced officers, normally working plainclothes and using unmarked cars, who do the follow-up investigations of cases initiated by other branches of the department. Through their networks of informants ("snitches") and contacts with officers of other agencies, investigators also initiate many cases themselves. When patrol or traffic officers are unable to "close" a case expeditiously with an arrest, the case is passed on to the bureau for the painstaking, systematic exploration of leads to help solve the case and, if possible, to identify and arrest the suspect and present the case for formal charging in court. Assignment to a particular detail (homicides, vice, narcotics, property crimes, etc.) allows an officer to become a skilled specialist in that particular field and increases the overall efficiency of the department.

The *traffic* division may include both motorcycle officers ("motors"), radar-equipped patrol cars, and accident investigators. These officers are specialists in the traffic laws, motor vehicle equipment and safety laws, and the investigation and "reconstruction" of traffic collisions. Size permitting, the traffic division may include a special enforcement team for driving under the influence.

Although the public frequently think that traffic officers issue citations under a "quota" system, this is not the case. Vehicle Code § 41602 prohibits the use of a quota system by any law enforcement agency, and § 41603 precludes reliance on an officer's citation totals for promotion or discipline, except in combination with other factors.

Administrative *support services* may include internal personnel, payroll and routine administration functions, as well as training, communications, crime lab, and internal affairs which investigates allegations of police misconduct within the department. Assignment to internal affairs division ("IAD") is rarely ever sought on a voluntary basis, for it pits officer against fellow officer. And while the overwhelming majority of allegations of misconduct are found to be unsupported, the prospect of one officer investigating another can present an emotional and troublesome conflict for both officers in an organization where team effort and esprit de corps are literally life-and-death matters. Still, most police agencies would prefer to police their own, rather than allowing the intrusion of an outside "review board" or other agency looking into complaints and allegations.

CRIME DETECTION

Information about criminal activity comes from a variety of sources. The three primary ways such information reaches police are *reports* from victims and witnesses, *observations* by patrolling officers, and *informant* tips.

When citizens discover that they have been victimized by criminals, their automatic reaction is to reach for the telephone and call the police. Responding patrol officers determine whether or not a crime has in fact been committed and whether a suspect can be readily identified.

Depending on the nature of the crime, patrol officers may take all statements and collect any physical evidence themselves, or they may simply stabilize the scene and summon technicians, detectives or other specialists to assume the investigation. Basic procedures, such as photography, measurements and fingerprinting, are often performed by a *crime scene investigation* ("CSI") officer; more extensive investigation falls to the detective bureau.

Many crimes come to light through the observations of vigilant officers. Police on night patrol may spot a burglary in progress, for example, or may identify narcotics and weapons offenses through routine contacts with pedestrians and motorists. Experienced officers develop a skill at noticing suspicious factors that may warrant a temporary detention of individuals, during the course of which additional information may be established, often leading to search and arrest.

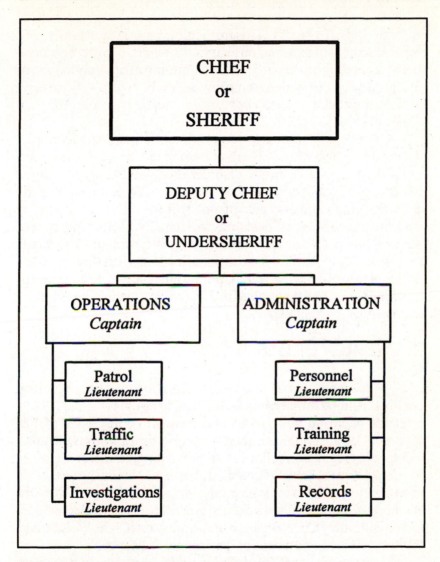

Typical law enforcement agency organization chart.

Informants also supply leads to the detection and solution of crimes. These individuals may be concerned citizens, anonymous tipsters, grudge informants (such as spouses, girlfriends or angry confederates), or confidential informants ("CI") who provide information to police for pay, or for leniency in their own criminal cases (known as "working off a beef"). Tips from informants are generally less-reliable sources of information than victim reports or officer observations; depending on the circumstances, informant tips may have to be independently corroborated somehow before they will justify intrusive police action (such as a search or arrest). See, for example, *Illinois v. Gates* (1983) 462 US 213.

Occasionally, the detection of crime will result inadvertently during the process of non-investigative police activity. For instance, police response to domestic disorder complaints may reveal the presence of narcotics or illegal weapons inside a home; fire suppression activities may yield evidence of arson; or the rescue of attempted suicides or drug overdose cases may incidentally disclose evidence of criminal conduct. Alert police officers, originally summoned for assistance in traffic collisions, medical aid situations, disturbances of the peace, landlord-tenant disputes, public nuisances, and a variety of other calls, may find themselves making arrests and seizing evidence unrelated to the original activity.

IS THERE A CRIME?

Whatever the initial source of information to police regarding possible criminal activity, how do officers determine whether or not a crime has occurred, and if so, what crime it is? As discussed earlier (Chapter 1), California has no common-law crimes. Unless a statute, ordinance or regulation defines a crime in writing, "no act or omission is criminal or punishable" (Penal Code § 6). This obviously means that investigating officers must be trained in the knowledge of literally hundreds of criminal offenses defined in the Penal Code, Vehicle Code, Health and Safety Code, Business and Professions Code, Welfare and Institutions Code, and municipal and county ordinances.

Every provision of law defining a crime contains two or more "elements" which must be present to constitute the offense. Thus, the officer must not only be aware that there *is* a particular crime relating to certain behavior, he must also be familiar with all of the requisite *elements* of that crime. Every citizen is aware that there is a crime of *burglary*, but few of them know the statutory elements (in fact, many burglary victims incorrectly report that they have been robbed); the public commonly think of *assault and battery* as a single offense, when they actually are two separate crimes. Unlike the uninformed citizen, the police officer must be able to determine, usually without reference to the statute books, whether or not a particular set of circumstances amount to criminal conduct.

To meet this need, police officers train many long hours during academies, in-service schools, and continuing education courses on the identification of crimes and their elements. The more commonly-committed offenses are memorized, and abbreviated codes are usually carried in the officer's field briefcase for quick reference as to less-common crimes. In addition, every written crime report, and every booking slip, serve as exercises in covering the elements of the identified crime; if an officer neglects to include an essential element in her report or booking slip, the supervisor, jailer or prosecutor may reject the item as incomplete.

So before an officer takes a crime report or makes an arrest, he will review either a mental checklist of memorized elements, or a written code section, to ascertain the commission or attempted commission of a specific offense. If in doubt, the officer may consult a supervisor or more experienced fellow officer for advice. If the available evidence fails to indicate the existence of all elements of an identifiable statutory crime, no enforcement action can be taken, despite the fact that the complaining citizen may have been treated unfairly by someone, or that an individual may have acted in a socially-unacceptable or offensive manner, or that some damage or injury may have been inflicted. It is the police officer's duty to distinguish between apparent crimes and noncriminal behavior that is merely rude, negligent or tortious (creating a civil wrong) in nature.

TESTIMONIAL EVIDENCE

All of the evidence presented in court in the trial of a criminal case will fall into one of three categories—*testimonial evidence* (the verbal statements and testimony of witnesses), *confession evidence* (statements made by the defendant that can be used to show his guilt), or *physical evidence* (tangible items that can be shown to the jury and examined by them for any evidentiary value). Any given case may or may not involve confession or physical evidence, but every case will depend, to a greater or lesser degree, on the testimony of witnesses.

Knowing the importance of testimonial evidence, the investigating police officer tries in every case to ascertain whether there are witnesses, to identify them, to interview them, and to preserve their statements as evidence in the case. And contrary to the popular misconception, "witness" does not merely mean an "eyewitness" to the actual commission of the crime. A person could become a potential *trial* witness without having seen the crime or even knowing of its commission. For example, such people as the custodians of bank records or telephone records, treating physicians, neighbors, laboratory personnel, psychiatrists or relatives of the accused might be called as witnesses, despite the fact that they have no firsthand knowledge as to who committed the crime.

In putting together a case, the police officer contacts and attempts to interview not only the crime victims and eyewitnesses, but also anyone else who might have relevant information about the planning of the crime such as information on the preparatory steps taken, the approach to the crime scene, presence at or near the scene, the getaway, the cover-up, the disposal of stolen property or dead bodies, etc. The officer also is concerned with collection, preservation, analysis and interpretation of physical evidence, anyone who overheard any incriminating statements made by the accused, and the presence or absence of any facts tending to establish a defense to the crime, among others. If the officer determines that a person may be a potential witness, she conducts either a *field interview* or a *stationhouse interview* of the witness to identify relevant information.

An interview of a witness generally follows one of two basic approaches. If the witness seems to be hostile to police and friendly to a suspected perpetrator, the interview will have many of the same characteristics as a cross-examination in court, including leading questions, a skeptical tone, a demand for explanations of inconsistencies, and a probing pursuit of small details that could not be quickly or easily fabricated. If the interview is not recorded on audio or video equipment, the hostile witness is *quoted* exactly (and frequently) in the written report of the witness's statement.

A witness who appears to be friendly to the victim and helpful to the police, on the other hand, is *not* influenced with leading questions, but is interviewed in a more objective, open-ended fashion ("What happened? How do you know? What did you see? What did you hear?"). With this witness, quotations are used sparingly in the written report.

In both kinds of interviews, the witness is separated from others (especially from the suspect and victim), so that the witness will give his or her independent account, uninfluenced and uninterrupted by others. With both kinds of witnesses, the careful officer avoids "translating" the statement into his own words, or recording what he *thinks* the witness *meant* to say. Reported statements will invariably be compared with courtroom testimony for consistency or inconsistency, and the lawyer with the most to benefit from this comparison will argue it forcefully to the jury in attacking, or supporting, the witness's credibility.

A thorough and complete criminal investigation will include reports of the interviews with all identified witnesses—both those who might appear to be potential prosecution witnesses, and those who seem favorable to the defense. The report should show the date, time, place and length of the interview, as well as a summary (if not recorded) of the essential information. To be most useful, this report should be factual and explanatory—not conclusionary or vague.

If a suspect is identified, arrested and charged, the prosecutor will use the witness reports as a basis for planning the presentation of the case in court. Where additional information is needed, the prosecutor may conduct further interviews herself, or may ask police or district attorney investigators to obtain further statements. In most cases, however, the accounts of witness statements contained in the police officer's crime and arrest reports will be expected to be sufficiently accurate and complete to make extensive re-interviews unnecessary.

CONFESSION EVIDENCE

Although the statements of all persons who may be potential witnesses are important to obtain and record, no category of evidence is more critical than the suspect's own statements. For while other witnesses may be disbelieved by a jury, whether due to bias, perception difficulties, poor memories, inconsistent statements or unconvincing performance on the witness stand, the incriminating statements of the defendant himself are rarely ever discredited by the jury. As numerous justices of the US Supreme Court have repeatedly observed, confession evidence will do more to convict a guilty defendant than either of the two other forms:

The defendant's own confession is probably the most probative and damaging evidence that can be admitted against him.

> *Bruton v. US* (1968) 391 US 123, 139
> (White dissenting.)

Admissions of guilt are more than merely desirable; they are essential to society's compelling interest in finding, convicting, and punishing those who violate the law.

> *Moran v. Burbine* (1986) 475 US 412

Triers of fact accord confessions such heavy weight in their determinations that the introduction of a confession makes the other aspects of a trial in court superfluous, and the real trial, for all practical purposes, occurs when the confession is obtained. No other class of evidence is so profoundly prejudicial.

> *Colorado v. Connelly* (1986) 479 US 157,182
> (Brennan dissenting.)

The relatively-greater convincing force of the suspect's own words connecting him with the crime makes it of paramount importance that officers attempt—in *every* kind of case, whether driving under the influence, shoplifting, rape or murder — to obtain some sort of statement from the suspect. If possible, a full *confession* should be taken. This would include an *admission as to every element of the crime*, and statements negating any legal defense. Where a complete confession cannot be obtained, officers should try for as many admissions as the suspect will make. And as a last resort (and far preferable to nothing at all), the police should ask the suspect to elaborate in detail on his denial, alibi, or other asserted defense or exculpatory (negating guilt) statements. If these can be shown to be false, they can be very damaging to the defendant as evidence of "consciousness of guilt".

Great care must be taken by investigative officers in the timing and techniques used in the interrogation of suspects, so as not to render any resulting statements inadmissible in court. A series of US Supreme Court decisions have defined four separate and distinct constitutional "exclusionary rules" applicable to confession evidence. If a suspect's statements were obtained in violation of the guidelines for any one of these constitutional rules, the statements may be excluded from trial— even though they may be true, and even though they are highly relevant.

The court long ago decided that the only effective way to enforce certain constitutional protections was to exclude from a defendant's trial any incriminating evidence the state obtained only by violating the defendant's rights. The manner in which police obtain a suspect's statement may implicate any of four constitutional amendments, each of which carries its own exclusionary remedy.

The *Fourth Amendment* forbids unreasonable searches and seizures. If the court rules that the acquisition of evidence was itself, or resulted from, an unreasonable search or seizure, the evidence is subject to suppression under the Fourth Amendment exclusionary rule. This holding dates to *Weeks v. US* (1913) 232 US 383, made applicable to the states in *Mapp v. Ohio* (1961) 367 US 643. The California Supreme Court has decided that the suppression of evidence from a trial in a California court due to allegedly-unreasonable search or seizure is to be governed by US Supreme Court rulings that apply the Fourth Amendment exclusionary rule. See *In re Lance W.* (1985) 37 C3d 873.

In *Wong Sun v. US* (1963) 371 US 471, the Supreme Court held that where a suspect's statement is obtained by "exploitation" of an illegal arrest, the statement is "fruit of the poison tree" (sometimes called "derivative evidence"), and is inadmissible under the Fourth Amendment exclusionary rule (except as possible impeachment evidence). And in *Dunaway v. New York* (1979) 442 US 200, the court held that a *Miranda* warning and waiver cannot be used by police to purge or "attenuate" the taint of an unreasonable search or seizure.

Together, the holdings of *Wong Sun* and *Dunaway* make it extremely important that police remain aware of, and in compliance with, the changing rules of search and seizure. For if the court should find that a suspect's statements had been obtained by exploitation of an unlawful *search, entry, detention* or *arrest*, the Fourth Amendment exclusionary rule may devour "the most probative and damaging evidence" of the defendant's guilt, and not even a *Miranda* waiver can save it. (Discussion of the mechanics of the suppression hearing is covered in Chapter 7.)

A *Fifth Amendment* exclusionary remedy was created by the Supreme Court in the well-known (though not well-understood)

"Miranda decision," *Miranda v. Arizona* (1966) 384 US 436. The court reasoned that a person taken into custody by police would be subjected to substantial mental pressures, just from the mere fact of the custodial restraints. When the additional pressures of police interrogation were added to the pressures inherent in custodial surroundings, the individual's ability to exercise his free will would presumptively be overcome, and he would be *compelled* by this coercive combination to make incriminating responses he might otherwise have chosen not to make. Since the Fifth Amendment forbids *compelled* self-incrimination, the use of such statements at trial would be unconstitutional.

To counterbalance the inherent compulsion thought to exist in the process of custodial interrogation, the Supreme Court devised the warning-and-waiver scheme now familiar to every television viewer. The court majority (*Miranda* was a 5-4 opinion) decided that the overbearing pressure of custodial interrogation could be neutralized by reminding the suspect of his right to remain silent, alerting him to the courtroom consequences of his decision to speak, and offering the free assistance of an attorney to advise him. Any statement or answers the suspect gave after this admonition of rights would then appear to be voluntary, and not compelled, and thus admissible in court without violating the Fifth Amendment.

In *People v. May* (1988) 44 C3d 309, the California Supreme court ruled that Proposition 8 required California courts to follow US Supreme Court decisions interpreting "rights to counsel and rights against self-incrimination." This development meant a radical departure from previous California decisions based on the "independent state grounds" of the state constitution.

These state decisions had extended the *Miranda* requirements to impose a duty to admonish suspects before questioning in *noncustodial* circumstances, on the basis of such factors as location of the interrogation, nature of the questioning (whether "accusatory" or "investigative"), whether or not suspicion had "focused" on the person being interrogated, and whether or not the suspect was no longer free to leave (i.e., being detained). See, for example, *People v. Herdan* (1974) 42 CA3d 300, 306.

By contrast, the US Supreme Court has ruled that police questioning need be preceded by *Miranda* warnings only where there has been "a formal arrest or restraint on freedom of movement of the degree associated with a formal arrest." *California v. Beheler* (1983)

463 US 1121, 1125. The High Court has rejected the notion that *Miranda* is triggered by location of the interrogation [*Oregon v. Mathiason* (1977) 429 US 492], or by the nature of the questioning [*Schneckloth v. Bustamonte* (1973) 412 US 218], or by the "focus" of suspicion [*Beckwith v. US* (1976) 426 US 341]; *Stansbury v. California* (1994) 511 US 318, or by the fact of detention [*Berkemer v. McCarty* (1984) 468 US 420]. Instead, under the US Supreme Court holdings, police questioning requires *Miranda* compliance only where the suspect is subjected to the "functional equivalent of formal arrest" (*Berkemer*, at 442).

If police questioning of a custodial suspect proceeds without *Miranda* compliance, any resulting statements he may make are inadmissible at his trial, except as impeachment or rebuttal evidence to his inconsistent testimony. *Harris v. New York* (1971) 401 US 222; *People v. May* (1988) 44 C3d 309. An exception to the *Miranda* rule applies in cases of imminent threat to the public safety or officer safety. If prompt, unwarned questioning of an arrestee may protect officers or others from the dangers of concealed firearms, explosives, hostile assailants or other potential safety threats, *Miranda* does not apply until critical information has been obtained and the questions turn to crime investigation. *New York v. Quarles* (1981) 467 US 647; *People v. West* (1980) 107 CA3d 987.

The *Sixth Amendment* exclusionary rule concerns the right of counsel. The Constitution guarantees every "accused" person the assistance of an attorney, beginning with the first court appearance, or the filing of an indictment or information, whichever occurs first. *US v. Gouveia* (1984) 467 US 180. Once this constitutional right to counsel has *attached* by formal court proceedings *and* the defendant has *asserted* the right by hiring or requesting appointment of an attorney, police may no longer deliberately elicit incriminating statements from the accused in the absence of his lawyer. *Massiah v. US* (1964) 377 US 201; *Michigan v. Jackson* (1966) 475 US 625.

This so-called "Massiah rule" is not violated where the defendant himself initiates discussions and waives his right to counsel [*Patterson v. Illinois* (1988) 108 S. Ct 2389]; nor where police question a suspect about an *uncharged* case [*Maine v. Moulton* (1985) 474 US 159], even though an attorney-client relationship may exist between the suspect and his lawyer at the time of questioning [*Moran v. Burbine* (1986) 475 US 412]. Any statements obtained by police in violation of the right to counsel are inadmissible in the prosecution case-in-chief; as with *Miranda*-violative statements, Massiah-violative statements are admissible for impeachment or rebuttal of the defendant's contrary testimony. *Michigan v. Harvey* (1990) 110 S. Ct 1176.

A body of *Fourteenth Amendment* exclusionary case law governs the admission of a suspect's statements claimed to be involuntary. Beginning with *Brown v. Mississippi* (1936) 297 US 278, the Supreme Court has held in a long line of decisions that the Fourteenth Amendment "due process" clause prohibits any courtroom use of involuntary statements. Not only are such statements considered inherently untrustworthy, but coercive police procedures employed to obtain involuntary statements are deemed offensive to the notion of due process. The courts will thus exclude any statements obtained from a suspect with severely impaired capacity (such as through mental retardation, physical exhaustion from lack of rest during prolonged interrogation, influence of hallucinogenic drugs, or traumatic injury), if police used coercive interrogation techniques against the impaired suspect. *Mincey v. Arizona* (1978) 437 US 385; *Colorado v. Connelly* (1987) 479 US 157. And even with a rational, unimpaired suspect of ordinary intelligence, police use of threats, force, or promises of leniency, "express or implied, however slight," may render a statement involuntary as a matter of law, and inadmissible under the Fourteenth Amendment due process clause. *Jackson v. Denno* (1964) 378 US 368.

Because the criminal defense attorney knows how devastating his client's admissions of guilt will be with the jury, he will examine very closely the circumstances under which police obtained the admissions. It is almost inevitable that every confession will be challenged by the defense in court, on grounds of violation of either the Fourth, Fifth, Sixth or Fourteenth Amendments, or some combination of these. Police interrogation procedure must obviously comply with all of these constitutional guidelines if the defendant's damaging statements are to be admissible as proof of his guilt. (See **Interrogation Checklist**, below.)

Ideally, a suspect's confession should be *videotaped*, and if possible, should include a video reenactment. Next best, the interrogation should be preserved on *audio* cassette. Less preferable as evidence would be a signed, *written* confession, in the suspect's handwriting. And least desirable, from the standpoint of courtroom proof, would be an officer's testimony relating the defendant's *oral* admissions.

Although an appellate decision, in *People v. Jones* (1983) 145 CA3d 751, once held that police officers were required to retain and preserve rough notes of their interviews with suspects for defense discovery, that decision was subsequently overruled in *People v. Tierce* (1985) 165 CA3d 256. *Tierce* held that *Jones* conflicted with the federal rule on preservation of rough notes, and that Proposition 8 compelled adherence to the federal guideline, set forth in *Killian v. US* (1961) 368 US 231, that rough notes could be destroyed once the data was incorporated into the formal report. If an officer's rough notes are still in existence when California *statutory* discovery is triggered (see Chapter 7), those notes become subject to disclosure and thereafter cannot be destroyed. *Thompson v. Superior Court* (1997) 53 CA4th 480.

INTERROGATION CHECKLIST

- Fourth Amendment (*Wong Sun*, etc.) Statements are *not* admissible if they result from *any* unreasonable...

  - Detention

  - Arrest

  - Search

  - Entry

- Fifth Amendment (*Miranda*, etc.) Warning and waiver is required with...

  - Custody (arrest or functional equivalent), and

  - Interrogation (questioning or functional equivalent)

- No warnings are required for...

  - Public/officer safety questions

- Detainees under "focus" of suspicion

- Voluntary station house interviews

● Sixth Amendment (*Massiah*, etc.) Police may not elicit statement if the right to counsel is...

- Attached (by arraignment or formal charge), and

- Asserted (by suspect's obtaining or requesting counsel)

● No violation occurs if...

- Suspect initiates discussions and waives counsel, or

- Interrogation relates to uncharged cases

● Fourteenth Amendment (*Brown*, etc.) Due process precludes use of involuntary statements from...

- Coercive questioning of severely impaired suspect, or

- Use of force, threats, or promises of leniency

PHYSICAL EVIDENCE

Items of physical evidence—such as weapons, narcotics, currency, fingerprints, fibers, fluids, documents and stolen property—are sought by police, as contraband, instrumentalities or fruits of the crime, to establish how the crime occurred, and who committed it. Much of the physical evidence associated with many kinds of crimes is known as "transfer evidence;" when the defendant was committing the crime at the crime scene, physical evidence may have been transferred *from* him to the scene or the victim, and other evidence may have been transferred *to* him.

For example, the burglar who shattered a window glass may have left his blood or tissue on the window pane, and may have picked up tiny glass fragments in his shoe soles or trouser cuffs. Or the rapist may have transferred semen and pubic hairs to his victim, at the same time that the victim's hair follicles were transferred to him. The thief who transferred his victim's stolen property to himself may have carelessly transferred his own fingerprints onto nearby objects. If scientific examination can match evidence transferred between the suspect and the crime scene, this can be powerfully incriminating circumstantial evidence of the suspect's guilt.

In order to identify, collect and preserve physical evidence, the investigating officer must be familiar with the *kinds* of evidence normally associated with specific crimes, the *places* where such evidence may be found, the *techniques* for logging, photographing, measuring, collecting and packaging various kinds of evidence, and the *procedures* for maintaining control of the custody of the evidence until it reaches the courtroom. Any errors in the collection, analysis or preservation of the evidence may be grounds for its exclusion from the trial.

For instance, a gunshot residue test sequence performed in the wrong order will give distorted results; a blood-alcohol sample placed in a glass vial without an anticoagulant agent will be useless; certain kinds of biological evidence must be kept in paper containers, while others require airtight plastic; some specimens must be stored at room temperature, and others must be frozen; identifying markings should be placed on all items or their containers, but should not obscure or destroy evidentiary characteristics; a "chain of custody" of collected items must be maintained (usually by written record on an evidence label) to disprove any tampering, alteration or substitution between collection and court; and when two or more officers or technicians are involved in collecting and analyzing evidence, each must be prepared to testify to the particular steps he or she took, and in what order.

Not only must police officers be highly trained in the *scientific* techniques of evidence collection, they must also be versed in the *legal* restrictions imposed on evidence acquisition by state and federal statute, and by the Fourth Amendment to the US Constitution. In the area of electronic surveillance, for example, officers must abide by provisions of California Penal Code §§ 29 through 636, as well as Title 18 of the US Code; voice prints are controlled by Penal Code § 637.3, and polygraph ("lie detector") examination by § 637.4; even the use of radar to obtain evidence of speeding violations is subject to the restrictions of Vehicle Code § 40802.

And whether or not statutory controls govern particular evidence acquisition, the Fourth Amendment prohibition of unreasonable searches and seizures is always present as a check on police practices that may infringe a suspect's possessory or privacy interests. As previously noted, the Fourth Amendment exclusionary rule bars admission in the prosecution case-in-chief of any evidence obtained through exploitation of an unreasonable search or seizure. This is not to say that police are bound by the Fourth Amendment in all acquisitions of evidence, but only those resulting from a "search" or a "seizure," as those terms have been defined by the Supreme Court:

> A "search" occurs when an expectation of privacy that society is prepared to consider reasonable is infringed. A "seizure" of property occurs when there is some meaningful interference with an individual's possessory interests in that property.
> *US v. Jacobsen* (1984) 466 US 109, 113.

> ...a person has been "seized" within the meaning of the Fourth Amendment only if, in view of all of the circumstances surrounding the incident, a reasonable person would have believed that he was not free to leave.
> *US v. Mendenhall* (1980) 446 US 544, 554.

Under these definitions, the collection and inspection of *abandoned property* by police is not subject to the Fourth Amendment. By definition, "abandoned property" would not support any legitimate expectation of privacy or any claimed possessory interest. *California v. Greenwood* (1988) 100 L Ed 2d 30; *People v. Patrick* (1982) 135 CA3d 290.

Likewise, evidence obtained through a *consensual encounter* between police and a citizen, involving no commands or official pressures on the citizen to remain or to respond, would not be governed by the Fourth Amendment. *Florida v. Royer* (1983) 460 US 491; *Wilson v. Superior Court* (1983) 34 C3d 777.

It has also been held that a person's *exposed characteristics* enjoy no protectible expectation of privacy, provided no unlawful search or seizure created the occasion for their collection. Such evidence includes handwriting exemplars [*US v. Euge* (1980) 444 US

707; *People v. Paine* (1973) 33 CA3d 1048], voice exemplars [*US v. Dionisio* (1973) 410 US 1], fingerprints [*Schmerber v. California* (1966) 384 US 757; *Perkey v. DMV* (1986) 42 C3d 185], and photographs of the face or person [*US v. Crews* (1980) 445 US 463; *People v. Mayoff* (1986) 42 C3d 1302].

Beyond these categories of "non-search" activities, the US Supreme Court has interpreted the Fourth Amendment as requiring that police searches and seizures be conducted with a judicially-authorized *search warrant*. The court noted, in *Katz v. US* (1967) 389 US 347, 257, that warrantless searches are "*per se* unreasonable," subject to certain approved exceptions. Although extended discussion of the many search warrant exceptions would be beyond the scope of an overview of investigation and arrest procedures, the following list contains the most common exceptions, and citations to leading US Supreme Court and/or California cases interpreting these exceptions:

Arrests. *US v. Watson* (1976) 423 US 411; *People v. Rios* (1956) 46 C3d 297.

Border Inspection. *US v. de Hernandez* (1985) 473 US 531; *People v. Matthews* (1980) 112 CA3d 11.

Consent. *US v. Watson* (1976) 423 US 411; *People v. Ratliff* (1986) 41 C3d 675.

Controlled Delivery. *Illinois v. Andreas (1983) 463 US 765*; *People v. Hampton* (1981) 115 A3d 515.

Detentions. *US v. Mendenhall* (1980) 446 US 544; *In re James D.* (1987) 43 C3d 903.

Evidence Destruction. *Ker v. California* (1963) 374 US 23; *People v. Johnson* (1981) 123 CA3d Supp. 26.

Fleeting Targets. *US v. Ross* (1982) 456 US 798; *People v. Chavers* (1983) 33 C3d 462.

Hot Pursuit. *US v. Santana* (1976) 427 US 38; *People v. Escudero* (1979) 23 C3d 800.

Instrumentality. *Cardwell v. Lewis* (1974) 417 US 583; *People v. Rogers* (1978) 21 C3d 542.

Inventory. *Illinois v. Lafayette* (1983) 462 US 640; *People v. Burch* (1987) 188 CA3d 172.

Jail/Prison. *Block v. Rutherford* (1984) 468 US 576; *People v. West* (1985) 170 CA3d 326.

Officer Safety. *Terry v. Ohio* (1968) 392 US 1; *People v. Williams* (1988) 45 C3d 1268.

Open Fields. *Oliver v. US* (1984) 466 US 170; *People v. Dumas* (1973) 9 C3d 871.

Plain Feel. *Minnesota v. Dickerson* (1993) 508 US 366; *People v. Chavers* (1983) 33 C3d 462.

Plain Shape. *Henry v. US* (1959) 361 US 98; *People v. Green* (1981) 115 CA3d 259.

Plain Smell. *US v. Place* (1983) 462 US 696; *People v. Cook* (1985) 16 C3d 663.

Plain View. *Harris v. US* (1968) 390 US 234; *People v. Kilpatrick* (1980) 105 CA3d 401.

Private Conduct. *Walter v. US* (1980) 447 US 649; *People v. Yackee* (1984) 161 CA3d 843.

Probation/Parole. *Griffin v. Wisconsin* (1987) 483 US 868; *People v. Bravo* (1987) 43 C3d 600.

Property Protection. *Michigan v. Tyler* (1978) 436 US 499; *People v. Duncan* (1986) 42 C3d 91.

Public Records. *US v. Miller* (1976) 425 US 435; *People v. Pearson* (1985) 169 CA3d 319.

Protective Sweep. *Maryland v. Buie* (1990) USLW 4281; *Tamborino v. Superior Court* (1986) 41 C3d 919.

Public Safety. *Cady v. Dumbrowski* (1973) 413 US 433; *People v. Superior Court* (1970) 6 CA3d 379.

Regulatory Inspection. *New York v. Burger* (1987) 482 US 691; *People v. Shope* (1982) 128 CA3d 816.

Rescue. *Warden v. Hayden* (1967) 387 US 294; *People v. Brown* (1970) 12 CA3d 600.

School Search. *New Jersey v. TLO* (1985) 469 US 325; *In re William G.* (1985) 40 C3d 550.

Search Incident to Arrest. *New York v. Belton* (1981) 453 US 454; *People v. Fay* (1986) 184 CA3d 882.

Work Inspection. *O'Connor v. Ortega* (1987) 480 US 709; *Tucker v. Superior Court* (1978) 84 CA3d 43.

If search-and-seizure activity does not fit within any of the established exceptions, or if an error occurred in the manner or timing of a search, the evidence may nevertheless remain admissible in court under one of the following doctrines:

Attenuated Taint. (Intervening acts overrode the causal connection between Fourth Amendment error and production of the disputed evidence.) *Segura v. US* (1984) 468 US 796; *People v. Cella* (1983) 139 CA3d 391.

Auxiliary Use. (Evidence inadmissible in the case-in-chief due to Fourth Amendment error may still be admitted for impeachment or rebuttal, at sentencing hearings, during probation/parole revocation proceedings, or in federal deportation hearings.) *US v. Havens* (1980) 446 US 620; *People v. Harrison* (1988) 199 CA3d 803.

Good Faith. (Objectively reasonable reliance by an officer on a flawed warrant, statute, probation condition, consent to search, or description of premises or persons does not mandate suppression of resulting evidence.) *US v. Leon* (1984) 468 US 897; *People v. Barbarick* (1985) 168 CA3d 731.

Independent Source. (If at least one lawful source of evidence was pursued, a separate, unlawful source does not make the evidence inadmissible.) *Castello v. US* (1961) 365 US 265; *People v. Teresinski* (1982) 30 C3d 822.

Inevitable Discovery. (If police "jumped the gun" in prematurely searching or seizing evidence they would inevitably have discovered later through proper means, no exclusion is required.) *Nix v. Williams* (1984) 467 US 431; *Green v. Superior Court* (1985) 40 C3d 126.

The vast body of California and federal case law on searches and seizures is sometimes conflicting, and constantly changing. Mastering the basic rules and staying current on the weekly refinements are two of the biggest training challenges for law enforcement.

IDENTIFICATION PROCEDURE

In some cases, the identity of the criminal is established by physical evidence (such as fingerprints or DNA genetic typing); in other cases, police may obtain the suspect's admission that he committed the crime. Where the physical or confession evidence is not available, or needs corroboration, officers will attempt to obtain a *pretrial identification* of the suspect from witnesses who may be able to recognize him, whether by photograph or in person. As with other evidence-acquisition activity, the pretrial identification procedure must follow certain guidelines and avoid certain errors in order to produce evidence of ID that will be admissible in court.

In particular, the ID procedure must not have been so "unnecessarily suggestive as to give rise to a substantial likelihood of irreparable misidentification." *Neil v. Biggers* (1972) 409 US 188; *People v. Sluts* (1968) 259 CA2d 886. This simply means that police should not say or do anything to suggest in advance that a witness should identify any particular person. If the court finds that the pretrial ID procedure was unnecessarily suggestive, the fact that the suspect was identified cannot be admitted into evidence, and the witnesses will be permitted to make an in-court ID only if it can be established that such ID is based on independent recollection, free of the tainted procedure. *Manson v. Brathwaite* (1977) 432 US 98; *People v. Pervoe* (1984) 161 CA3d 342.

A pretrial ID may result from any of four different processes, one of which has no police involvement, and the other three of which are established and controlled by the police. As long as they are conducted properly, resulting identifications can be used in court.

A *confrontation* ID involves a chance encounter between the suspect and the victim or other witness in an uncontrolled, unplanned setting. For example, a rape victim might see her assailant in the supermarket, and notify police. It is obvious that this kind of ID could not have been suggested by police, and it is therefore admissible in evidence. *People v. Hunt* (1977) 19 C3d 888.

The *field showup* is used by police when a suspect is apprehended near the crime scene, shortly after occurrence. Its purpose is to quickly confirm that the right person has been detained, or to dispel suspicion and allow the detainee to go on his way. Because of the importance of prompt, on-the-scene identification or exoneration, the courts have held that this procedure, properly conducted, is not unnecessarily suggestive—even though only a single suspect may be presented, in a custodial setting, for viewing by the witness.

As safeguards against suggestiveness, police should be careful not to tell the witness that they believe the person being detained is the perpetrator, or that he has admitted his guilt, or that he had the victim's property when stopped, etc. Although some police officers virtually discourage the witness from making an ID (by giving a lengthy and gratuitous "witness admonition" about the dangers of misidentification, the importance of clearing the innocent, the lack of significance in the fact of the suspect's detention, and so on), all the law actually requires is that police avoid suggesting that the detainee is the guilty party. No cautionary admonition is required; it is sufficient to tell the witness, "We have someone detained. Look at him carefully and tell us whether or not you recognize him."

In *People v. Harris* (1975) 15 C3d 384, the California Supreme Court held that a person detained for showup ID should normally not be transported to the witness's location; instead, the witness should be taken to the suspect's location. This restriction would not apply, said the court, if police already had probable cause to arrest the suspect, or if the suspect consented to be moved, or if the witness was incapacitated, or where the circumstances were such that transporting the suspect to the witness's location would be less intrusive and less inconvenient for the suspect.

A *photo display* can be used when police have a booking photo or other picture of the person they believe to be the perpetrator. Observing the same precautions against suggestiveness that apply to the field showup, the officer simply presents the suspect's photo to the witness to see whether or not recognition occurs. While a single-photo ID is not per se improper [*Manson v. Brathwaite* (1977) 432 US 98], most officers compose a photo lineup, consisting of two to six photos of similar individuals. If an ID is made, the photo lineup is preserved or photocopied as evidence of its balanced composition. As with the field showup, no special witness admonition is legally required, though some officers apparently feel compelled to read the witness a long list of warnings and precautions.

When an arrest has been made, the suspect can be compelled to stand in a jailhouse *lineup* (or his refusal to participate can be revealed to a jury as evidence of consciousness of guilt). Witnesses can be assembled to view the lineup and give their independent responses (usually in writing, to avoid influencing one another). At any lineup conducted after the defendant's Sixth Amendment right to counsel has attached, the defendant's attorney is entitled to be notified and to be present (as a silent observer only). *Kirby v. Illinois* (1972) 406 US 682. There is no right to have counsel present for field showup or photo display ID. *US v. Ash* (1973) 413 US 300.

In cases where a victim or eyewitness seems unable to recall ID features in sufficient detail to establish a description, law enforcement officers have sometimes used hypnosis to enhance the memory. The California Supreme Court, voicing skepticism as to the scientific reliability of hypnosis and concern as to the possibility of improper suggestiveness, has ruled that post-hypnotic identifications are inadmissible in court. *People v. Shirley* (1982) 31 C3d 18. The holding of *Shirley* has since been essentially codified by the legislature in Evidence Code § 795. (Any statements given by a witness *before* being hypnotized are still acceptable, if otherwise admissible in evidence.)

ARREST PROCEDURE

An "arrest" is defined as "taking a person into custody, in a case and in the manner authorized by law." Penal Code § 834. An arrest is made by "actual restraint of the person, or by submission to the custody of an officer," and may be effected with reasonable force. Penal Code §§ 835 and 835a.

A peace officer's authority to arrest is defined by statute and is derived in one of four ways: the officer may arrest on the basis of her own initiative, whenever any crime is committed in her presence, or when she has probable cause to believe the arrestee has committed a felony (Penal Code § 836); an officer may arrest in obedience to an arrest warrant (Penal Code § 836); an officer may arrest in obedience to an oral order by a magistrate for offenses in the magistrate's presence (Penal Code § 838); and an officer must accept custody of a person apprehended by a citizen's arrest (Penal Code §§ 142, 847).

Penal Code § 840 places time limits on the making of arrests, limiting arrests for infractions and misdemeanors to the hours of 6 a.m. to 10 p.m. in the home, except where specifically otherwise authorized by arrest warrant. Any lawful arrest for any offense can be made in a public place at anytime.

The Fourth Amendment has been interpreted to require an *arrest warrant* to justify a nonconsensual entry into a person's residence to make any arrest, in the absence of exigent circumstances. *People v. Ramey* (1976) 16 C3d 263; *Payton v. New York* (1980) 445 US 573. And if the person named in the arrest warrant is believed to be in a third person's residence, a separate *search warrant* must be obtained for the third party's premises, in order to search for the subject of the arrest warrant. *Steagald v. US* (1981) 451 US 204.

The courts have also construed the Fourth Amendment as placing a limitation on the use of deadly force by police in making an arrest:

> Where the officer has probable cause to believe that the suspect poses a threat of serious physical harm, either to the officer or to others, it is not constitutionally unreasonable to prevent escape by using deadly force. Thus, if the suspect threatens the officer with a weapon or there is probable cause to believe that he has committed a crime involving the infliction or threatened infliction of serious physical harm, deadly force may be used if necessary to prevent escape, and if, where feasible, some warning has been given.
>
> *Tennessee v. Garner* (1985) 471 US 1, 11.

See also:

Kortum v. Alkire (1977) 69 CA3d 325, 333.

Any person who knows or should know that he is being arrested by a peace officer has a duty not to resist with force or weapons (Penal Code § 834a). Depending on the nature and extent of resistance, a person who delays or obstructs an officer in making an arrest or performing any official duty may be guilty of either a misdemeanor or a felony (Penal Code §§ 148 and 69; Vehicle Code §§ 2800-2800.3).

In order to obtain an arrest warrant for a suspect, a peace officer submits complete crime and investigation reports to the prosecutor and requests the filing of a criminal complaint. If the prosecutor files a criminal complaint with the court and the magistrate is satisfied that reasonable grounds exist to believe the defendant guilty, the magistrate will issue an arrest warrant, commanding any peace officer in the state to arrest the defendant (Penal Code §§ 813-816).

To serve an arrest warrant at private premises, the officer must comply with the "knock-notice" law of Penal code § 844 (similar provisions apply to search warrant service, under § 1531). Unless compliance would increase peril to officers or frustrate service of the warrant, police must knock loudly, state their identity, purpose and authority, demand admittance, and wait a reasonable time to be admitted. If necessary, forcible entry may be made thereafter. *Duke v. Superior Court* (1969) 1 C3d 314.

If an arrest is made under authority of a warrant, the arresting officer must proceed as directed by the warrant (Penal Code § 848). This usually means either producing the arrestee before the magistrate, or booking him into jail to be held pending arraignment on the prosecutor's complaint. In specified cases, misdemeanor arrestees may be released on a citation by written promise to appear in court (Penal Code § 827.1). If the arrest was made without a warrant, the officer may take the arrestee before the nearest magistrate, or may "unarrest" the person where it is determined that no criminal complaint is warranted (Penal Code § 849).

Arrest and disposition records are kept at the local level, and are reported to the California Department of Justice, Criminal Identification and Investigation (CII), and in the more serious cases to the FBI. These reports and subsequent court-reported dispositions become entries on the offender's criminal record, or "rap sheet."

OFFICIAL VIOLATIONS

To control police behavior and to protect the rights of prisoners, the legislature has enacted a variety of statutes creating duties or imposing restrictions on police. Included among these are the following:

- Refusing to accept a citizen's arrest is punishable by state prison and fine of up to $10,000. Penal Code § 142. (Police are protected from civil liability for receiving a citizen's false arrest by Penal Code § 847.)

- Delaying to take an arrestee before a magistrate is a misdemeanor. Penal Code § 145.

- Making an arrest without lawful authority is a misdemeanor. Penal Code § 146.

- Inhumanity to prisoners is punishable by fine of $4,000 and removal from office. Penal Code § 147.

- Refusal or neglect to diligently pursue gaming violations is a misdemeanor. Penal Code § 335.

- Refusing to suppress a riot is a misdemeanor. Penal Code § 410.

- It is a felony to eavesdrop on a confidential communication between a prisoner and his attorney, physician or religious advisor. Penal Code § 636.

- An officer who refuses to permit a retained attorney to visit a prisoner is guilty of a misdemeanor, and must pay the prisoner $500. Penal Code § 825.

- Depriving an arrestee of his right to three phone calls within three hours of arrest is a misdemeanor. Penal Code § 851.5.

- Alteration or cancellation of a citation, after it has been issued and delivered to the person cited, is a misdemeanor. Penal Code § 853.6(j).

- Misdelivery of an extradited prisoner is a misdemeanor. Penal Code § 1550.2.

- Any violation of official duty not otherwise specifically covered is a misdemeanor. Government Code § 1222.

In addition to the possibility of criminal prosecution for an official violation, police officers are subject to civil suit for damages in either state or federal court under Title 42, § 1983, of the United States Code. That statute provides for an officer's civil liability for depriving any person of any constitutional right or other right secured by the laws of the United States.

Operating on the investigating officer, therefore, is the combination of his own internal controls, his oath to enforce the laws, departmental policies, the evidentiary exclusionary rules, misdemeanor and felony criminal sanctions for proscribed conduct, and the possibility of civil liability for mistakes. The professional peace officer is expected to investigate crime and apprehend criminals within the bounds of all of these constraints, while risking his own life, if necessary, to protect the lives and security of the citizenry (on average, 90 officers are killed each year in the line of duty in the USA, and thousands are injured).

It is not difficult to see that law enforcement is among the most challenging professions in society, requiring the greatest possible dedication, training, discipline, skill and commitment, and deserving the public's deepest gratitude and respect.

SUMMARY

√   The principal components of a typical police agency are command, patrol, investigation, traffic and administrative support.

√   The three primary sources of information about crimes are reports from victims and witnesses, observations of officers, and informant tips.

√   To recognize potential criminal behavior, the police officer must be familiar with the elements of many statutory offenses, defined in a number of state codes and local ordinances.

√ The three categories of evidence in criminal cases are testimonial, physical, and confession.

√ Testimonial evidence is the most common, and includes the statements of victims, eyewitnesses and other persons with relevant knowledge.

√ Confession evidence is considered to be the most probative evidence of guilt. In obtaining confession evidence, police must abide by court-created rules under the Fourth, Fifth, Sixth and Fourteenth Amendments.

√ *Miranda* warnings, designed to neutralize the inherently compelling atmosphere of custodial interrogations, serve to protect a suspect's Fifth Amendment rights. Warnings are required prior to interrogation of a person who has been formally arrested, or subjected to restraints amounting to the functional equivalent of arrest.

√ The Sixth Amendment right to counsel as embodied in the Massiah rule precludes police-initiated questioning in a charged case after the right has attached by court proceedings and been asserted by obtaining or requesting counsel.

√ The due process clause of the Fourteenth Amendment forbids coercive questioning of a seriously-impaired suspect, or the use of force, threats or promises of leniency to obtain an involuntary statement.

√ Physical evidence may be the fruits or instrumentalities of a crime, or contraband, or identifying "transfer evidence."

√ Police collection of physical evidence requires proper preservation and "chain of custody" to preserve evidentiary integrity.

√ The constitutional rules of search and seizure generally require a warrant, or a recognized exception for warrantless search or seizure.

√ Despite a search or seizure error, evidence may still be admissible by application of the doctrines of attenuated taint, independent source, inevitable discovery, good faith and auxiliary use.

√ A pretrial ID of a suspect may result from a chance confrontation, or from field showup, photo display or lineup activities. To be admissible in court, a pretrial ID must not have resulted from unnecessarily suggestive procedures.

√ Police arrest powers are statutory, and may derive from police initiative, judicial order, arrest warrant, or citizen's arrest.

√ To obtain an arrest warrant, an officer submits crime reports to the prosecutor for issuance of a criminal complaint. When this complaint is filed in court, the magistrate will issue an arrest warrant.

√ Absent consent or exigent circumstances, an officer must have an arrest warrant in order to enter private premises to make an arrest. With a warrant, an officer must usually comply with "knock-notice" requirements before nonconsensual entry.

√ Numerous statutes provide misdemeanor or felony sanctions for specified violations by public officers, and federal civil liability may also arise from infringement of civil rights.

ISSUES FOR DISCUSSION

1. Given all the technical rules a police officer must observe while investigating crimes, has the officer's job become so complicated that no one could possibly master it? Do all the court-created exclusionary rules deter people from entering this dangerous profession? Is this good for law enforcement professionalism?

2. Why might the legislature have decided to allow police to arrest for felonies based on probable cause, but not allow arrests for misdemeanors unless committed in the officer's presence? Exhibiting a firearm in a threatening manner is a misdemeanor

(PC § 417(a)(1); bigamy is an alternative felony ("wobbler") (PC § 283). Does it make sense that an officer cannot arrest for the former *not* committed in his presence, but can for the latter?

3. The *Miranda* presumption is that a suspect subjected to custodial interrogation is compelled to make incriminating statements. When police are dealing with robbers, rapists, murderers and drug dealers, is it realistic to presume these suspects are intimidated by police questioning? Was the *Miranda* opinion based on empirical evidence, or just on the personal preferences of the five justices distrustful of police? In a democracy, should any five unelected individuals have the unchecked power to impose their will on society?

CHAPTER 5

CRIME CHARGING PROCEDURE

Learning Goals: After studying this chapter, you will be able to correctly answer the following questions:

√   Who makes the decision to prosecute a criminal case?

√   What are the controls on the prosecutor's crime-charging discretion?

√   What basic inquiries does the prosecutor make in deciding whether to charge a case under the *Uniform Crime Charging Standards*?

√   Why might a prosecutor sometimes decline to charge an arrested person whose guilt appears to be obvious?

√   What are eight legitimate reasons for refusing prosecution of cases that could be successfully prosecuted to conviction?

√   What factors influence the prosecutor's selection of particular charges?

√   What are the three classifications of crimes in California, and how do they affect the charging decision?

√   What are the four kinds of charging documents, who files them, and in what kinds of cases?

√   What are three common grounds of defense attacks on the crime-charging decision?

√   What alternatives to charging may the prosecutor exercise?

√   How may charges be dismissed after charging? Who makes the decision?

THE DECISION TO PROSECUTE

Just as it is true that not every criminal investigation results in an arrest, it is also true that not every arrest results in a prosecution. The decision as to which cases will be formally charged in court, and which will not, is within the discretion of the prosecuting attorney (Government Code § 26500). After the police have completed their investigation and have identified the suspected criminal, they will present the evidence to the prosecutor, who may be either a city attorney, district attorney or attorney general (Penal Code § 691.5). Whether the suspect has already been arrested and jailed, or whether police are seeking an arrest warrant for his apprehension, it will be the prosecutor's decision whether or not to proceed against the suspect in court.

This is another area of criminal procedure that is often misunderstood by the public, the media and the script writers. One popular notion is that the *victim* initiates criminal prosecutions by way of some Hollywood process known as "pressing charges" against the defendant. Another common report is that *police* "have charged the suspect with three counts of murder." Whether such assumptions reflect misconceptions of the crime-charging process, or merely careless use of the technical term "charge," the fact is that neither concept is accurate in California.

Although a victim's report of crime is important in initiating certain kinds of investigations, and the victim's cooperation will certainly facilitate a prosecution, the decision of whether or not the State of California will commit its resources to a public prosecution cannot be made by a victim: some crimes have no victim who could make such a decision (e.g., murder, child abuse, prostitution, sale of narcotics, gambling, cruelty to animals); nor are victims likely to be sufficiently schooled in the laws of evidence and procedure to determine whether a prosecution could legally proceed to successful conclusion, or to select the appropriate charge or make appropriate special allegations, etc.

The crime-charging decision is made in the prosecutor's office.

Moreover, even where the victim does not request prosecution (as from intimidation or fear), the state may have a strong interest in enforcement of the law. Penal Code § 684 provides that "A criminal action is prosecuted in the name of the people of the State of California, as a party, against the person charged with the offense." (If a victim's concurrence were necessary to support a prosecution, crimes resulting from gang rivalry or prison violence might never be charged, for lack of cooperation.) Accordingly, there is no device in California procedure known as "pressing charges," and the decision to prosecute is not delegated to crime victims.

For some of the same reasons, crime charging authority is not vested in the police [although police officers may initiate court proceedings in *infraction* cases by filing a citation with the magistrate, per Penal Code § 853.6(e)]. While it is true that experienced police officers gain a great deal of legal knowledge in the course of their careers, the focus of their information is on investigating and solving crimes and apprehending criminals.

By contrast, the prosecuting attorney is trained in the intricacies of courtroom evidence and procedure, including the assessment of issues of charge selection, rules of pleading, enhancement allegations, joinder and severance of counts and codefendants, admissibility questions, discovery, confrontation rights, venue, affirmative defenses, and dozens of other legal issues that may affect the prospects of successful prosecution. This specialized knowledge is presumed to make the prosecutor the best-qualified individual in the system to exercise the state's crime-charging authority. And it is the prosecutor, after all, who will be representing the state at trial.

Police spokespersons sometimes announce to the media that a suspect has been "arrested on charges of arson and murder," for example, or "booked on charges of spousal abuse and child endangerment." If such an arrest or booking has been preceded by the filing of a complaint by the prosecutor, charging the suspect with those offenses, the announcement would be correct. If such an announcement were made in connection with a warrantless arrest before complaint issuance, however, it would be inaccurate.

And in either kind of case, a police statement to the effect that "we are charging Mr. Ramirez with thirteen counts of first-degree murder" would not be technically correct. More accurate terminology might be "We have arrested Mr. Morris for arson," or "Mr. Lucas has been booked for murder." Misuse of such phrases as "pressing charges," "arrested on charges," and "booked on charges" merely contributes to misunderstanding of the actual charging procedure.

The independence of the prosecutor in matters of crime charging is considered sufficiently important in the scheme of separation of powers that not even the courts may intervene to control the exercise of this discretion:

> The powers of state government are legislative, executive and judicial. Persons charged with the exercise of one power may not exercise either of the others except as permitted by this Constitution.
>
> *California Constitution* art. III, sec. 3

As the district attorney (or other prosecutor) is an official of the executive branch of government, "The prosecution of a case by the district attorney involves an exercise of executive power." *Esteybar v. Municipal Court* (1971) 5 C3d 119, 127.

> It is well established that, except where a statute clearly makes prosecution mandatory, a district attorney is vested with discretionary power in the investigation and prosecution of charges and a court cannot control this discretionary power by mandamus.
> *Ascherman v. Bales* (1969) 273 CA3d 707, 708

> The discretionary power vested in the district attorney to control the institution of criminal proceedings may not be controlled by the courts, and it may not be conferred on another by the board of supervisors.
> *Hicks v. Board of Supervisors*
> (1977) 69 CA3d 228, 240

Thus, a judge has no power to order the district attorney to file charges, to add charges to a complaint, or to refrain from charging a defendant. Nor can a judge agree with a defendant to accept a guilty plea to an uncharged, lesser offense, since this would usurp the prosecutor's crime-charging power. *People v. Smith* (1975) 53 CA3 655, 459. While it is certainly true that the ultimate disposition of a charged case is within the court's jurisdiction [*People v. Superior Court (On Tai Ho)* (1974) 11 C3d 59], the decision on whether or not to invoke the court's jurisdiction by filing charges—and if so, what charges to file — is an executive decision beyond the reach of the judicial branch, and independent of the preferences of individual victims or even of the police.

LIMITATIONS ON PROSECUTORIAL DISCRETION

The preceding discussion is not to suggest that the district attorney's crime-charging authority is absolute, or that it is not subject to other checks and balances:

The Attorney General has direct supervision over the district attorneys of the several counties of the State....

> When he deems it advisable or necessary in the public interest, or when directed to do so by the Governor, he shall assist any district attorney in the discharge of his duties, and may, where he deems it necessary, take full charge of any investigation or prosecution of violations of law of which the superior court has jurisdiction. In this respect he has all the powers of a district attorney, including the power to issue or cause to be issued subpoenas or other process.
>
> *Government Code* § 12550

> Whenever the Attorney General considers the public interest requires, he may, with or without the concurrence of the district attorney, direct the grand jury to convene for the investigation and consideration of such matters of a criminal nature as he desires to submit to it. He may take full charge of the presentation of such matters to the grand jury, issue subpoenas, prepare indictments, and do all other things incident thereto to the same extent as the district attorney may do.
>
> Penal Code § 923

In addition to the supervisory role of the attorney general over the prosecutorial function, the county grand jury's powers to investigate and indict can serve an oversight role:

> The grand jury may inquire into all public of-
> fenses committed or triable within the county and
> present them to the court by indictment.
>
> Penal Code § 917

And as an elected official, the district attorney is subject to removal at the ballot box if his crime-charging policies or prosecutorial performance do not meet with public approval. "In the final analysis, the district attorney, like a judge, is answerable to the electorate for the manner in which he conducts his office." *People v. Municipal Court (Bishop)* (1972) 27 CA3d 193, 208.

(*After* the prosecutor has exercised his discretion in favor of charging a defendant, any perceived irregularities in his charging decision may be reviewed by the court on motion of the defense. The three most common motions used for this purpose alleging vindictive prosecution, discriminatory prosecution, or grounds for recusal are discussed separately, later in this chapter.)

CRIME-CHARGING STANDARDS

Given that the Fourteenth Amendment's command of equal protection of the laws applies to the states, it would seem unacceptable for crime-charging decisions to vary from county to county, or from one judicial district to the next within a county, or from one deputy district attorney to another within the same office. Theoretically, at least, a person who steals a car in Alpine County should not face felony charges of grand theft auto, if identical conduct in Los Angeles would be prosecuted as a misdemeanor joyriding. Nor should a woman who is raped in Orange County find her allegations insufficient to support a complaint, if a similar case would be prosecuted in Fresno.

In an effort to standardize, to the extent humanly possible, the evaluation of cases presented for prosecution, the district attorneys of all California counties and their deputies use the charging criteria and guidelines set forth in the *Uniform Crime Charging Standards* and *Uniform Crime Charging Manual*, published by the California District Attorneys Association. Under the UCCS, a prosecutor's primary charging responsibility is "to determine whether or not there is sufficient evidence to convict the accused of the particular crime in question." This determination involves consideration of three basic inquiries:

1. Does the evidence satisfactorily show the suspect's moral guilt? (Is he *actually* guilty?)

2. Is there legally sufficient, admissible evidence to establish a corpus delicti and the perpetrator's identity? (Can he be proven *legally* guilty?)

3. Considering the quality and quantity of the admissible evidence, together with any reasonably foreseeable defenses, is it probable that an objective fact-finder would find the suspect guilty? (Can he be *convicted*?)

Only if the charging attorney is satisfied that all three of these inquiries are answerable in the affirmative can she exercise her discretion to charge. In some instances, unfortunately, the first of these inquiries is answered "yes," but the second or third questions must be answered "no." In these cases, despite the suspect's evident moral guilt, the prosecutor is ethically bound not to file formal charges, unless and until the admissible evidence can be sufficiently strengthened to warrant a verdict of guilt.

The distinction between *moral* guilt and provable *legal* guilt is one of three explanations for the troublesome fact that prosecutors sometimes must deciine to file charges in cases where police have already arrested and booked an obviously-guilty person. Such person will then be released from jail, to the disappointment of police and the bewilderment of victims.

"The DA refused to file!" is a common complaint of police court-liaison officers who have the uncomfortable duty of advising the arresting officers their cases have been "rejected" for prosecution. But such a decision by the prosecutor is not necessarily an indication that the person arrested is not believed to be guilty; it may simply be an assessment of the insurmountable difference between *knowing* it and *proving* it.

Another possible explanation for a prosecutor's refusal to file a case may be found in the distinction between *available* evidence and *admissible* evidence. The police officer may legitimately rely on all available evidence without regard to its admissibility in court in solving crimes and making arrests:

> It is well settled that an arrest may be made upon hearsay evidence; and indeed, the "reasonable cause" necessary to support an arrest cannot demand the same strictness of proof as the accused's guilt upon a trial....
>
> *US v. Heitner* (1945) 149 F2d 105, 106

> It is settled...that reasonable cause to justify an arrest may consist of information obtained from others and is not limited to evidence that would be admissible at the trial on the issue of guilt.
>
> *People v. Boyles* (1955) 45 C2d 652, 656

The prosecutor, on the other hand, cannot evaluate the case on the basis of all available evidence, but must consider only the evidence that will be admissible in court. This means setting aside any evidence that will be inadmissible under the many exclusionary provisions in the Evidence Code, or under constitutional rules of exclusion, or under the corpus delicti rule, for example. If the residue of admissible evidence is then insufficient to establish jurisdiction, elements and ID, prosecution must be declined.

A third factor in the differentiation of arrests from prosecutions is the gap between the respective levels of justification. A police officer may lawfully arrest a suspect on the basis of *probable cause* to believe him guilty of a felony. This standard requires only a "fair probability," or a "strong suspicion" of guilt. *Illinois v. Gates* (1983) 462 US 213, 232. Conviction in court, on the other hand, requires proof beyond a reasonable doubt a far greater burden of proof than probable cause. Penal Code § 1096. Therefore, a police officer's decision to arrest might be perfectly valid as supported by probable cause, based on all available evidence, even though prosecution might be declined because the admissible evidence was deemed insufficient to convince a jury of the defendant's guilt beyond a reasonable doubt.

Further, there are some cases in which prosecution may be declined even though the basic criteria have been met and a conviction could likely be obtained. The UCCS lists eight bases on which the prosecutor might properly exercise his discretion not to charge:

1. **Contrary to legislative intent**. Penal Code § 4 states that its statutory provisions "are to be construed according to the fair import of their terms, with a view to effect its objects and to promote justice." (Example: A person who enters his own home intending to write an NSF check for $500 is technically guilty of burglary, but such a prosecution would not further the legislative intent. See *People v. Gauze* (1975) 15 C3d 709.)

2. **Antiquated statute**. If a law has gone unenforced for many years and no longer serves a deterrent purpose in modern society, its technical violation need not be prosecuted. (Example: Penal Code § 273g, a statute enacted in 1907, making it a misdemeanor for a parent to be habitually drunk in a child's presence.)

3. **Contrary to victim's best interest**. Even though crimes are prosecuted on behalf of the state, it is appropriate to take the individual victim's situation into consideration. (Example: Husband was the victim of a minor assault, has reconciled with his wife who is in counseling, and insists that family harmony would be disrupted by prosecution.)

4. **Grant of immunity is necessary**. When one criminal's testimony is essential to convict a more serious offender, immunity may have to be granted to obtain his cooperation and testimony. (Example: Immunity may be granted to the getaway driver if necessary to bring the robber-murderer to justice.)

5. *De minimus* **violation**. Some violations carry low fines and no incarceration. The prospect of a three-day trial at an average courtroom cost of $7,000 per day might not justify enforcement. (Example: Business and Professions Code § 13652, setting a $50 fine for service stations that fail to provide an air pressure gauge for customers.)

6. **Present confinement on other charges**. If the defendant is already sentenced to harsher punishment than he could possibly receive on the new case, no point would be served by prosecution. [Example: Vehicle Code § 41500(a) provides for dismissal of traffic tickets when a felon is sentenced to state prison.]

7. **Pending conviction on other charges**. If defendant is in trial in another case where his conviction appears inevitable and his probable sentence will be so substantial that the new case would not add significant consecutive punishment, prosecution may be declined. (Example: Serial murder defendant facing overwhelming cases is also suspected of an unrelated trespass.)

8. **Highly disproportionate cost of prosecution**. (Example: Petty theft from a tourist, who would have to be flown to trial from her home in England, and the defendant extradited from his place of arrest in New Hampshire.)

CHARGE SELECTION

If the prosecutor decides to file charges, he must decide which charges to file, and the appropriate charging level. This decision is fairly straightforward in some cases, such as where a single, clearly-identifiable offense occurred. For example, if the evidence indicates the defendant possessed a usable quantity of cocaine without prescription and there is no evidence of possession for sale, the prosecutor can simply file one felony charge of violation of Health and Safety Code § 11350(a).

Other cases present charging options among which the prosecutor must choose. A person arrested in possession of another's vehicle without permission might be charged with a misdemeanor or felony *driving or taking* (Vehicle Code § 10851), or a misdemeanor or felony *grand theft auto* (Penal Code § 487h). The maximum punishments for these offenses range from jail to three years in prison.

A physical attack by one person upon another might amount to assault and battery (Penal Code §§ 240-242), an assault with a deadly weapon (Penal Code § 245), an assault to commit mayhem (Penal Code § 220), or even an attempted murder (Penal Code § 664/187). The punishment could range from six months in jail to life in prison.

How does the prosecutor select among the possible charging alternatives? As a general proposition, she files those charges that most accurately describe the most serious offense supported by the evidence. Where the defendant has committed a series of crimes, every offense that would be separately punishable is charged. For example, a defendant who broke into a house at night, robbed and then pistol-whipped a man inside, and then raped a woman before leaving, would be charged with first degree burglary, first degree robbery, assault with a deadly weapon, forcible rape, and special allegations of being armed with a firearm, use of a dangerous or deadly weapon, and infliction of great bodily injury.

This is not to suggest that it is the prosecutor's duty to "throw the book at" the defendant. In some cases, however, it may not be possible for the prosecutor to predict how the evidence will develop at trial. Alternative charges can be pled in such cases, and the jury can decide, after determining the facts, which of the charged offenses have been satisfactorily proven.

When a course of conduct is punishable under two or more provisions of law, only one punishment can be imposed. Penal Code § 654. This section has been interpreted to require a single prosecution for all of the defendant's related acts during one criminal transaction.

Kellet v. Superior Court (1966) 63 C2d 822. This protects against such prosecutorial abuses as charging first the burglary, for example, and after that charge is tried, the robbery, then the rape, etc., until the state has worn down the defendant and bankrupted him with legal defense fees.

Under *Kellet*, a prosecution for any of the offenses bars any subsequent prosecution for other offenses from the same course of conduct. At charging, therefore, the prosecutor must elect the charges to be pursued, and exclude any to be forever barred under *Kellet* and 654.

In choosing the appropriate charge, the prosecutor must also consider the charge *level*. Public offenses in California are classified as felonies, misdemeanors and infractions (Penal Code § 16). With few exceptions, *infractions* (which includes most traffic offenses and some cases of trespass and disturbing the peace see Penal Code § 19e) are punishable only by fine of up to $250. *Misdemeanors* (minor crimes, such as petty theft, assault, driving under the influence and disorderly conduct) are generally punishable by maximums of $1000 fine and six months in jail (though some are subject to one year in jail). *Felonies* (serious offenses, such as robbery, rape, arson, child molestation and murder) are punishable by specified fines (usually $5000 to $10,000) and state prison terms ranging from a year and a day to life. Certain categories of murder are punishable by death.

The legislature has determined which crimes fall into which of these three categories, in most instances. In a significant number of cases, however, the legislature has recognized that a particular kind of crime might most fairly be treated as a misdemeanor in some circumstances and as a felony in more aggravated cases. In this category of crimes, unofficially referred to as "wobblers" (technically, "alternative misdemeanor/felonies"), the legislature has provided for charging discretion by the prosecutor, and final disposition discretion by the judge, by making these crimes punishable *either* by county jail (as misdemeanors) *or* by state prison (as felonies). This "wobbler" category includes such crimes as commercial burglary, ADW, grand theft, possession of methamphetamine, and many others.

As provided in Penal Code § 17, the prosecutor initially has the discretion to charge any "wobbler" as either a misdemeanor or a felony. If he charges a misdemeanor, the case remains a misdemeanor unless the defendant at arraignment requests to be charged as a felon [see § 17(b)(4)]. If the prosecutor initially charges the "wobbler" as a felony, it remains a felony unless the magistrate or judge later determines that it should be a misdemeanor [see Penal Code § 17(b)(1), (3) and (5)].

Factors the prosecutor considers in deciding the appropriate charging level and the particular crimes to be charged include the following:

→ Seriousness of defendant's conduct.

→ Nature and extent of injuries, loss or damage.

→ Defendant's prior criminal record.

→ Probability of continued criminal conduct.

→ Eligibility for probation.

→ Particular vulnerability of the victim.

→ Use of firearms or deadly weapons.

→ Baseness of motive.

→ Societal need for deterrence.

→ Apparent affirmative defenses.

→ Proof problems.

→ Severity of this case as compared with like crimes previously prosecuted as felonies or misdemeanors.

Taking all relevant circumstances into consideration, the prosecutor has a duty to charge all punishable offenses, at the highest level reasonably supported by the admissible evidence. She may ethically neither undercharge the case to "give the defendant a break," nor overcharge the case to pressure the defendant into pleading to a lesser charge.

In making the charging decision, as in all her official duties, the prosecutor is to be guided by her responsibility not merely to win convictions, but to seek justice. *People v. Ruthford* (1975) 14 C3d 399; American Bar Association Code of Professional Responsibility Canon 7, Disciplinary Rule 7-103.

THE PLEADINGS

Documents filed with a court to invoke the court's jurisdiction to grant some form of relief are known as "pleadings." The initial pleadings in a criminal case are the charging documents, and these are of four basic kinds:

1. **Citation**. In infraction cases (and some misdemeanors, with the prosecutor's prior approval) a police officer can summon a defendant to court and initiate proceedings before a magistrate by means of a "citation." Penal Code § 853.6. The citation must be subscribed under oath, and "verified on information and belief." Penal Code § 740. This means that the issuing officer must sign an oath on the citation, such as "I declare under penalty of perjury, based on information and belief, that the offense described on this citation was committed by the named defendant, as specified above."

2. **Complaint**. The charging document in *misdemeanor* cases is the "complaint." This pleading must also be sworn to, by the prosecutor who files the charges (or his designee). A complaint is also used to initiate preliminary hearing proceedings before a magistrate of the justice or municipal court in *felony* cases (see Chapter 6).

3. **Information**. After a felony case has been bound over for superior court trial following a preliminary hearing, the complaint that was used to initiate proceedings is replaced with a similar

document, called an "information." The information contains the
charges to be tried in superior court.

4. **Indictment**. If the grand jury exercises its power to charge a
suspected criminal, it files with the clerk of the superior court a
charging document called an "indictment," which is similar to an
information. Penal Code §§ 944, 951.

The contents of any accusatory pleading must include the title of
the action, the name of the court, names of the parties, and a statement
of the offenses (including dates, crimes charged, charge level, and any
special allegations, such as prior convictions or "sentence enhancements" for aggravating circumstances). Penal Code § 950. The
language of the pleading may be in the words of the statute or in any
ordinary words "sufficient to give the accused notice of the offense of
which he is accused." Penal Code § 952.

A single pleading may charge multiple defendants with the same
crimes (Penal Code § 1098), and may charge a single defendant with
two or more connected offenses. Penal Code §§ 954, 970. If a single
defendant believes a consolidated trial of his several crimes would deny
him justice, he may move for a *severance* of counts. *People v. Bean*
(1988) 46 C3d 919. Or, if one defendant feels that his right to a fair
trial will be prejudiced by a joint trial with codefendants, he may move
for a severance of defendants. *People v. Aranda* (1965) 63 C2d 518.
If the court grants a severance motion, separate trials must be held as
to the different crimes, or the different defendants.

An accusatory pleading may be *amended* to correct clerical
errors or other defects or insufficiency at any time before the defendant
has entered his plea. After plea, an amendment can be made only by
leave of court, where the defendant's substantial rights would not be
impaired. Penal Code § 1009; *People v. Hernandez* (1961) 197
CA2d 25.

```
1        TONY RACKAUKAS, DISTRICT ATTORNEY
         COUNTY OF ORANGE, STATE OF CALIFORNIA
2        POST OFFICE BOX 808
         SANTA ANA, CA 92702
3        TELEPHONE: (714) 834-3600
4        Filed this 27th day of April, 1999
5        IN THE SUPERIOR COURT OF THE STATE OF CALIFORNIA
6                IN AND FOR THE COUNTY OF ORANGE
7             THE PEOPLE OF THE STATE OF CALIFORNIA,
8
                   Plaintiff,              ) Case No. C-12345
9                                          )
10                 vs.                     )
                   John Doe,               )       Information
                   Defendant (s)           )
11
12
```

The District Attorney of Orange County hereby accuses the aforenamed defendant(s) of violating the law at and within the County of Orange as follows:

COUNT 1: On or about March 1, 1999, John Doe, in violation of section 459/460.2/461 of the Penal Code (BURGLARY OF VEHICLE - 2nd DEGREE), a FELONY did willfully and unlawfully enter a motor vehicle, to wit, 1990 Geo Storm, the property of John Q. Public, the doors of said vehicle being locked, with the intent to commit larceny and any felony.

COUNT 2: On or about March 1, 1999, JOHN DOE, in violation of Section 451(d) of the Penal Code (ARSON OF PROPERTY OF ANOTHER), a FELONY, did willfully, unlawfully, and maliciously set fire to and burn and cause to be burned the property of another, to wit, John Q. Public, located at Disneyland Parking lot.

It is further alleged that the above offense is a serious felony within the meaning of Penal Code Section 1192.7(c)(14).

Contrary to the form, force and effect of the statute in such cases made and provided, and against the peace and dignity of the People of the State of California.

Pursuant to Penal Code Section 1054.5(b), the People are hereby informally requesting that defense counsel provide discovery to the People as required by Penal Code Section 1054.3.

Dated: April 27, 1999

                   TONY RACKAUKAS, DISTRICT ATTORNEY
                   COUNTY OF ORANGE, STATE OF CALIFORNIA
         BY: _____
                   DEPUTY DISTRICT ATTORNEY

The charging document in Superior Court is the "information."

ATTACKS ON CHARGING

As discussed earlier, a court may not act to control the prosecutor's crime-charging decision; however, once charges have been filed and the court acquires jurisdiction of them, it may evaluate the charging decision for compliance with constitutional standards of due process and equal protection. This review normally occurs on the defendant's motion for dismissal due to *vindictive prosecution* or *discriminatory prosecution*, or a defense motion to *recuse* the prosecutor.

The prosecutor is required to use his charging authority only for legitimate purposes, in legitimate ways. His use of added charges or increased charges in retaliation for a defendant's successful appeal of a conviction would raise a presumption of *vindictiveness*, which would deny a defendant due process. *Blackledge v. Perry* (1974) 417 US 21; *Twiggs v. Superior Court* (1983) 34 C3d 360. Thus, when a conviction is reversed on a charge of manslaughter, the prosecutor cannot "up the ante" by charging the defendant with murder for his retrial.

By contrast, a prosecutor may legitimately add new counts, or move to amend to increase the severity of existing counts, at any time before jeopardy has attached, such as where the defendant refuses to agree to a plea bargain on the original counts. *US v. Goodwin* (1982) 457 US 368; *In re Bower* (1985) 38 C3d 865. According to the US and California Supreme Courts, this tactic does not amount to penalizing a defendant for exercising his right of appeal, when the "ante" is increased prior to trial.

The defense allegation of *discriminatory prosecution*, sometimes known as a "Murgia motion," involves a claim that the prosecutor brought charges in an arbitrary or discriminatory manner, such as for political or racial reasons. If the defendant can show that he was singled out for selective prosecution on the basis of his status while others who engage in similar conduct are not prosecuted, he may be entitled to a dismissal of the charges for denial of equal protection of laws. *Murgia v. Municipal Court* (1975) 15 C3d 286.

And even though no vindictive or discriminatory prosecution may be present, a defendant may move for *recusal* of the prosecutor (having him disqualified and replaced) on a showing that an apparent conflict of interest is likely to prevent the defendant from receiving a fair trial. Penal Code § 1425; *People v. Superior Court (Greer)* (1977) 19 C3d 255. This motion might be made, for example, where the district attorney was formerly a defense attorney who once represented the defendant or his witnesses [*Lowe v. Superior Court* (1980) 111 CA3d 367; *People v. Lepe* (1985) 164 CA3d 685], or where the victim of the crime was a member of the district attorney's office (*Greer*, supra). However, the entire district attorney staff need not be recused where the appearance of conflict relates only to a single deputy, who might be subpoenaed by the defense [*People v. Superior Court (Rabaca)* (1978) 86 CA3d 180].

If a defendant's recusal motion is granted, it does not mean that the case will not be prosecuted, but just that a substitution of prosecuting attorneys will be made to insure due process. If the recusal is only of an individual attorney, any other prosecutor in the office can assume the prosecution. Where the entire staff must be recused to avoid the unfairness of conflict, the Attorney General prosecutes the case. Penal Code § 1424; Government Code § 12550. If necessary, the court can appoint an attorney to prosecute. Penal Code § 1130.

ALTERNATIVES TO CHARGING

Instead of initiating formal charges, the prosecutor can choose other alternatives:

- Decline to charge. For any of the reasons previously discussed, the prosecutor might decide no charges were warranted.

- Conduct an office "hearing" to arrange voluntary resolution (simple assaults, bad checks, noisy dogs, etc.).

- Refer to other enforcement agencies (such as agencies of the federal government, or state licensing authorities).

- Return for further investigation. If the crime warrants prosecution but the admissible proof is inadequate for conviction, additional police work may be indicated.

- Present to the grand jury. The prosecutor may take the case to the grand jury for their examination and decision on whether or not to indict in the following cases: (1) Where a crime scheme is complicated, or (2) where offenses involve public figures, or (3) secrecy must be maintained to prevent flight or destruction of evidence, or (4) witnesses require special protection, or (5) very controversial issues are involved, or (6) the statute of limitations must be tolled (suspended) by indictment of a "John Doe" defendant. Penal Code §§ 917, 935.

DISMISSAL OF CHARGES

Once criminal charges have been filed and at anytime before judgment, the charges may be subject to dismissal. Penal Code § 1378 provides for the *civil compromise* of certain misdemeanor crimes, on payment of court costs, where the injured victim appears in court and acknowledges that he has "received satisfaction" for his injuries. The court may then stay all further proceedings and discharge the defendant. This procedure is not available for felonies or where a felonious intent was present, nor for riotous acts, assaults on peace officers, or violations of domestic violence restraining orders. Penal Code § 1377.

In addition, any action may be dismissed on motion of the prosecuting attorney, or on the court's own motion, in the furtherance of justice, per Penal Code § 1385. This provision permits termination of the prosecution where it is discovered the wrong person was accused, or indispensable evidence or witnesses are no longer available, or immunity is to be granted, etc. A dismissal under this section is a bar to any further prosecution of the same case. Penal Code § 1387. A court ordering a 1385 dismissal must state the reasons for doing so, in the minutes (court record).

(Other than the civil compromise procedure under section 1378, there is no provision in California law for a victim to "drop charges."

For the same reasons that the victim is not delegated the authority to make a decision to charge a criminal case, he is not given the power to dismiss it. The victim who calls the police or prosecutor and announces, "I'm dropping the charges," is often surprised to learn that the State of California is not.)

SUMMARY

√ The decision to charge a suspect with a crime in California is made either by the prosecuting attorney, the attorney general, or the grand jury. Victims do not "press charges."

√ Court proceedings in infraction cases may be initiated by police citation.

√ The prosecutor's crime-charging discretion cannot be directed by the courts.

√ The attorney general has supervisory power over all district attorneys and may take charge of any prosecution, if necessary.

√ California prosecutors utilize the *Uniform Crime Charging Standards* to maintain consistent filing decisions.

√ Under the UCCS, not only must a suspect's moral guilt be evident, but it must also appear that the admissible evidence is sufficient to establish all necessary facts and justify a conviction.

√ The prosecutor's decision not to prosecute an apparently guilty party might be based on the differences between *moral* and *legal* guilt, between *available* and *admissible* evidence, and between the *probable cause* standard of arrest and the standard of proof *beyond a reasonable doubt* for conviction.

√ Prosecution may legitimately be declined, based on such factors as legislative intent, antiquated statute, victim's interests, immunity to testify, *de minimus* nature, present confinement, pending conviction, or inordinate cost.

√ Charge selection should result in a prosecution for all punishable offenses reasonably supported by the evidence.

√ A "654/Kellet" problem concerns the need to include all intended charges in a consolidated prosecution, to avoid repetitive, harassing prosecutions.

√ The prosecutor must initially decide the appropriate available charge level, whether infraction, misdemeanor or felony.

√ A "wobbler" may be charged as either a misdemeanor or a felony, in the prosecutor's discretion, subject to judicial reduction.

√ Prosecutions may be commenced in four ways: by police citation for infractions; by complaint filed by the prosecutor for misdemeanors and felony preliminary hearings; by information filed by the prosecutor in superior court felony proceedings; and by indictment filed by the grand jury.

√ Subject to defense motion to sever, a pleading may charge a defendant with multiple, related counts, or multiple defendants with a single crime.

√ An accusatory pleading may be amended routinely before plea, and afterward by leave of court.

√ Three common defense attacks on the charging decision are motion to dismiss for vindictive prosecution, motion to dismiss for discriminatory prosecution, and motion to recuse the prosecutor for conflict of interest.

√ As alternatives to charging, the prosecutor may decline prosecution, use mediation, refer to other agencies, return for investigation, or present the case to the grand jury for their charging decision.

√ Some misdemeanor cases can be civilly compromised, with court costs.

√   Either the prosecutor or court may move for dismissal of charges in furtherance of justice, for reasons stated in the minutes. Crime victims do not "drop charges."

ISSUES FOR DISCUSSION

1. When the prosecutor reviews a case to decide whether or not to charge a crime, is she too likely to "play devil's advocate," looking for potential trial problems? Is this a necessary approach?

2. Is the grand jury used too little in California, as compared with other jurisdictions? Would a grand jury indictment be a more reliable way of making crime-charging decisions than relying on the judgment of individual prosecutors?

3. Is a motion to recuse a prosecutor for conflict of interest really just a way of claiming that the prosecutor may be *too* committed to enforcing the law? Isn't that his job?

4. As a practical matter, should the prosecutor be allowed to dismiss criminal cases without the court's concurrence? If the prosecutor determines that a case should be discontinued, how can a judge effectively require the prosecutor to continue? Can the prosecutor be told which witnesses to call at trial, and what questions to ask them?

CHAPTER 6

PRELIMINARY PROCEDURE

Learning Goals: After studying this chapter, you will be able to correctly answer the following questions:

√ What are the various procedures for securing the defendant's presence in court, and when is each used?

√ What is a bench warrant? When is it issued?

√ What takes place at arraignment?

√ What is a demurrer? What are the grounds for demurring? When must a demurrer be made?

√ What are the six pleas that a defendant may enter, and when is each appropriate?

√ How and when is bail set? Posted? Forfeited? Exonerated?

√ What is a preliminary hearing? What is its purpose? How does it differ from a trial?

√ In what category of cases is a preliminary hearing required?

SECURING DEFENDANT'S APPEARANCE

The defendant is required to appear either personally or through counsel at all misdemeanor proceedings, and is required to be present for felony proceedings, except for certain procedural matters for which he may execute a written waiver of personal appearance and be represented by counsel. Penal Code § 977. How is his attendance secured?

If criminal proceedings were initiated by issuance of a citation (infractions and some misdemeanors), the defendant will have given his written promise to appear at the time and place designated for arraignment. Penal Code § 853.6(d). Where proceedings were initiated by issuance of complaint and arrest warrant, the defendant will be brought before the magistrate by the custodial officer, Penal Code § 978; if the defendant was previously released on bail or on his own recognizance ("OR," meaning bound by his own word to appear as ordered), he must voluntarily appear for arraignment or suffer forfeiture of bail and prosecution for the additional charge of violating a promise to appear. Penal Code §§ 853.7, 1320, 1320.5.

Except in certain cases of violent crimes, the prosecutor may have initiated the proceedings by complaint and *summons*, instead of arrest warrant. Penal Code § 813. Essentially, a summons is a written order for the defendant to "arrest" himself and present himself in court to answer charges on a specified date. This procedure would not be used with an accused who is a flight risk, or where his criminal record makes his voluntary appearance unlikely.

In any case where a defendant fails to appear as promised or as summoned, the court will issue a *bench warrant* for his arrest. Penal Code §§ 853.8, 978.5, 979. The distinction between arrest warrants and bench warrants is basically that an *arrest* warrant is issued in connection with a charged criminal offense, while a *bench* warrant is issued to secure the courtroom attendance of a non-appearing defendant (or witness). Both warrants are served in the same manner. Penal Code § 983.

Whenever a convicted person is sentenced to more than 90 days in jail or to any prison term at a time when he has outstanding charges pending against him in any county in California, he may file a written *demand for trial* with the district attorney of that county. The district attorney then has 90 days to bring the prisoner to trial, or the case may be dismissed. Penal Code § 381. Out-of-state prisoners must be tried within 180 days of demand. Penal Code § 1389. If a trial is scheduled, the prisoner's appearance is secured by removal order and transportation order issued by the court.

California has entered into the Uniform Criminal Extradition Act with other states to accomplish the interstate extradition of prisoners guaranteed by article IV, § 2, of the US Constitution. See Penal Code § 1547-1556.2. Provisions of this act allow the district attorney in California to make a written request to the governor for a *requisition* of the fugitive from the "asylum state." Penal Code § 1554.2. If approved, the governor then submits a demand for the fugitive to the governor of the asylum state, and issues a "governor's warrant" to an officer in this state to receive custody of the fugitive and present him to the prosecuting county. Penal Code § 1554.1.

Thus, whether an accused is on some sort of pretrial release, or is in custody under arrest, or is a sentenced prisoner, or is an interstate fugitive, mechanisms exist to compel his attendance in court provided he can be located and apprehended.

ARRAIGNMENT

The first judicial appearance for the defendant in California is the *arraignment*. Penal Code § 976. To prevent a lengthy detention of an arrestee in custody without judicial review by a neutral magistrate, Penal Code § 825 requires that an arrested person be brought before a magistrate "without unnecessary delay, and in any event, within 48 hours after his arrest," excluding weekends and holidays.

When the 48 hours expire at a time when the court in which the magistrate is sitting is not in session, that time shall be extended to include the duration of the next regular court session on the judicial day immediately following. If the 48-hour period expires at a time when the court in which the magistrate is sitting is in session, the arraignment may take place any time during that session. However, when the defendant's arrest occurs on a Wednesday after the conclusion of the day's regular court session, and provided that the Wednesday is not a court holiday, the defendant shall be taken before the magistrate not later than the following Friday, provided that Friday is not a court holiday.

Penal Code § 825(a)(2)

In addition to the state statutory rules, the US Supreme Court has held that the Fourth Amendment requires a prompt judicial determination of the propriety of any *warrantless* arrest (if a warrant was issued, a magistrate will already have determined that there is probable cause for arrest). *Gerstein v. Pugh* (1975) 420 US 103.

In *Riverside County v. McLaughlin* (1991) 500 US 44, the US Supreme Court decided that the outside limit of the "promptness" required by *Gerstein* and the Fourth Amendment would be 48 hours, barring extraordinary circumstances (examples might include illness, injury, death or public insurrection). Unlike PC § 825, *McLaughlin* specifically declined to make any exception for holidays or weekends.

Therefore, even in cases where a suspect's *arraignment* can lawfully be delayed beyond 48 clock hours due to the court being closed, the probable cause *determination* cannot. As noted in Chapter 3, *McLaughlin* essentially requires counties either to have a magistrate available at all hours to review the PC for warrantless arrests within the 48-hour period, or to provide a judicial hearing officer for this purpose. As *Gerstein* had already established, the PC review can be based on written reports and declarations, and need not provide other procedural protections normally associated with a full-blown adversarial hearing (no right to counsel, or confrontation of witnesses, or cross-examination, for example).

Failure to present the defendant for arraignment within prescribed limits does not result in dismissal of the case. *In re Walters* (1975) 15 C3d 738. Such failure may, however, subject the custodial officials to civil liability and criminal prosecution. Title 42, § 1983, United States Code; Penal Code § 145.

At arraignment, a number of significant events occur:

- **Reading and advisement**. The defendant's name is called and he must identify himself by his true name, or be prosecuted by the name on the accusatory pleading. Penal Code § 989. The court then gives him a copy of the accusation and reads it to him. Penal Code § 988. The court then advises the defendant of his statutory and constitutional rights, including the right to appointed counsel if indigent, and the time limits for speedy trial. All defendants being arraigned each day may be given a single, mass advisement of rights, to save court time. *Mills v. Municipal Court* (1973) 10 C3d 288. A defendant appearing with counsel at arraignment may waive reading of the complaint and advisement of his rights. *People v. Emigh* (1959) 174 CA2d 391.

- **Appointment of counsel**. If the defendant appears without counsel, he is advised of the right to counsel. Penal Code § 987. If he is unable to employ counsel and so requests, the court must appoint counsel to defend him. If he has already retained counsel, the court must give him reasonable time to send for his counsel.

- **Waiver of counsel**. An accused has the right to waive counsel and represent himself, if he is capable of doing so. *Faretta v. California* (1975) 422 US 806. This does not mean that he must have legal training, but only that he must have the mental capacity to effectively waive his right to counsel and conduct his own defense. An unrepresented defendant is said to be proceeding "pro per" (*in propria persona*: through himself). A pro per defendant is not entitled to have "co-counsel" appointed. *People v. Davis* (1984) 161 CA3d 796. In its discretion, the court may appoint "stand-by counsel" to take over the defense if defendant ceases to represent himself. *McKaskle v. Wiggins* (1984) 465

US 168. Before allowing a defendant to continue pro per, the court must take "Faretta waivers," inquiring into the defendant's awareness of his rights and consequences, and making a finding of a knowing and voluntary waiver of the right to counsel.

- **Inquiry into mental competence.** At any time during a criminal case, from arraignment to judgment, the court must suspend criminal proceedings and order a competency hearing if "a doubt arises in the mind of the judge" that the defendant is mentally competent to understand the proceedings or assist his counsel in his defense. Penal Code §§ 1367, 1368. A competency hearing is then held in superior court, and criminal proceedings are suspended, if necessary, during treatment, to be resumed, if ever, after the defendant's restoration to competency. Penal Code § 1372. If the underlying charge is a misdemeanor, the superior court judge may order it dismissed if defendant is adjudged incompetent. Penal Code § 1370.2

- **Demurrer.** Once the defendant has been informed of the charges against him, he is required to enter a responsive pleading. He has two choices to demur, or to enter a plea. Penal Code § 1002. A "demurrer" is an attack on the legal sufficiency of the accusatory pleading. A defendant who demurs to the state's pleading is essentially saying that the accusatory pleading has a facial or technical defect that renders it inadequate to require him to defend. A demurrer must be made in writing, before any plea is entered. Penal Code §§ 1004, 1005. It may be based on any of five grounds:

1. The indicting grand jury exceeded its authority, or the court has no jurisdiction of the offense in the complaint or information. (Example: Crime is alleged to have occurred in Mexico.)

2. Charging document does not conform to legal requirements. (Example: Statement of the offense is so vague and ambiguous that defendant cannot tell what he is accused of.)

3. Misjoinder. (Example: Unrelated crimes are charged in a single pleading, contrary to the rule in Penal Code § 954.)

4. No offense stated. (Example: Stated description of defendant's conduct does not amount to a violation of law.)

5. Prosecution barred. (Example: The date of alleged violation is beyond the applicable statute of limitations).

If the defendant demurs, the court conducts a hearing on the matter and either sustains or overrules the demurrer. Penal Code § s 1006, 1007. If the demurrer is overruled, the defendant must enter a plea. If the demurrer is sustained, the charging authority must remedy the defect (if possible) by amendment or new accusation in the time allowed by the court, or the matter must be dismissed. Penal Code §§ 1007, 1008. The failure to demur is a waiver of any defects, except for lack of jurisdiction or failure to state an offense, which may be reviewed in a post-conviction motion. Penal Code § 1012.

● **Entry of plea.** The most significant event to occur at arraignment is the defendant's plea. Per Penal Code § 1016, six kinds of pleas are possible:

1. *Guilty*. This plea admits all charges and results in conviction, making the defendant subject to the penalties prescribed by law. (See further discussion in Chapter 8 as to procedure on guilty plea.)

2. *Not guilty*. This plea puts in issue every material allegation, except the validity of charged prior convictions, and places on the state the burden of proving the accused guilty beyond a reasonable doubt. Penal Code §§ 1019, 1096.

3. *Nolo contendere* ("no contest"). In felonies, a nolo plea is tantamount to a plea of guilty for all purposes. For infractions and misdemeanors, a nolo plea is essentially

a guilty plea for criminal court purposes, but may not be used to prove liability in any civil suit.

4. **Former judgment**. If the accused was either convicted or acquitted in a proceeding involving the same acts, he cannot be prosecuted again for them.

5. **Double jeopardy**. If a previous trial placed the defendant in jeopardy (a jury was sworn) and jeopardy was not waived (such as by motion for mistrial or filing an appeal) and whether or not the prior trial proceeded to conviction or acquittal the defendant cannot be retried. Penal Code § 1023.

6. **Not guilty by reason of insanity** ("*NGI*"). Any defendant who does *not* plead NGI is conclusively presumed to have been sane. A defendant who pleads *only* NGI is admitting he committed the acts charged, and placing only his sanity (at time of the offense) in issue. A defendant who pleads *both* NGI and not guilty is denying he committed the offense, while maintaining that if he did, he was insane.

On such a plea, two trials must be conducted—one as to guilt, and if convicted, one as to sanity. A convicted defendant found sane by the trier of fact is liable to punishment; one found insane is committed for treatment, for the same maximum term as he might have been imprisoned (though extensions may be made as long as he remains dangerous). Penal Code §§ 1026-1026.5.

Except in misdemeanor cases where counsel is authorized to plead for the accused, all pleas must be made personally by the defendant in open court and recorded in the minutes. Penal Code §§ 1017, 1018. If defendant refuses to enter a plea, the court must enter a plea of not guilty for him. Penal Code § 1024. If the accusatory pleading contains allegations of previous convictions, defendant must admit or deny the allegations. Penal Code § 1025.

RELEASE FROM CUSTODY

While criminal proceedings are pending, a determination must be made as to the defendant's custodial status. Three basic options are possible:

1) The defendant may be released on his own recognizance.

2) The defendant may be released on bail.

3) The defendant may be confined.

Compelling arguments can be made for the pre-conviction release of accused persons. One such argument is that until guilt has been shown at trial, it is possible that an innocent person may stand falsely accused; any incarceration of an innocent person is naturally repugnant to principles of justice. Also, a custodial defendant is limited in his ability to assist in preparing his defense, is unable to earn a livelihood to support his family and pay for his own attorney, and is a financial burden on the taxpayers while incarcerated. Many jails are overcrowded, and safety of prisoners may be a significant concern, especially where youthful, minor offenders may be exposed to more violent criminals.

At the same time, compelling arguments can also be made for detention of persons accused of crime. If there is probable cause to suspect that a person has offended once, there is reason to fear that he may continue to do so if permitted to remain at liberty. The safety of his alleged victims, witnesses, arresting officers and others involved in his apprehension might be threatened by his release. He might flee from justice and not be apprehended until he again preys on society. Or, an accused who knows he is facing a lengthy prison term may feel he has nothing to lose by going on a crime spree while awaiting trial or sentence.

Attempting to reconcile these conflicting concerns, the law has generally favored the least-restrictive method of insuring the defendant's presence at future court proceedings that is consistent with protection of the public safety, considering the circumstances of the offense and characteristics of the defendant. *People v. Arnold* (1976) 58 CA3d Supp.1; *Van Atta v. Scott* (1980) 27 C3d 424.

Release on OR. A release of the defendant on his *own recognizance* is obviously the least-restrictive arrangement (many people admitted to bail may be unable to post the required amount, and so remain in custody). All persons who are charged with *misdemeanors* are entitled to be released OR, "unless the court makes a finding upon the record that an own recognizance release will not reasonably assure the appearance of the defendant as required." Penal Code § 1270. If the court makes such a finding, bail must then be set. Thus, OR release in misdemeanor cases is a matter of qualified statutory right, subject to the state constitutional proviso that "A person may be released on his or her own recognizance in the court's discretion." Cal. Const. Art. I, Sec. 12. Defendants charged with non-capital *felony* offenses have no presumptive right to OR release, but may be released OR in the court's discretion. Penal Code § 1270.

Factors the court considers in exercising its discretion include the defendant's ties to the community, employment status, family attachments, parole or immigration status, record of appearances or failures to appear in the past, and severity of the sentence the defendant may be facing. The court may also consider whether the defendant is alleged to have injured a victim, used a firearm or other dangerous weapon, or threatened a victim or witness. *Van Atta v. Scott, supra.*

To be released OR, the defendant must sign a written agreement, promising to (1) appear in court as ordered, (2) obey conditions of his release, (3) remain in California, (4) waive extradition if apprehended elsewhere, and also (5) acknowledging the penalties for violating his agreement. Penal Code § 1318. Any wilful failure to appear in violation of an OR release agreement is punishable as a misdemeanor if the defendant was originally charged with a misdemeanor, or as a felony if on felony OR release. This is true, even if the defendant is ultimately found not guilty on the original charges. Penal Code § 1320.

Release on bail. If the defendant is not deemed eligible for OR release, the next consideration is setting a reasonable *bail*. The posting of bail by a defendant or his surety involves the deposit of money, or bond for the payment of money (defendant can usually obtain a bond for 10 percent of the bail amount, which is nonrefundable), or other "undertaking" (such as security of real estate equity or government bonds), as a guarantee the defendant will make all ordered court appearances. Penal Code § 1269, 1278, 1287, 1295, 1298. If he does so, the bail will be "exonerated" after the court proceedings, and returned to the defendant or his bondsman. If he wilfully fails to make an ordered appearance, the bail will be forfeited to the county treasurer (Penal Code § 1305, 1307), defendant's release on bail will be revoked (§ 1310), and a bench warrant will issue for his arrest (§ 979).

Both the US Constitution (Eighth Amendment) and the California Constitution (Article I, § 12) forbid requiring "excessive bail." This term does not refer to the defendant's financial ability to post a certain amount, but to the reasonableness of the amount in view of all relevant circumstances. *In re Burnette* (1939) 35 CA2d 358.

The courts of each county meet annually to revise and adopt a uniform bail schedule for bailable offenses, based on the seriousness of the charge and any enhancing allegations. Penal Code § 1269b. Upon arrest and booking for most offenses subject to this schedule, the defendant can obtain his release by posting the appropriate bail. A magistrate may order either a higher or lower amount in an individual case, based on information supplied by a peace officer or the defendant. Penal Code § 1269.c.

A person arrested for a "violent felony," as defined in Penal Code § 667.5 (including such crimes as murder, manslaughter, mayhem, rape, robbery, arson, child molestation and forcible sex crimes), cannot be released on bail until so ordered by a magistrate after a bail hearing. Penal Code § 1270.1.

Bail-bond offices are often located near a jail or courthouse.

Although the California Supreme Court once ruled, *In re Underwood* (1973) 9 C3d 345, that a court could not consider the suspect's dangerousness or the public safety in setting bail, that decision was overruled by popular vote in 1982 with the electorate's enactment of Proposition 4, amending the bail provisions of article I, § 12, of the California Constitution. As a result, a court in setting or denying bail in felony cases must consider the circumstances of the crime, risks to victims and witnesses, allegations of violence, the defendant's prior criminal record, the likelihood of failure to appear, the alleged use of weapons, and seriousness of charges. *"The public safety shall be the primary consideration."* Penal Code § 1275.

Retention in custody. The Eighth Amendment prohibition of excessive bail does not mean that all arrests must be bailable. *Carlson v. Landon* (1952) 342 US 524. An accused charged with an offense punishable by death cannot be granted bail "when the facts are evident or the presumption great" that he committed the charged crime. Calif. Const. art. I, sec. 12; California Penal Code § 1270.5. In addition, defendants charged with felonies cannot be released on bail when their guilt is evident and the court finds a "substantial likelihood" that release would result in great bodily harm to another. Art. I, sec. 12.

PRELIMINARY HEARINGS

Being charged with a felony would be a serious disruption of most people's lives. Such an event may carry with it pretrial detention, separation from family, loss of earnings or loss of employment, public embarrassment, social stigma, the financial burdens of bail and defense, the loss of professional license, the prospect of lengthy incarceration and fine, a lifelong record of felony conviction or even, in capital cases, execution. The formal charging and trial of an accused felon is therefore an awesome exercise of the state's power, and requires careful, independent review against abuse or mistake.

Under Article I, § 14, of the California Constitution, this independent determination may be provided either by the grand jury inquiry that precedes an indictment, or by a preliminary hearing before a magistrate prior to the filing of an information in superior court. Thus, the felony cases initiated by the prosecutor's filing of a complaint to which the defendant does not plead guilty must proceed by way of preliminary hearing. Penal Code § 738. The purpose of this hearing (also called a "preliminary examination," or simply "prelim") is to determine whether there is probable cause to believe that a crime was committed and that the defendant committed it, before subjecting both the defendant and the state to a trial. *People v. Encerti* (1982) 130 CA3d 791.

The preliminary hearing must be held within 10 court days of arraignment or plea, unless good cause justifies a continuance, or the parties waive this time limit and agree to a later date. If the preliminary hearing is continued more than 60 days without the defendant's waiver, the complaint must be dismissed. Penal Code § 859b.

A preliminary hearing is held before a magistrate (there is no jury involved in this proceeding). It is not a full-blown trial and does not require that the prosecution present all the witnesses or evidence of the defendant's guilt only sufficient proof to meet the probable cause requirement. Hearsay is admissible to establish probable cause.

At this hearing, the defendant has a right to counsel or to self-representation [Penal Code § 858; *People v. Lopez* (1977) 71 CA3d 568]; a right to confront and cross-examine prosecution witnesses (Penal Code § 865); a right to present evidence and call witnesses in his own behalf (§ 866); a right to exclude non-testifying witnesses during testimony, except the investigating officer (§ 867); and a conditional right to close the hearing to the public, where necessary to a fair adjudication (§ 868).

Once a preliminary hearing begins, it must proceed continuously until completion, except for the "conduct of brief court matters" during temporary recesses. This requirement of continuous prelim may be waived by the defendant or excused for good cause. Penal Code § 861. The defendant must be personally present at the prelim and may not appear through counsel. Penal Code §§ 977(b), 1043.5(a); *People v. Green* (1979) 95 CA 3d 991.

If he chooses, a defendant may waive his right to a preliminary hearing and go directly to superior court. Penal Code § 860; *In re Watson* (1972) 6 C3d 831. As a practical matter, however, few defendants elect to do this. The preliminary hearing provides the defense with an opportunity to evaluate and test the prosecution witnesses, to commit their testimony to a transcript that may be used to impeach any inconsistent testimony at a later trial, to obtain early discovery of the people's case, to make various motions affecting the admissibility of evidence, to convince the magistrate to make critical findings of fact that could lead to dismissal in superior court, to obtain a reduction of "wobbler" felonies to misdemeanor charges following the prelim, and to delay the trial in hopes that prosecution witnesses may become forgetful, uncooperative or unavailable.

Because of the potential for impeachment of trial witnesses with the transcript of their preliminary hearing testimony, it is extremely important that peace officers and civilian witnesses alike be fully prepared to testify accurately, in detail, at the prelim. The witness who neglects such preparation often finds himself "eating his own words" at the trial, and losing credibility with the jury.

After both the prosecution and defense have made their presentations to the prelim magistrate, the prosecutor will move to "hold the defendant to answer" the charges in superior court. The parties may then either argue the sufficiency of the evidence, or merely submit the matter to the magistrate. If the magistrate is not satisfied that the required showing of probable cause has been made, she must order the complaint dismissed and the defendant discharged. The prosecutor may appeal the dismissal order to the superior court, or may re-file the same matter for a second and final preliminary examination. In some "violent felony" cases, the same matter may be filed a third time. Penal Code §§ 871, 871.5, 1387, 1387.1.

If the preliminary hearing magistrate finds sufficient evidence to believe the defendant committed any charged "wobblers," she then has two options: she may reduce any "wobblers" to misdemeanors for plea or trial in misdemeanor court [Penal Code § 17(b)(5)], or may hold the defendant to answer them as felony charges in superior court. Penal Code § 872. Felony charges which are not "wobblers" must, on a finding of probable cause, be bound over to superior court. Following a "hold to answer" order, the district attorney must file an information in the superior court within 15 days setting forth the felony accusations (and any related misdemeanor counts bound over for trial with the felonies). Penal Code § 739. Superior Court proceedings will then begin with a new arraignment on the information. Penal Code §§ 976, 977.

Occasionally, in order to obtain a sentence reduction in consideration of early admission of guilt, a defendant will waive prelim and agree to plead guilty to the charges, or some of them, in superior court. When he chooses this course, the magistrate will take a "certified plea" of his guilt, with appropriate waivers (see Chapter 8), and order the defendant to superior court. Penal Code §§ 859a, 877a. The prosecutor will file an information, and the superior court judge will take the defendant's plea again, with waivers, and set sentencing proceedings. Or, if the magistrate is an actual or designated superior court judge, the judge may simply sit as a superior court and take the plea directly.

Preliminary hearings apply only in *felony* cases. If a person charged only with misdemeanors appears at arraignment in custody and requests a "probable cause hearing," the magistrate must promptly examine the police reports and other documents supporting the complaint and determine whether there is probable cause to believe the defendant committed the charged offenses. If probable cause is lacking, the complaint is dismissed and the defendant discharged. The prosecutor may re-file the case once, within 15 days. Penal Code § 991; *In re Walters* (1975) 15 C3d 738.

SUMMARY

√ The defendant's appearance in court may be secured by his promise to appear on a citation, his voluntary compliance with a summons, or his arrest.

√ If a defendant fails to appear as promised or as ordered by process of the court, a bench warrant will issue for his arrest.

√ A fugitive may be returned to California from another state by the process known as *extradition*.

√ The first court appearance of the defendant is the arraignment. Defendants in custody must be arraigned within 48 hours after arrest.

√ At arraignment, the defendant must be advised of the charges and of his legal rights.

√ If the defendant believes the accusatory pleading is legally defective on its face, he enters a response known as a *demurrer*.

√ If no demurrer is entered or sustained, the defendant may enter any of six pleas: guilty, not guilty, *nolo contendere*, former judgment, double jeopardy, or not guilty by reason of insanity.

√ While proceedings are had, defendant may be released on his own recognizance, or may be admitted to bail or denied bail.

√ Non-dangerous offenders who are not flight risks may be released OR on their written promise to appear. A violation of such promise is a new crime.

√ Reasonable bail may be required of defendants who pose no threat and are not facing capital charges. The primary consideration in setting bail is protection of the public safety.

√ Preliminary hearings are held in felony cases to screen out groundless charges. A magistrate who finds probable cause to believe the offense occurred and the defendant committed it will hold the defendant to answer in superior court. A "wobbler" not judged to rise to felony level may be reduced by the magistrate to a misdemeanor.

√ A defendant may waive his right to preliminary hearing; he may also enter a "certified plea" to the charges.

√ A defendant may use the preliminary hearing as a "preview" of the prosecution case, and as groundwork for the impeachment of unprepared witnesses.

ISSUES FOR DISCUSSION

1. Is the plea of "not guilty by reason of insanity" overused, or just overpublicized? Should insanity be an excuse for committing criminal acts? Can psychiatrists inform a jury about a defendant's prior mental state, based on subsequent clinical evaluation?

2. Should the practice of granting *OR* releases be discontinued in all felony cases? In all cases? Would increased pretrial detention result in shorter delays in the justice system, or perhaps more guilty pleas?

3. Could the preliminary hearing be eliminated without compromising justice? Would it be adequate to have a magistrate review the sworn arrest records in any challenged case and determine whether a defendant was being improperly subjected to trial?

CHAPTER 7

PRETRIAL PROCEDURE

Learning Goals: After studying this chapter, you will be able to correctly answer the following questions:

√   What is change of venue, and when is it appropriate?

√   What is the difference between a due process motion and a speedy trial motion? When is each used?

√   What is a discovery motion? What information is discoverable?

√   What is "attorney work product"? May it be discovered?

√   In what cases would a motion to disclose informant be brought? When should it be granted? Denied?

√   What is a Pitchess motion? In what kinds of cases is it used? What is the procedure on the motion?

√   If the defendant claims an unreasonable search or seizure produced evidence against him, what is his procedure for litigating this issue?

√   What is a Harvey-Whiteley motion? How can police meet this attack on their actions?

√   When can a party petition for relief by writ of mandate?

√   What is a writ of prohibition?

IMPORTANCE OF PRETRIAL PROCEDURE

It is normal to think of the jury trial as the process by which *the* important issue in a criminal case—guilt or innocence—is resolved. And while that small minority of criminal cases which actually do result in a jury trial may bear out that notion, the fact is that most criminal litigation occurs in the *pretrial* phase.

During the period following filing of the initial accusatory pleading, the parties embark on an often-lengthy process of challenges to the posture of the case pending trial. Depending on all of the circumstances, the parties may challenge the court's jurisdiction, the venue, the judge, the prosecutor, the defense attorney, timing of trial, the admissibility of evidence, defendant's competence, prior convictions, joinder of parties, joinder of counts, nondisclosure of evidence, and the fairness of the investigation and all preliminary proceedings, among other matters.

These pretrial maneuvers, which may take several months or several years, are the result of the dictates of due process and equal protection. Their aim is to insure that both the state and the defendant have a fair opportunity to prepare their cases, to obtain appropriate sanctions for any unfairness that may be established to have occurred, to define the triable issues, and to obtain rulings on the admissibility of contested evidence, so that both sides will know what may and may not be presented to the jury.

In the process of conducting the various pretrial examinations, both parties will normally acquire an appreciation of the strengths and weaknesses of the prosecution and defense posture. The result, very often (in fact, in more than 90% of the cases charged), is that the pretrial sifting will result in a realization by one side or the other (or both) that a particular result is so likely from any jury trial as to render trial superfluous. The case is then disposed of by entry of a plea to the charges, or dismissal of the charges, or a plea to reduced charges, as appropriate under the law.

Since less than 10 percent of all criminal cases filed in California actually go to trial, it is easy to see the relative importance of the pretrial procedures. The outcome of various motions and initiatives during this phase not only determines the final disposition of 90% of the cases, it also defines the trial parameters of the remaining 10% of cases.

There are at least four dozen different motions and actions the parties can use to shape the case for trial or disposition. Some are based on constitutional provisions, some are statutorily defined, and others are judicially declared. The ones most commonly brought and litigated are discussed below.

ATTACKS ON THE FORUM

Before the defense will agree to have other issues decided by a particular court, there may first be a challenge to the court itself.

Peremptory Challenge. Under Code of Civil Procedure §170.6, either party to a case has a right to exercise one peremptory challenge to a judge. Such a challenge is one that need not be supported by any particular evidence of bias or incompetence; the challenging party simply files an "affidavit of prejudice," asserting that she believes she cannot obtain fairness from a particular judge. If the challenge is timely filed, it is effective to disqualify that judge from presiding over any further proceedings in the case. *People v. Rodgers* (1975) 47 CA3d 992.

Challenge for Cause. If a party believes he can show actual cause for the disqualification of a particular judge, he can file a challenge under Code of Civil Procedure §§ 170.1 and 170.5. Reasons for challenging a judge for cause could include such things as the judge's personal interest in the outcome of a case, family or business relationship with one of the lawyers or parties or witnesses, or any other fact that might indicate that the judge might have a reason to favor one side or the other. An affidavit setting forth such allegations must be filed, and unless the judge then disqualifies herself, another judge must hold a hearing and decide the disqualification issue. Unlike the single peremptory challenge allowed, there is no limit to the number of challenges for cause that may be made.

Change of Venue. A motion for change of venue is a request to move the trial from one place to another. In misdemeanor cases, a change of venue may be granted for the convenience of the witnesses and parties. Penal Code §1035. In all cases, change of venue must be ordered whenever there is a "reasonable likelihood that a fair and impartial trial cannot be had" in the original venue. Penal Code §§ 1033, 1034.

This motion is most frequently litigated in high-publicity cases, such as the Charles Ng serial murder trial, and the notorious "Manson family" murder cases [*People v. Manson* (1976) 61 CA3d 102]. A case need not be as well-publicized as these examples, however; change of venue might be necessary in any case where juror bias might exist due to the outrageous nature of the crime, local reputation of the victim, or continuous, inflammatory press coverage. *People v. Tidwell* (1970) 3 C3d 62.

On the other hand, venue need not be changed, despite such factors, if it appears that an unbiased jury can still be obtained in the local venue. *People v. Harris* (1981) 28 C3d 935. And there is little justification for ordering a change of venue when publicity and outrage are widespread throughout the state, such as in the "Unabomber" or O. J. Simpson cases.

A change of venue, if granted, applies only to the trial itself. All pretrial legal issues are litigated in the original court. Penal Code § s 1033, 1034. The costs of trying a case in the new venue are paid by the county where the matter was originally prosecuted. Penal Code §1037.

ATTACKS ON THE PLEADINGS

In addition to the demurrer, or attack on the sufficiency of the pleading, discussed in Chapter 6, there are other challenges to the complaint or information relating to multiple charges or defendants.

Motion to Consolidate. A defendant is entitled to a single proceeding to litigate his guilt or innocence arising from a particular transaction or indivisible course of conduct. This prevents harassment and waste of public resources by repetitive prosecution. Penal Code § 654, 954; *Kellett v. Superior Court* (1966) 63 C2d 822. Therefore, if the defendant broke into a home, destroyed and vandalized the contents, and stole car keys and a car from the garage, he should be prosecuted by a single pleading, charging burglary, malicious mischief and grand theft; if the prosecutor filed multiple complaints, each charging a separate offense, the defendant could move to consolidate all charges in a single pleading, for a single trial.

Motion to Sever Counts. Many criminals commit numerous crimes, against numerous victims, before apprehension. For efficiency, the prosecutor prefers to charge all known crimes of the same class in a single pleading, for a single trial. Thus, a serial rapist might be charged with several, or several dozen, counts of raping numerous victims. Such a defendant would almost invariably move to sever the counts for separate trials: he would not want any one jury to be aware that he was suspected of multiple crimes, and he might wish to burden the prosecution with multiple trials, in the hope some cases might eventually be abandoned.

Since the law favors a joinder of all known cases, as permitted by Penal Code § 954, a defendant moving to sever the charges against him has the burden of showing unfair prejudice would result from a single trial. *People v. Bean* (1988) 46 C3d 919. Factors to be considered on a motion to sever include the cross-admissibility of evidence (defendant used the same knife and made the same threats in all rapes, for example), comparative strength of the cases (weak cases should not be "reinforced" by joinder with strong cases), inflammatory nature of some of the cases that might prejudice the jury as to others, and the possibility of the death penalty for any charge (non-death penalty cases usually should not be joined with death cases for trial, although they could be brought out at the penalty phase). *People v. Balderas* (1985) 41 C3d 144, 173.

Motion to Sever Defendants. Penal Code §1098 establishes a legislative preference for the joint trial of two or more defendants charged with the same crimes. Thus, both the robber and getaway driver should be jointly tried, or the gang members involved in a drive-by shooting, or the principals in any other cases where all share criminal liability.

For tactical reasons, jointly-charged defendants often move to sever their cases from each other. The least-culpable defendants obviously do not want "guilt by association" with hardened codefendants, and all defendants would prefer to be tried last, giving them a free look at the prosecution case and maximum time to fashion their defense.

In some cases, criminal defendants agree among themselves to try to continue the trial of the ones against whom the prosecution has the strongest case (this can be accomplished by repeatedly developing "conflicts" with their attorneys, so that new attorneys must be brought in and given time to prepare). At the same time, the defendant against whom the prosecution has the weakest case refuses to waive his speedy trial rights and insists on severing his case for prompt trial. If he is acquitted at his severed trial, he is then free to become a defense witness for his codefendants, leading the jury to believe that he was the responsible party, and that his codefendants are innocent. This ploy frequently works well with successive juries, who have been known to acquit everyone involved in a murder, each jury believing that "the other guy did it."

Severed trials may be necessary where one defendant has given a confession that implicates his codefendants. Since the Sixth Amendment guarantees that each defendant have the right to confront and cross-examine the witnesses against him, an out-of-court confession by Defendant A which implicates Defendant B is inadmissible as to B in their joint trial; unless A becomes a witness at trial, B has no opportunity to cross-examine him as to his statements, and is thus denied confrontation rights. In such cases, the prosecutor must either edit the confession to eliminate any references to B, or must not offer the confession into evidence at their joint trial. If the confession cannot be effectively edited and is necessary to insure conviction of A, joint trials must be ordered. *People v. Aranda* (1965) 63 C2d 518, 530; *Bruton v. US* (1968) 391 US 123.

TIME OF TRIAL

The parties to a criminal prosecution may litigate several pretrial issues relating to timing, seeking either to delay the trial, or to obtain sanctions because it has already been delayed too much.

Motion to Continue. This is very likely the single most common pretrial motion. It is made by the prosecution when police officers or civilian witnesses are unavailable, or when evidence examination is incomplete, or when the assigned prosecuting attorney is otherwise engaged, or under other circumstances when more time is needed to prepare the case or avoid conflicts. The defense may move to continue following the substitution of attorneys, where additional preparation is required, pending the outcome of other cases, pending appellate litigation, or even pending payment of retainer by the defendant.

When both parties can agree that a continuance is necessary, they may stipulate to continue the matter to a certain date, subject to the court's approval. If the motion to continue is contested, the court hears evidence and argument on the motion, and either grants or denies the motion.

Because delays are costly, frustrating and inefficient to the administration of justice, continuances are disfavored, and a court must find "good cause" to order a continuance (examples: prosecutor in a domestic violence case is in another trial; codefendant's attorney is engaged elsewhere). Sanctions may be imposed on an unprepared party, ranging from monetary assessments to dismissal of the case. *People v. Rubaum* (1980) 110 CA3d 930.

Due Process Motion to Dismiss. When the defendant believes that the state delayed too long *between the commission of the crime and the initiation of formal charges*, he may move to dismiss for denial of due process. *Scherling v. Superior Court* (1978)

22 C3d 493, 505. On this motion, the defendant is essentially maintaining that the government unjustifiably delayed in bringing charges, and that because of the delay, his case has been unfairly prejudiced, such as by loss of witnesses or lapse of memory. If the prejudicial effect on the defendant's ability to put on a defense outweighs the prosecution's asserted justification for the delay, the defendant's right to due process has been violated, and dismissal is the appropriate remedy. *People v. Pellegrino* (1978) 86 CA3d 776.

Speedy Trial Motion to Dismiss. The Sixth Amendment right to speedy trial commences with formal accusation, such as the filing of a criminal complaint, or indictment. *US v. Marion* (1971) 404 US 307, 320. By virtue of the Fourteenth Amendment, this provision of the federal constitution is applicable to the states. *Klopfer v. North Carolina* (1966) 386 US 213.

Whereas the *due process* motion concerns the time delay between *crime and charging*, the *speedy trial* motion concerns the delay between *charging and trial*. Once a complaint has been filed by the prosecutor and an arrest warrant issued, police must show diligence in attempting to serve the warrant to bring the defendant before the court. If the length of time between charging and arrest is longer than the applicable statute of limitations period, the court will presume that the defendant has been prejudiced; unless the prosecution shows a countervailing justification for such lengthy delay (such as defendant's flight from the jurisdiction), the case must be dismissed. *Serna v. Superior Court* (1985) 40 C3d 239, 254.

If any delay between charging and trial is shorter than the statute of limitations, the court must then balance four factors to see whether speedy trial has been denied. These are (1) length of the delay; (2) reason for the delay; (3) defendant's assertion of his rights; and (4) prejudice to the defendant. *Barker v. Wingo* (1972) 407 US 514, 530.

Frequently, an out-of-custody defendant is charged by complaint and an arrest warrant is issued, but remains unserved for many months or years. This may be due to personnel shortages in the warrant bureau of the responsible law enforcement agency, or relocation of the defendant without readily-ascertainable forwarding address. When, as in a typical scenario, the defendant is contacted by police during a routine traffic stop or other unrelated activity and a warrant check reveals the outstanding warrant, the defendant will then be arrested and will usually file a "Serna motion" or speedy trial motion for dismissal. The prosecution must then show "due diligence" by the police in attempting to serve the warrant, or suffer dismissal. *Strunk v. US* (1973) 412 US 434, 439.

Due diligence may be established by a record of repeated attempts to serve the warrant at defendant's last known address, by contact with neighbors or employers, by roll-call announcement to other officers, and by entry of the warrant into the automated system, to alert officers statewide. *People v. Hannon* (1977) 19 C3d 588. If the department's warrant log does not disclose such efforts at due diligence, a prejudiced defendant can obtain dismissal of the case. *Heathman v. Superior Court* (1989) 207 CA3d 888.

Statutory Motion to Dismiss. In addition to the constitutional due process and speedy trial provisions, California statutory law sets time limits for commencing trial once the defendant appears in court. In misdemeanor cases, a defendant must be brought to trial within 30 days if he is arraigned in custody, or within 45 days of non-custodial arraignment. In felony cases, the defendant must be brought to trial within 60 days of the filing of an information in superior court.

These deadlines can be waived by the defendant, or can be exceeded if the court finds good cause for delay. Otherwise, if trial is not commenced within the statutory time, defendant can move for a dismissal, which must be granted. Penal Code § 1382.

An order of dismissal for violation of due process or speedy trial rights is a bar to further prosecution for the same case. *People v. Glover* (1974) 40 CA3d 1006. A dismissal based only on violation of the deadlines in Penal Code § 1382 is also a bar to further prosecution for misdemeanors (unless the people successfully appeal); however, felonies dismissed on 1382 grounds can be re-filed one additional time (or twice more for specified "violent felonies"), as long as the deadlines are met on this subsequent prosecution. Penal Code §§ 1387, 1387.1.

DISCOVERY MOTIONS

Per *Brady v. Maryland* (1963) 373 US 83, the prosecution has an affirmative duty to disclose material, favorable evidence to the defense, without request. Examples might be information that a witness has identified someone else from a photo spread or lineup, or that a witness is now recanting or changing a statement, or that a prosecution witness has prior criminal convictions that are admissible to impeach his or her testimony.

Under the reciprocal discovery statutes (Penal Code §§ 1054-1054.8), both the prosecution and defense are entitled to specified discovery, including the names and addresses of intended witnesses, investigative reports, physical evidence, and scientific test results. Disclosure may be obtained by informal request or, if necessary, court order, and must generally be provided at least 30 days before trial. This statutory scheme is the exclusive means of obtaining discovery in a criminal case in California.

Sanctions the court may impose against a party for failing to furnish mandated discovery include contempt proceedings, prohibiting the introduction of concealed evidence or the testimony of an undisclosed witness, granting the opposing party a continuance to investigate and prepare, and informing the jury of the failure or refusal to provide timely disclosure. (Penal Code §1054.5)

Not all information is discoverable. Any evidence that is constitutionally or statutorily privileged need not be disclosed, nor can one party discover the "work product" of the other. *In re Misener* (1985) 38 C3d 543. Work product includes the trial strategy of counsel, internal memos, research, attorney's evaluation of the case and its problems, and the general preparation of the case for trial:

> ...it is essential that a lawyer work with a certain degree of privacy, free from unnecessary intrusion by opposing parties and their counsel. Proper preparation of a client's cases demands that he assemble

information, sift what he considers to be the relevant from the irrelevant facts, prepare his legal theories and plan his strategy without undue and needless interference.

Hickman v. Taylor (1947) 329 US 495, 510

Although the work product doctrine most frequently is asserted as a bar to discovery in civil litigation, its role in assuring the proper functioning of the criminal justice system is even more vital. The interests of society and the accused in obtaining a fair and accurate resolution of the questions of guilt or innocence demand that adequate safeguards assure the thorough preparation and presentation of each side of the case.

At its core, the work product doctrine shelters the mental processes of the attorney....

US v. Nobles (1975) 422 US 225, 238

General discovery motions usually seek the identity and statements of parties and witnesses, access to physical evidence, scientific test results, reports prepared by expert witnesses, notes used by witnesses to prompt their testimony, and evidence of pretrial identifications. Depending on the nature of the case and the potential defenses, a defendant may make certain special discovery motions aimed at particular evidence or information.

Motion to Disclose Informant. As discussed in Chapter 4, one method of investigation used by police to detect and solve crime is the use of confidential informants. Recognizing the practical necessity of such technique, particularly in such clandestine crimes as vice and narcotics offenses, the legislature has created a special statutory privilege to shelter confidential information. Evidence Code § 1041 establishes a governmental privilege to refuse to disclose the identity of a person who has furnished information in confidence to a law enforcement officer.

However, the Supremacy Clause of the US Constitution mandates that federal due process rights of discovery take precedence over state privilege statutes. Therefore, if a defendant's right to a fair trial would be prejudiced by nondisclosure of an informant, the statutory privilege must yield. This fact forms the basis for the defense motion to disclose the informant.

If the defendant can demonstrate a due process right to discovery, the prosecution must either divulge the informant's identity (thereby rendering him or her useless for future investigations, and possibly endangering the informant's safety), or suffer sanctions, including dismissal. Thus, in any case where police relied on information from a CI, the defense routinely makes a motion to disclose, hoping that if the motion is granted, the prosecutor may choose to suffer a dismissal rather than to "give up" the informant. See *Roviaro v. US* (1957) 353 US 53; *Eleazer v. Superior Court* (1970) 1 C3d 847.

In order to be entitled to disclosure of a CI's identity and whereabouts, the defendant must show that the informant's testimony is material on the issue of the defendant's guilt, and thus necessary to a fair trial. The informant might be a material witness by virtue of being a co-participant in the crime, or a percipient witness, or a decoy used to entrap defendant, for example. *Twiggs v. Superior Court* (1983) 34 C3d 360; *Theodor v. Superior Court* (1972) 8 C3d 77.

Pitchess Motion. Another statutory privilege that may sometimes be at odds with a defendant's due process rights is the one contained in Penal Code § 832.7, relating to confidentiality of peace officer personnel records. To protect the privacy of personal data and to encourage thorough internal investigations, the legislature has shielded peace officer personnel records, including records of citizen complaints against officers. Penal Code § 832.8. The procedure for disclosure of such information is provided by Evidence Code § s 1043 and 1045.

These several statutes essentially codify the holding of *Pitchess v. Superior Court* (1974) 11 C3d 531. *Pitchess* held that a defendant charged with such offenses as resisting arrest and battery on a peace officer has a due process right to learn whether the peace officer is the subject of citizen complaints for excessive force or biased behavior. If the defendant plans to allege self-defense in resisting an errant officer, he should be entitled to contact other citizens who might testify to the officer's mistreatment of them. To do this, he would need to discover portions of the officer's confidential personnel records.

Once a *Pitchess* motion is brought, the city or county attorney, attorney general or other legal representative of the peace officer responds to the motion. To be sufficient, a *Pitchess* motion must show what is being sought and why it is needed for the defense. *People v. Memro* (1985) 38 C3d 658.

If the requisite showing is made, the judge hearing the motion conducts an in-camera review (in chambers, not in open court) of the personnel file. Neither the prosecutor nor defense attorney may be present at this review. If the judge finds discoverable material, she will order it disclosed to the defense, on pain of sanctions that may include dismissal. *Dell M. v. Superior Court* (1977) 70 CA3d 782.

Hitch/Trombetta/Youngblood Motions. A defendant's due process rights include the right not to have the state deliberately suppress or destroy material evidence that might have significantly aided in the suspect's defense. In *People v. Hitch* (1974) 12 C3d 641, the California Supreme Court indicated that deliberate destruction of potentially favorable evidence would warrant dismissal of charges, since it would deprive the defendant of a fair trial.

For several years thereafter, "Hitch motions" were used to limit or dismiss the prosecution of cases where police lost or destroyed blood samples, tape-recorded confessions, test results, physical evidence, writings, or even opportunities to produce exculpatory (justified) evidence [e.g., *Brown v. Municipal Court* (1978) 86 CA3d 357, suppressing Breathalyzer results because police denied the arrestee's request for an independent blood test].

The *Hitch* rationale came under critical scrutiny after it was carried to such extremes as to suppress photographs of shoplifted merchandise simply because the merchandise had been returned to the shelf and sold [*People v. Brown* (1982) 138 CA3d 832], and to require a judge to "invent" evidence and instruct the jury to consider it in their deliberations [*People v. Zamora* (1980) 28 C3d 88]. In *California v. Trombetta* (1984) 467 US 479, the US Supreme Court questioned the validity of *Hitch* (footnote 5), and unanimously held that no due process violation was to be found in the loss of evidence unless two conditions were met:

> The evidence must both possess an exculpatory value that was apparent before the evidence was destroyed, and be of such a nature that the defendant would be unable to obtain comparable evidence by other reasonably available means.
>
> *California v. Trombetta*
> (1984) 467 US 479, 489

The Court went further a few years later, chastising Arizona courts for imposing sanctions on the state due to the failure to preserve biological samples of speculative value to the defense:

> We think the Due Process Clause requires a different result when we deal with the failure of the State to preserve evidentiary material of which no more can be said than that it could have been subjected to tests, the results of which might have exonerated the defendant.... We therefore hold that unless a criminal defendant can show bad faith on the part of the police, failure to preserve potentially useful evidence does not constitute a denial of due process of law.

> ...The presence or absence of bad faith by the police for purposes of the Due Process Clause must necessarily turn on the police's knowledge of the exculpatory value of the evidence at the time it was lost or destroyed.
>
> *Arizona v. Youngblood*
> (1988) 488 US 51

After reviewing *Hitch, Trombetta* and *Youngblood*, the California Supreme Court subsequently declared: "Based on the foregoing, we conclude that *Hitch* has not survived *Trombetta*." *People v. Johnson* (1989) 47 C3d 1194, 1233. Though *Trombetta-Youngblood* motions are occasionally made, they no longer provide criminal defendants with the license granted by *Hitch* to invoke sanctions for virtually any omission by police to perpetually warehouse all possible evidence in a case.

Mejia Motion. A similar history describes the *Mejia* motion. In *People v. Mejia* (1976) 57 CA3d 574, the Court of Appeal ruled that the deportation of a potentially material defense witness by virtue of governmental action (or inaction) deprived the defendant of due process and warranted dismissal. This holding was repudiated by the US Supreme Court in *US v. Valenzuela-Bernal* (1982) 458 US 858, ruling that deportation infringed due process only where the state was aware of the deportee's value as an exculpatory witness. This holding is now followed in California. *People v. Lopez* (1988) 198 CA3d 135.

Lineup Motion. The defense can move for a court-ordered lineup if such motion is made promptly after arrest or arraignment, and if eyewitness identification is a material issue in the case, and if there is a reasonable likelihood of mistaken identification which could be resolved by a lineup. *Evans v. Superior Court* (1974) 11 C3d 617, 625. A charged defendant has a right to have his attorney present at the lineup, as a silent observer, to witness the fairness of the procedure. *US v. Wade* (1967) 388 US 218; *Gilbert v. California* (1967) 388 US 263.

Motion to Compel Exemplars. Although the Fifth Amendment forbids compelling the defendant to make any incriminating statements, it does not prohibit compelling the production of physical evidence. *Schmerber v. California* (1966) 384 US 757. The prosecution thus may move for court-ordered production of non-testimonial evidence from the accused. For example:

Handwriting exemplars. *US v. Mara* (1973) 410 US 19; *People v. Paine* (1973) 33 CA3d 1048.

Voice exemplars. *US v. Dionisio* (1973) 410 US 1.

Fingerprints. *Hayes v. Florida* (1985) 470 US 811; *Perkey v. DMV* (1986) 42 C3d 185.

Photographs. *US v. Crews* (1980) 445 US 463; *People v. Teresinski* (1982) 30 C3d 822.

Blood samples. *South Dakota v. Neville* (1983) 459 US 553, 563.

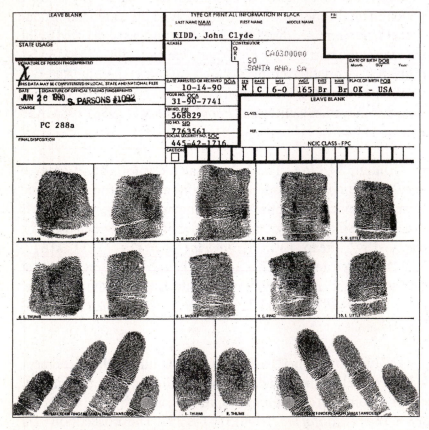

The court can order the defendant to submit to fingerprinting.

MARSDEN MOTION

A defendant who becomes dissatisfied with his appointed counsel and who believes that the attorney cannot or will not provide effective representation can move for dismissal of the attorney and substitution of new counsel. *People v. Marsden* (1970) 2 C3d 118. On the defendant's motion, the court must conduct an in-camera hearing, from which the prosecutor is excluded, to inquire into the reasons for the defendant's allegations and any evidence of the attorney's position. *People v. Young* (1981) 118 CA3d 959; *People v. Stephens* (1984) 156 CA3d 1119. If the court finds that defendant's right to effective representation is substantially impaired, counsel must be discharged and substitute counsel appointed. *People v. Walker* (1976) 18 C3d 232.

EVIDENTIARY MOTIONS

Several specific motions are available to the parties to attempt to limit the admissibility of evidence at trial:

Motion to Declare Priors Unconstitutional. Some crimes (such as petty theft, prostitution and driving under the influence) can be punished more severely if it is alleged and proved that the defendant has been previously convicted of the same crime. A defendant facing such allegation may attempt to limit his exposure on the subsequent case by attacking his prior convictions as unconstitutional. This usually involves a challenge to a guilty plea the defendant entered on his earlier case, on grounds that he did not knowingly and intelligently waive his constitutional rights. *Boykin v. Alabama* (1969) 395 US 238; *In re Tahl* (1969) 1 C3d 122.

The defendant moving to declare a prior guilty plea invalid on constitutional grounds must show that it was not voluntarily and intelligently made under the federal test applicable to such issues. *People v. Howard* (1992) 1 C4th 1168. To rebut such a showing, the prosecution may present evidence of the conviction. This may be done by certified copies of the prior judgment and, if a guilty plea was entered, a certified copy of the "Tahl form" completed by the defendant when he entered his plea. (This form contains a recitation of the defendant's rights, notice of the consequences of a guilty plea, and the defendant's statement of waiver of his rights and admission of guilt. See Chapter 8.) Special statutory procedures for deciding challenges to prior convictions of driving under the influence are outlined in Vehicle Code §§ 23209 and 41403.

Penal Code § 1538.5 Motion to Suppress. In *Mapp v. Ohio* (1961) 367 US 643, the US Supreme Court ruled that the federal exclusionary rule adopted to deter violations of Fourth Amendment rights against unreasonable search and seizure was binding on the states. The procedure for implementing the *Mapp* rule is set forth in Penal Code § 1538.5.

Prior to trial, a defendant who claims that any evidence against him resulted from an unreasonable search or seizure may move for its "suppression," or exclusion from trial. The defendant files a written notice of motion, specifying the evidence sought to be suppressed, and the grounds for its suppression. The prosecution files a response, and a hearing is held before the court to determine the propriety of the search or seizure. *People v. Manning* (1973) 33 CA3d 586.

The 1538.5 hearing is not used to litigate the legality of ID procedures [*People v. Stearns* (1973) 35 CA3d 304]; nor to decide questions of *Miranda* compliance [*People v. Edelbacher* (1989) 47 C3d 983]; nor to address due process issues [*People v. Ahern* (1984) 157 CA3d 27]. It is used only to decide the admissibility of any evidence claimed to be the product of an illegal search or seizure. *People v. Jennings* (1988) 46 C3d 963.

For a number of years, California courts relied on the "independent state grounds" of the California Constitution to suppress evidence that would have been admissible under the federal exclusionary rule. Subsequent to enactment of Proposition 8 in 1982, however, a 1538.5 hearing may not be used to suppress federally-admissible evidence. *In re Lance W*. (1985) 37 C3d 873, 896.

In order to maintain a motion to suppress, a moving defendant must establish that he has "standing" to do so based on a violation of his own legitimate expectation of privacy or possessory interests. He is not entitled to litigate a claimed violation of another's rights, even though such alleged violation produced evidence against him. *People v. Hamilton* (1985) 168 CA3d 1058.

In ruling on a motion to suppress, the court must determine whether any unreasonable search or seizure occurred, and if so, whether the challenged evidence resulted from an "exploitation" of the illegality. In making this determination, the court does not apply a "but for" test of causation ("but for the unlawful detention, defendant would not have been arrested on outstanding warrants, searched incident to arrest, and found to be in possession of contraband"). Instead, the court must inquire as to whether the evidence was discovered by direct exploitation of the initial illegality (search did not occur during unlawful detention, but after lawful arrest). *People v. Williams* (1988) 45 C3d 1268, 1300; *New York v. Harris* (1990) 110 S. Ct. 1640.

Evidence suppressed following a 1538.5 hearing may not be used by the prosecution in its case-in-chief, but may be used to impeach the defendant [*US v. Havens* (1980) 446 US 620, 628], to revoke his probation or parole [*People v. Harrison* (1988) 199 CA3d 803, 812], and to determine appropriate sentence [*People v. Baumann* (1985) 176 CA3d 67, 81]. If the defendant testifies during a 1538.5 hearing, his testimony may be used to impeach him at trial. *Simmons v. US* (1968) 390 US 377, 394.

Harvey-Whiteley Motion. A particular variation of the 1538.5 motion is the "Harvey-Whiteley motion." This motion is a challenge to the *authenticity* of official information relied on by police to detain or arrest the defendant.

For example, if the arresting officer reads a "wanted flyer," or hears an announcement about a wanted person at roll call, or receives information by radio or computer from the police dispatcher, this information can be used to justify a detention or arrest of a suspect. However, if the defense questions the *source* of the information relayed by flyer or roll-call announcement or dispatch, the prosecution must show that there was in fact a source *outside the police station*, and that police did not fabricate phony information to justify detention or arrest. *People v. Harvey* (1958) 156 CA2d 516, 523; *Whiteley v. Warden* (1971) 401 US 560.

To meet Harvey-Whiteley objections, most police agencies tape record all incoming calls, and retain the tapes of such calls as proof that a citizen informant really did supply information that was relayed to the arresting officer. At the hearing on the motion, the police dispatcher is often called to testify to authenticate the report.

As a practical matter, defendants rarely seriously question the authenticity of official information transmitted within the police department to the arresting officer. However, if the agency has failed to adequately document the source of outside information, the defendant may be able to suppress such information as evidence of suspicion or probable cause. Unless the officer's independent observations were sufficient to justify the action taken, any resulting evidence would then be suppressed. *People v. Remers* (1970) 2 C3d 659, 667; *People v. Madden* (1970) 2 C3d 1017. In practice, therefore, the Harvey-Whiteley motion is not so much a challenge to the legitimacy of the underlying information as it is to the ability of the police to *prove* the information was actually received, and not fabricated. In *dicta*, the US Supreme Court has questioned whether *Whitely* provides any ground for suppressing evidence, saying, "Its precedential value regarding application of the exclusionary rule is dubious." *Arizona v. Evans* (1995) 514 US 1.

Motion to Traverse a Search Warrant. Another particular variety of search-and-seizure motion is the "motion to traverse," sometimes also called a "Theodor motion." *Theodor v. Superior Court* (1972) 8 C3d 77. If police seized evidence under authority of a warrant, Penal Code §1538.5(a)(2) permits suppression if it can be shown that the warrant was improperly issued on the basis of deliberately false or misleading statements in the supporting affidavit.

In order to "traverse," or controvert, the warrant, the defendant must give notice in writing of the claimed errors, and must produce evidence at a hearing that material errors did exist in the affidavit. If successful, he may be able to "quash" the warrant, and suppress any evidence seized under its authority.

Like the Harvey-Whiteley Motion, the motion to traverse is less likely to be made to test the validity of the information in the affidavit than to put the police and prosecution to a test of proof: many affidavits contain material information supplied by confidential informants; if the defendant contradicts information supplied by the CI, the prosecution might have to reveal the CI by calling him as a witness to support the affidavit, or protect him by conceding that material errors may have occurred. Thus, the typical motion to traverse was more an attempt to force the prosecutor into the difficult position of choosing to "give up" the CI, or suffer loss of critical evidence and likely dismissal. *People v. Rivas* (1985) 170 CA3d 312.

The California Supreme Court essentially returned the traversal motion to its intended purpose, in *People v. Luttenberger* (1989) 50 C3d 1, by adopting the federal standard of *Franks v. Delaware* (1978) 438 US 154. Under *Luttenberger*, a defendant cannot merely allege that the CI's identity is necessary to permit a fair opportunity to traverse; he must make a "substantial preliminary showing" that the CI possesses information critical to traversal, and he must raise a reasonable doubt about the truthfulness of the CI's statements in the affidavits. Unless the defendant meets this considerable burden, the prosecution is spared the difficult choice. The practical effect of the *Luttenberger* decision is to significantly reduce the number of expeditionary traversal motions.

Evidence Code § 402 Motion. Motions made preliminarily, at the beginning of trial, are known as motions "in limine." One such motion is a 402 motion, challenging the *foundation* for admission of certain evidence. For example, before the prosecution may offer a defendant's custodial confession into evidence, the foundational fact of *Miranda* compliance must be established. A defendant who wishes to exclude evidence of his statements from the trial would therefore make a "402 motion in limine," which would place the burden of establishing *Miranda* compliance on the prosecution.

Likewise, if the defendant sought to exclude his confession as involuntary under the Fourteenth Amendment Due Process Clause, he would make a 402 motion addressed to this issue. The burden would then be on the prosecution to show voluntariness, by preponderance of the evidence, as a foundation to admissibility of the confession. *People v. Markham* (1989) 49 C3d 63.

By contrast, if the defendant wanted to challenge admissibility of his confession on grounds that it was the product of illegal arrest, detention or other search-or-seizure activity, this issue would be litigated by 1538.5 motion. *People v. Superior Court* (*Zolnay*) (1975) 15 C3d 729, 734.

The 402 hearing on foundational facts can be made by either the prosecution or defense, to challenge the admissibility of any evidence for which the law requires "laying a foundation" of preliminary facts. This could include not only such issues as *Miranda* compliance and voluntariness of statements, but also right-to-counsel issues, lineup or ID irregularities, wiretap violations, speed trap violations, and compliance with administrative regulations governing laboratory analysis of blood-alcohol samples, for example.

Kelly-Frye Motion. A special variety of 402 motion is the "Kelly-Frye" motion, used to challenge the foundation for evidence acquired by a scientific procedure. Whenever a new technique is developed for investigation of crime or analysis of evidence, the results of such technique are not admissible in trial until it can be preliminarily shown that the technique is scientifically reliable. *People v. Kelly* (1976) 17 C3d 24; *Frye v. US* (DC Cir. 1923) 293 F 1013. Fingerprint science has met the Kelly-Frye test; polygraph (lie detector) science has not. Whenever a new method is developed, whether it be the "lateral gaze nystagmus" test for drug and alcohol influence, or the analysis of DNA for genetic identification, admissibility of resulting evidence must await acceptance by the scientific community of reliability of the procedure. *People v. Brown* (1985) 40 C3d 512.

When a Kelly-Frye motion is made, the proponent of the evidence must produce satisfactory proof of scientific acceptance and reliability. This may be done through the testimony of expert witnesses, judicial notice of articles in scientific publications, the results of experiments, tests and demonstrations, and proof that other courts have found the new methods acceptable. *People v. Leahy* (1994) 8 C4th 587.

Evidence Code § 352 Motion. Even though evidence might be relevant in a case, there still must be some restrictions on its admissibility. Otherwise, cumulative (repetitive) evidence might be offered at trial long after a fact was sufficiently proven (for example, calling all 25 witnesses to a crime to testify to the same essential facts would be an unnecessary repetition of relevant evidence). Also, evidence of a highly-inflammatory nature might be relevant, but so likely to distract the jury from consideration of other evidence as to be disproportionately influential in the assessment of all the evidence (for example, graphic photographs of a murder victim's wounds might be relevant to show cause of death, but so shocking and gruesome as to divert an outraged jury from fairly considering the defendant's assertion of self-defense).

To permit the trial judge to exercise reasonable control over the presentation of evidence, the legislature enacted Evidence Code §352, which provides as follows:

> The Court in its discretion may exclude evidence if its probative value is substantially outweighed by the probability that its admission will (a) necessitate undue consumption of time or (b) create substantial danger of undue prejudice, of confusing the issues, or of misleading the jury.
>
> Evidence Code § 352.

If either party is aware that the adverse party intends to offer evidence at trial that might be subject to exclusion under 352, a "352 motion in limine" may be brought to obtain an admissibility ruling (the motion may also be brought during trial, when the evidence is proffered).

The 352 motion is used most often by the defense, to suppress gruesome photographs or evidence of a defendant's prior criminal convictions. The motion is sometimes used by the prosecution to exclude evidence that other people have committed similar crimes, or to prohibit the defense from calling an uncharged "scapegoat" witness to take the stand and invoke the privilege against self-incrimination, thereby suggesting indirectly to the jury that he, not the defendant, is the guilty party, without being subject to cross-examination.

PENAL CODE § 995 MOTION

After a felony defendant has been held to answer charges following preliminary hearing, or has been indicted by the grand jury, he may obtain a review of the legality of his formal charging by filing a motion to set aside the information or quash the indictment, under Penal Code § 995. In essence, a 995 motion is like an appeal of the preliminary hearing magistrate's holding order, or the grand jury's indictment, to a superior court judge. If the defendant can convince the judge that he was improperly indicted or held to answer, the charges are dismissed.

To meet his burden, the defendant must show that the grand jury did not adhere to proper procedure for finding the indictment (e.g., wrong number of jurors, unauthorized persons present in the proceedings, or grossly incompetent evidence presented to the jury violated due process standards). If the preliminary hearing procedure was used, the defendant must establish a legal irregularity (such as violation of time limits within which to hold preliminary hearings), or insufficient admissible evidence to support the order to hold him to answer (for example, the magistrate erroneously admitted illegally-obtained evidence).

At the superior court hearing on a defendant's 995 motion, both parties usually submit written briefs and may also make oral arguments. The superior court judge reviews the transcript of the preliminary hearing or grand jury proceedings and issues an order either granting the motion and dismissing the charges, or denying the motion. If the 995 motion is granted, the prosecution may either file an appeal, or reinitiate grand jury or preliminary hearing proceedings for a second attempt (three attempts are permitted if the charges are "violent felonies" specified in Penal Code § 667.5). If a 995 motion is denied, the defendant may seek review by application for writ of prohibition in the court of appeal. Penal Code § 999a.

PRETRIAL WRITS

In some instances, a party may disagree with a lower court ruling on a motion or other request for relief, and yet have no right to appeal the ruling. If the aggrieved party believes the lower court's erroneous ruling will irreparably impair his case, he may apply to the next higher court for an order to correct the perceived error. This order is termed a "writ:"

> The word "writ" signifies an order or precept in writing, issued in the name of the people, or of a court or judicial officer, and the word "process" a writ or summons issued in the course of judicial proceedings.
>
> *Penal Code* § 7(15)

A *writ of mandate* issues to compel the lower court (or an individual) to perform a legal duty. Code of Civil Procedure § 1085. A *writ of prohibition* is used to prohibit the lower court (or other party) from proceeding with a particular course of conduct. Code of Civil Procedure § 1102. (The *writ of habeas corpus* is discussed in Chapter 13.)

In order to obtain a writ, the applying party (petitioner) must show that the lower court has acted beyond its jurisdiction, that there is no "plain, speedy and adequate remedy at law" to correct the error, and that the petitioner made timely assertion of his objections in the respondent court. *Ballard v. Superior Court* (1966) 64 C2d 159, 168.

Although a writ cannot be used to correct an evidentiary ruling (such as *Miranda* admissibility issue), it may be sought to reverse rulings on such matters as right to counsel, discovery, joinder and severance, speedy trial, and change of venue.

SUMMARY

√ The pretrial phase of a criminal case is often vital in shaping the issues and evidence for trial.

√ Any judge assigned to a case may be challenged for cause if he cannot be fair.

√ Either party may make one peremptory challenge to an objectionable judge, without establishing cause.

√ Change of venue must be ordered when a fair trial cannot be had at the location of the charged crime. Only the trial, and not pretrial proceedings, is relocated.

√ A defendant charged in multiple complaints with crimes based on the same acts may file a motion to consolidate all cases for a single prosecution.

√ If unfair prejudice would result from the joinder of multiple crimes in a single trial, the defendant may file a motion to sever counts for separate trials.

√ Two or more defendants prosecuted together may make a motion to sever defendants where one of them would be prejudiced by a joint trial.

√ Violation of a non-confessing defendant's right of confrontation through introduction of his codefendant's confession at their joint trial is known as Aranda-Bruton error.

√ A motion to continue should only be granted where the court finds good cause for the delay.

√ A defendant's claim of prejudicial delay between crime and formal accusation is litigated by a due process motion.

√ Where delay occurs between accusation and trial, the defendant may bring a speedy trial motion to dismiss.

√ By statute, California has imposed strict deadlines for commencement of a trial once the defendant has been arraigned, ranging from 30 to 45 days in misdemeanors to 60 days in felonies. The defendant can waive these deadlines and continue his case for good cause.

√ Discovery of information held by the adversary party is by formal motion or informal request. It does not extend to the opposing attorney's "work product."

√ If the defendant can show that a confidential informant's identity and whereabouts are necessary to insure a fair trial, he can prevail on a motion to disclose *informant*, and obtain either the disclosure, or sanctions which may include dismissal.

√ A Pitchess motion is a request for reports of citizen complaints from a peace officer's confidential personnel file, usually brought by a defendant charged with resisting or assaulting an officer.

√ The Hitch motion, long used by defendants to obtain sanctions for the state's failure to preserve potential defense evidence, has not survived the US Supreme Court's Trombetta-Youngblood test of bad-faith destruction of obviously-exculpatory evidence.

√ A Mejia motion concerns the unavailability of a potential defense witness because the government deported him. No sanction is warranted under the federal rule unless the state should have known of the deportee's value as a defense witness.

√ If mistaken ID may be at issue, defendant can move promptly for a lineup to test eyewitness identification of him.

√ The state may make a motion to compel exemplars of the defendant's characteristics for evidentiary comparison.

√ A Marsden motion is made by a defendant who wishes to discharge his appointed attorney for inadequate representation. The prosecutor is not a party to this action.

√ A defendant whose previous guilty plea is now being used to increase his liability for a subsequent offense may make a motion to declare priors *unconstitutional*.

√ A motion to suppress evidence under Penal Code § 1538.5 is based on allegations of unreasonable search or seizure, based on federal constitutional standards, by a party whose personal deprivation gives him "standing" to complain. The contested evidence must have been gained by police exploitation of unlawful conduct, not merely as a "but for" by-product.

√ To test the authenticity of information transmitted through official channels to the arresting officer, a defendant makes a Harvey-Whiteley motion, requiring proof of outside sources of probable cause.

√ An attack on the legal sufficiency of a search warrant is made by motion to traverse, though such motion is often aimed at forcing disclosure of a confidential informant or dismissal of the charges.

√ A 402 motion is a challenge to the existence of preliminary, or foundational, facts that must be established before particular evidence can be admitted. This is usually an "in limine" motion used to address *Miranda* and voluntariness issues.

√ New methods of acquiring or analyzing evidence must meet the Kelly-Frye test of demonstrated reliability and scientific acceptance before resulting evidence is admissible.

√ A 352 motion by either party attempts to convince the judge to exercise her discretion to exclude relevant evidence if its probative value is outweighed by its risk of prejudice or misuse of time. This is the motion used to exclude shocking evidence and information about the defendant's criminal history.

√ The Penal Code § 995 motion is used to obtain superior court review of the grand jury's indictment or preliminary hearing magistrate's order that the defendant be held to answer felony charges.

√ To obtain relief from an adverse ruling or conduct by the trial court, a party may petition the higher court for a writ of mandate or prohibition, ordering or prohibiting certain acts.

ISSUES FOR DISCUSSION

1. Is the pretrial phase of a prosecution devoted to too many technical procedures that delay trial of guilt or innocence? Should all pretrial motions be heard together?

2. How much pretrial litigation now devoted to attempts to suppress relevant evidence from the jury is justified? What would be better?

3. Do you agree with the legislature that special privileges should be enacted to shield confidential police informants from discovery and scrutiny? What are the risks in such an arrangement? How else could this dilemma be resolved?

4. How has the move away from independent state grounds and toward the federal rules of procedure affected criminal prosecutions in California? From society's point of view, is this an improvement? Why? Why not?

CHAP
8 TE
R

ALTERNATIVES TO TRIAL

―――――――――――――――――

Learning Goals: After studying this chapter, you will be able to correctly answer the following questions:

√   What is the most common disposition of criminal cases? When can *plea bargaining* be used?

√   What is meant by the term *slow plea*? How does it work? What are *Tahl/Boykin* waivers?

√   When can *diversion* be used as an alternative to trial? How does it work?

√   What is a *civil compromise*? When can it be used? What are the conditions?

√   What options are available to the court for handling cases involving *mentally impaired* defendants?

√   Under what circumstances may a court order a *dismissal* of a criminal case?

√   Can the prosecutor lawfully require a defendant to sign a *liability release* in exchange for dismissal of charges?

NON-TRIAL DISPOSITION

California is known for being the most litigious state in the Union. We reportedly have more law schools, lawyers and lawsuits per capita than any other place. One result of the crush of litigation activity is that it places an enormous strain on the justice system. Many civil lawsuits, for example, remain pending in superior court for five years before being assigned to a courtroom for trial. This backlog problem is so acute that retired judges have formed successful "judicial arbitration" services to provide a forum for the settlement of civil lawsuits between parties who will agree to be bound by the unofficial "rulings."

The spillover effect of civil backlogs is to put pressure on the criminal caseload. And conversely, since criminal cases take precedence for trial over civil cases, the increasing criminal caseload further logjams the civil process. In such a situation, it is easy to see that not all criminal cases can possibly be tried, and other means must be utilized to resolve criminal cases where possible, consistent with the aims of justice.

Once the pretrial discovery and litigation have been completed, the parties reassess the relative strengths and weaknesses of their respective positions to determine whether a trial will be necessary, or whether some alternative disposition of the case is appropriate. In the most serious cases, such as murder, rape, arson, robbery, kidnap and child molest, non-trial dispositions are less likely to be sought by either party. In most cases, however, conscientious attorneys will explore a variety of alternatives before proceeding to trial.

GUILTY PLEA

The most common disposition of cases is by entry of a plea by the defendant. Statistics vary, but range up to more than 80 percent of cases settled by plea in some jurisdictions. In many cases, both sides have substantial incentives to resolve the case in this manner, if possible.

The prosecution has limited staff and resources for the trial of cases, and cannot try every case charged, within the applicable time limits. Priorities must be observed when pending cases may run the gamut from barking dog violations to drunk driving manslaughter, and from insufficient-fund check cases to serial murder. In addition, every case has its own unique trial problems, every jury its own peculiar uncertainties. If the prosecution can be assured of a conviction by guilty plea to an appropriate charge, a jury trial with its cost, time consumption and unpredictable outcome may not be a wise course to pursue.

The prosecution must also consider the impact of a trial on the victims and witnesses in a case. Especially where trial testimony would prove emotionally difficult, humiliating, embarrassing or painful to witnesses (such as in rape, child molest and death cases), the prosecutor must weigh the uncertain benefits of a trial against the certain advantages and disadvantages of disposition by plea.

Likewise, the defendant and his counsel may have incentives to conclude the case by plea. If a defendant is facing a strong case with multiple charges, he may be able to limit his prison time exposure by arranging to plead to some of the charges and obtain reduction or dismissal of others. By policy, sentencing courts try to encourage early settlement of cases by recognizing a prompt admission of guilt as an important first step toward rehabilitation, thereby justifying a more lenient sentence choice.

If a defendant has retained private counsel in a case where his guilt is evident and a conviction likely, he may have an economic incentive for entry of a guilty plea. Even moderately-priced criminal trial lawyers may charge several thousand dollars for misdemeanor trial representation, and from $20,000 to $100,000 to handle felony cases through trial. Where a defendant is not conscientiously maintaining his moral innocence of the charges, the expense of a futile trial could simply compound his losses.

Defendants in some kinds of cases may also wish to spare themselves and their families the embarrassment and stress of a public trial. Where, for example, an otherwise-reputable citizen is charged with an act of prostitution, indecent exposure, lewd conduct or child molestation, entry of a plea to the charges might be an attractive' alternative to having a jury of strangers hear intimate and humiliating details of aberrant behavior.

IN THE SUPERIOR COURT OF THE STATE OF CALIFORNIA
AND FOR THE COUNTY OF ORANGE

C. **76733** .PEOPLE VS. **KIDD**

GUILTY PLEA IN THE SUPERIOR COURT

1. My true full name is **JOHN CLYDE KIDD**   am represented
   by **LEONARD BARRISTER**   who is my attorney.

2. I understand that I am pleading guilty and admitting the following offenses, prior convictions and special punishment allegations, carrying possible penalties as follows:

Charge	Sentence Range in Years (Circle if a particular sentence has been agreed on)	Enhancements	Term for Priors	yrs	Total Penal Years
I PC 459 2°	16-2-3				3

Maximum Total Punishment   3

2a. ☒ understand that I am ineligible for probation and will serve a state prison sentence for count(s) _____ of the information to which I am pleading guilty.

2b. ☒ I understand for persons sentenced to state prison the following terms of parole apply after expiration of the prison term.

    ☒ Determinate sentence: 3 years parole plus 1 year maximum confinement on revocation. An additional year of confinement can be imposed for my misconduct during the year of my revocation confinement. P.C. 3057

    ☒ Life sentence non-murder case: 5 years parole plus 1 year maximum confinement on each revocation. (Maximum total revocation confinement is 2 years.)

    ☒ Life sentence murder conviction:
        1st degree murder: 7 years to life parole.
        2nd degree murder: 5 years to life parole.

2c. ☒ I understand that it is absolutely necessary all plea agreements, promises of particular sentences or sentence recommendations be completely disclosed to the court on this form.

3. ☒ I understand that I have the right to be represented by an attorney at all stages of the proceedings until the case is terminated and that if I cannot afford an attorney, one will be appointed free of charge.

4. ☒ understand that I have a right to a speedy and public trial by jury. hereby waive and give up this right.

5. ☒ I understand that I have the right to be confronted by the witnesses against me and to cross examine them myself or through an attorney. I hereby waive and give up these rights.

6. ☒ I understand that I have the right to testify on my own behalf but that I cannot be compelled to be a witness against myself, and may remain silent if I so choose. I hereby waive and give up these rights.

7. ☒ I understand that I have the right to call witnesses to testify in my behalf and to invoke the compulsory process of the court to subpoena those witnesses. I hereby waive and give up these rights.

8. ☒ I understand that if I am not a citizen of the United States the conviction for the offense charged may have the consequence of deportation, exclusion from admission to the United States, or denial of naturalization pursuant to the laws of the United States.

9. ☒ understand that I will be required to register as a sex offender pursuant to Section 290 of the Penal Code.

10. ☒ I understand that I will be required to register as a narcotic offender pursuant to Section 11590 of the Health and Safety Code.

11. ☒ understand that I have the right to appeal the Superior Court's denial of my Penal Code Section 1538.5 motion suppression of evidence motion) in this case. I hereby waive and give up this right.

12. ☒ I understand that I have the right to receive credit for all time I have spent in custody prior to my sentencing in this case (both work time and good time). I hereby waive and give up this right.

F0232-412.5 (R 12/87)   FILE COPY

Defendant completes a "waiver of rights" (Tahl) form in order to plead guilty (page 1 of 2 pages).

A disposition of a case by entry of guilty plea may come about through a number of means:

Pre-plea Report. Where the only disputed issue is the severity of the appropriate punishment, the court may order the probation officer to prepare a pre-plea report. To do so, the probation officer may interview the victims, police officers and defendant, to obtain details of the crime and the defendant's background. The probation officer then submits a written report to the court with sentence recommendations, including an opinion as to whether or not the defendant should be granted probation. (For tactical reasons, either party might not wish to have a pre-plea report prepared.)

Once the pre-plea report has been reviewed by the court and the parties, the defendant may decide that the recommended sentence is acceptable and offer to change his plea to guilty for the specified sentence. If the court accepts, the case can be promptly settled. The prosecutor's concurrence is not required where the defendant is pleading guilty as charged. *People v. West* (1970) 3 C3d 595.

Plea Bargaining. Where permitted by law and local policy, the parties may be able to reach an agreed disposition by negotiated settlement, often referred to as "plea bargaining." In this process, the defendant agrees to enter a guilty plea to some of the charges in exchange for the prosecutor's agreement to move to dismiss the others, or agrees to plead guilty to a reduction from more-serious to less-serious charges. While such a process has little outward appeal to most of society and especially to the individual victims in a given case, its practical justification has been acknowledged even by the Supreme Court:

> For a defendant who sees slight possibility of acquittal, the advantages of pleading guilty and limiting the probable penalty are obvious—his exposure is reduced, the correctional processes can begin immediately, and the practical burdens of a trial are eliminated. For the State there are advantages—the more promptly imposed punishment after an admission of guilt may more effectively attain the objectives of punishment; and with the avoidance of trial, scarce

judicial and prosecutorial resources are conserved for those cases in which there is a substantial issue of the defendant's guilt or in which there is substantial doubt that the State can sustain its burden of proof.

It is this mutuality of advantage which perhaps explains the fact that at present well over three-fourths of the criminal convictions in this country rest on pleas of guilty, a great many of them no doubt motivated at least in part by the hope or assurance of a lesser penalty than might be imposed if there were a guilty verdict after a trial to judge or jury.

Brady v. US (1970) 397 US 742, 752

Plea bargaining is prohibited in "serious felony" cases and DUI cases, except where the prosecution case cannot be proven, or a material witness cannot be obtained, or a reduction in charge would not substantially change the sentence. Penal Code § 1192.7. In addition, some prosecutorial offices refuse to plea bargain other cases, or any cases at all. Although a court can compel the prosecutor to attend plea negotiation proceedings in cases other than those specified in 1192.7, it cannot compel the prosecutor to reduce or dismiss charges, to add new charges, or to acquiesce in an unacceptable disposition. *Bryce v. Superior Court* (1988) 205 CA3d 671.

Indicated Sentence. In cases where plea bargaining is not legally prohibited but the prosecutor either declines to participate or does not reach an agreement with defense counsel, a court may resort to "sentence bargaining." This involves an indication to the defendant of the maximum sentence the court is considering; if the defendant agrees to plead guilty on condition that the indicated sentence will be imposed, he is entitled to withdraw his plea if the judge changes her mind after receiving the sentence report. Penal Code § 1192.5; *People v. Delles* (1968) 69 C2d 906.

Slow Plea. To preserve appellate rights under Penal Code § 1237.5, and sometimes simply because he does not want to openly admit his evident guilt, a defendant may sometimes waive jury trial and agree to submit the issue of guilt to a judge on the basis of preliminary hearing transcripts, police reports, or other stipulated evidence. Since a finding of guilt is a foregone conclusion, such submission is tantamount to a plea of guilty. *Bunnell v. Superior Court* (1975) 13 C3d 592. This procedure is commonly referred to as a "slow plea." *In re Steven H.* (1982) 130 CA3d 449.

Tahl/Boykin **Waivers**. Whether a guilty plea is entered without inducement, or results from negotiations, or is based on a submission of stipulated records, the defendant who pleads guilty is giving up significant constitutional rights by foregoing a jury trial. Both the California and US Supreme Courts have held that a plea of guilty must therefore be accompanied by knowing and voluntary waivers of certain trial rights. *In re Tahl* (1969) 1 C3d 122; *Boykin v. Alabama* (1969) 395 US 238.

Specifically, the defendant must be advised of and waive the right to trial by jury, the right to confront the witnesses against him, and the right against self-incrimination. If the defendant is not represented by counsel, he must also waive the right to have appointed counsel to represent him. The court record of a defendant's plea of guilty must contain an explicit waiver of these rights, in both misdemeanor and felony cases. *Mills v. Municipal Court* (1973) 10 C3d 288.

In addition to the waiver of rights, a plea of guilty must also be accompanied by an advisement of the direct consequences it may have. *Bunnell v. Superior Court* (1975) 13 C3d 592, 605. Such consequences may include maximum and minimum punishments, probation ineligibility, parole liability, registration as a sex or narcotics offender, and loss of driving privilege. Per Penal Code § 1016.5, the defendant must also be informed that if he is not a citizen, his plea of guilty may result in deportation or other adverse immigration action.

A judge accepting a guilty plea to a felony is required to take a "factual basis" for the plea. Penal Code § 1192.5. This usually means having the defendant state the essential facts constituting guilt ("On

March 8, 1999, in Los Angeles County, I entered the inhabited dwelling of another at 482 Holly Drive with intent to commit theft inside."). Although a factual basis is often taken in misdemeanor cases, it is not required. *In re Gross* (1983) 33 C3d 561.

To avoid inadvertent error or omission in taking the waivers required for a guilty plea, courts commonly use a printed "Tahl form" containing a full advisement of rights, statements of waiver, advice on consequences, and questions about the factual basis. Once the defendant and his attorney complete this form and it is verified by the prosecutor, the court then takes the defendant's explicit waivers and makes a finding of a knowing and intelligent plea. *In re Johnson* (1965) 62 C2d 325.

DIVERSION

Certain classes of crimes viewed as amounting to special social problems, as well as public offenses, are sometimes subject to being diverted from the normal criminal process and into a treatment, rehabilitation or other correctional program. These cases include the following:

- Specified narcotics and drug abuse offenses. Penal Code § 1000.

- Domestic violence cases. Penal Code § 1000.6.

- Child abuse and neglect. Penal Code § 1000.12.

- Misdemeanors. Penal Code § 1001, § 1001.50.

- Mentally retarded misdemeanants. Penal Code § 1001.20.

- Bad checks. Penal Code § 1001.60.

- Parental contributing to the delinquency of a minor. Penal Code § 1001.70.

Diversion programs are subject to various restrictions, are not all available in every jurisdiction, and apply only in designated kinds of cases. Most require the prosecutor's determination of eligibility and court referral to probation or counseling for final evaluation. If diversion is granted, further criminal proceedings are suspended, to be dismissed on successful completion, or to be reinstated if diversion is not completed.

OFFICE HEARING

An informal, nonstatutory procedure for disposing of minor offenses without trial may be an *office hearing* conducted by the prosecutor to try to reach accord between the defendant and the complainant. This procedure might be used to settle neighborhood disputes, husband-wife disputes, chronic trespass problems, disturbance of the peace, and simple assault cases. The prosecutor attempts to mediate the dispute and arrange voluntary compliance with the law, subject to the threat of prosecution if the problem persists. This procedure is a pre-charging device used to avoid filing the case in court, if possible.

DA'S "PROBATION"

Once a comparatively minor case has been filed but is not considered appropriate for full criminal sanctions, the prosecutor may (usually with the concurrence of the complainant, if any) agree to a six-month continuance of the case. The understanding is that if no further problems occur, the matter will be dismissed at the end of six months; if the problem persists, prosecution will proceed. This is simply a means of holding the threat of prosecution over the defendant to keep him on his best behavior.

CIVIL COMPROMISE

When the victim of a *misdemeanor* has a remedy by civil action (e.g., assault, trespass, theft, joyriding), the case can be disposed of by *civil compromise* if the injured party appears in court and acknowledges satisfaction for her loss or injury. Penal Code §§ 1377, 1378. On payment of court costs, the defendant can be discharged and the case dismissed.

This procedure is discretionary with the judge, and cannot be used when the victim was an officer of justice on duty, or when the crime was committed riotously or with felonious intent, or in violation of a domestic violence restraining order.

IMMUNITY TO TESTIFY

When the state's interest in obtaining the testimony of a defendant to "catch a bigger fish" is greater than its interest in punishing the defendant for his lesser culpability, the defendant may be granted immunity to testify. If immunity proceedings are initiated by the prosecutor and approved by the court, the defendant will be ordered to testify. If he does so, he is not thereafter subject to prosecution for the transaction he gives testimony about (this is called "transactional immunity," and is contrasted with so-called "use immunity," which only prevents prosecutorial use of the compelled testimony, but not prosecution based on other evidence).

In felony cases, the granting of immunity involves a formal procedure, including a hearing after the defendant has been questioned and has claimed his Fifth Amendment privilege. Penal Code § 1324. The procedure is informal in misdemeanor cases, consisting of a written agreement between the prosecutor and defendant. Penal Code § 1324.1.

If a defendant who has been ordered to testify on condition of immunity refuses to do so, he may be punished for contempt, and his original prosecution may proceed. A person who testifies under grant of immunity must testify truthfully, for he can be prosecuted for perjury otherwise.

MENTAL TREATMENT ALTERNATIVES

Where it appears that a criminal defendant suffers from mental disorders, it is sometimes appropriate to suspend criminal proceedings and pursue treatment. As discussed in Chapter 6, any defendant whose mental competency to stand trial is in question must have a competency hearing in superior court. Penal Code § s 1367, 1368. If he is determined to be mentally incompetent to be dealt with in the criminal system, he can be committed to a state hospital or other facility for inpatient treatment. This commitment can last as long as the defendant might have been imprisoned, up to a maximum of three years, and may be extended on a showing of the defendant's continued dangerousness.

After competency is restored, the defendant can be returned to court for resumption of criminal proceedings. If he is convicted, he is entitled to credit against his prison term for time spent in treatment. Penal Code § 1375.5.

Provisions also exist for *civil commitment* of dangerous offenders who cannot be confined on incompetency grounds. The Lanterman-Petris-Short Act, comprising Welfare and Institutions Code §§ 5000-5579, establishes procedures for involuntary psychiatric commitment, with scheduled, periodic reviews.

One particular provision of the LPS Act commonly used by police, is the 72-hour evaluation detention prescribed in Welfare and Institutions Code § 5150. A peace officer who has probable cause to believe a person is dangerous to himself or to others may deliver the person to a designated professional practitioner; with professional certification, the person can be detained for 72 hours (usually in county hospital lock-down) for observation and evaluation. This is the procedure most likely to be used in cases of attempted suicide or other aberrational behavior. Depending on the evaluation results, further involuntary detention can then be imposed. Welfare and Institutions Code §§ 5250, 5260, 5300.

TRAILING GREATER OFFENSE

Many criminals have several cases pending at any given time, often in several jurisdictions, including federal court. When this is the case, the various prosecutors involved may identify the most serious case with the strongest chance of conviction and move it to trial. All other cases will then trail (follow behind). If the defendant is acquitted, the next priority case is readied for trial. Once a conviction is obtained, the trailing cases are usually disposed of by guilty plea with concurrent sentences, or are dismissed, if the defendant is given a substantial sentence on his convicted case and the trailing case is comparatively minor. (Example: Most pending traffic matters must be dismissed when a defendant is sentenced to prison. Vehicle Code § 41500.)

DEPORTATION

If the defendant in a case is an alien who is subject to deportation, this alternative is sometimes chosen in lieu of prosecution. In serious cases, the defendant would first be tried and, if convicted, sentenced to serve his punishment before then being deported. In other cases, the defendant may enter a guilty plea, or have his case dismissed, on the understanding that he will be delivered in custody to the Immigration and Naturalization Service for deportation. In relatively minor cases, this alternative may have greater deterrent effect than the weekend in jail or $500 fine that would probably be imposed.

DISMISSAL

Historically, the prosecutor who, for whatever reason, no longer desired to press his case against a defendant could appear in court and enter a *nolle prosequi* ("no further prosecution"). The case would then simply be in indefinite suspension, abandoned by the state but still technically pending. In 1872, the California Legislature abolished the nolle prosequi in this state. Penal Code § 1386. Once a case is charged, it must either be lawfully diverted, civilly compromised, prosecuted to conclusion, or dismissed.

Legitimate reasons for discontinuing a case are many: witnesses may disappear or die; physical evidence may be lost or destroyed, or ordered suppressed; statutes may be repealed or declared unconstitutional; the defendant may be sentenced on a more serious case, or become a witness for the state, or become disabled, or die, or be shown by new evidence to have been wrongly accused. Whenever a compelling, legitimate justification exists to discontinue a prosecution, the judge may, either on his own motion or on motion of the prosecutor, order the case dismissed "in furtherance of justice." Penal Code § 1385.

The decision as to whether or not to dismiss a case is in the judge's sole discretion. *People v. Johnson* (1966) 247 CA2d 331. Thus, it is inaccurate to speak of the prosecutor or police "dismissing" a case, or of the victim "dropping charges." Just as there is no such thing in California as a complainant "pressing charges" (Chapter 5), there is no such thing as a complainant "dropping charges." The judge's exclusive authority over motions to dismiss includes the power to deny the prosecutor's 1385 motion [*People v. Parks* (1964) 230 CA2d 805], or to order a 1385 dismissal over the prosecutor's objections [*People v. Superior Court (Howard)* (1968) 69 C2d 491].

While the judge's authority is exclusive, it is not absolute. The judge must set forth her reasons for dismissing a case, in the minutes. Failure to do so invalidates the dismissal order. *People v. Andrade* (1978) 86 CA3d 963. And the reasons stated in justification for dismissal must show that the "furtherance of justice" was involved, *People v. Ritchie* (1971) 17 CA3d 1098, and not merely the convenience of the judge or the parties, or other improper motive. *People v. Superior Court (Long)* (1976) 56 CA3d 374.

If the furtherance of justice requires, the court may dismiss portions of a case, such as separate counts of penalty enhancement allegations (except serious felony priors, per Penal Code § 1385(b), or DUI-related priors, per Vehicle Code § 23200). However, the judge may not engage in "plea bargaining" with a defendant by agreeing to order some of the charges dismissed under 1385 with defendant's plea to others where the prosecutor objects to the proposed disposition. *People v. Orin* (1975) 13 C3d 937.

If a court's dismissal under 1385 is improper, either because the reasons are not stated in the minutes, or due to improper grounds, the dismissal may be reversed on appeal taken by the people and the charges reinstated. *Bellizzi v. Superior Court* (1974) 12 C3d 33. Otherwise, a 1385 dismissal is a bar to any further prosecution for that offense. Penal Code §1387. (An erroneously-granted 1385 dismissal also prevents retrial if granted after jeopardy has attached.)

DISMISSAL-RELEASE

Whenever the prosecutor decides to move for dismissal under 1385, she must consider the potential civil liability of arresting officers and other officials who may be exposed to suit once the matter is dismissed. A defendant emboldened by obtaining a dismissal of a criminal charge may take that decision as an indication that the charges were unfounded from the beginning, especially where the crime was charged as resisting or assaulting an officer. Fortified with the prosecutor's decision, the defendant may then file civil actions for false arrest and false imprisonment against the law enforcement officers and their agencies.

To avoid creating an inducement to sue, the prosecutor often conditions her motion to dismiss on the defendant's execution of a written and signed *stipulation to probable cause* for his arrest and incarceration. Although this stipulation would not preclude damages for any official misconduct, such as unlawful use of force against the defendant, it would remove the basis for suit alleging illegal arrest or false imprisonment.

It is sometimes contended that such a dismissal-release agreement might run afoul of Penal Code § 153 (compounding or concealing a crime), or could violate Rule 5-100 of the Rules of Professional Conduct for lawyers (improper to threaten criminal prosecution to obtain consideration in a civil case). In fact, however, both the California and US Supreme Courts have sanctioned this procedure:

...the state may reasonably elect to forego the imposition of any criminal proceedings or sanctions. However, in doing so it must protect those who because the charges are to be dismissed might be improperly exposed to claims of civil liabilities due to their involvement in apprehending the accused.

We conclude that the time-honored practice of discharging misdemeanants on condition of a release of civil liabilities or stipulation of probable cause for arrest, does not contravene public policy when the prosecutor acts in the interests of justice.

Hoines v. Barney's Club (1980)
28 C3d 603, 610-614.

Although *Hoines* involved a misdemeanor charge, the US Supreme Court adopted a similar rationale to approve of the same kind of dismissal-release agreement in a felony case, in *Newton v. Rumery* (1987) 480 US 386.

SUMMARY

√ Incentives to resolve cases without trial include proof problems, restrictive priorities, and the guarantee of a particular outcome.

√ As many as 80% of criminal cases are resolved by entry of a guilty plea by the accused.

√ A pre-plea probation report may be useful to the court and the parties in determining the appropriateness of a guilty plea.

√ Plea bargaining involves an agreement by the defendant to plead guilty to specified charges in exchange for the prosecutor's motion to dismiss or reduce charges. Plea bargaining is not permissible in serious felony cases or charges of driving under the influence.

√ If the court believes that uncertainty of the sentence to be imposed is all that is preventing the defendant from pleading guilty, the court may give an indicated sentence to let the defendant know what he is facing.

√ Submission of a case to the court on the preliminary hearing transcripts or police reports is considered a slow plea of guilty, and must be treated as a guilty plea for purposes of waiver of rights.

√ By court decisions, a defendant entering a guilty plea must be advised of his rights and the consequences of conviction, and must waive his Tahl/Boykin rights on the record. In felony cases, the court must also take a factual basis for the finding of guilt.

√ Narcotics offenses and other specified crimes may be subject to diversion for treatment outside the criminal process.

√ Some prosecutors conduct an informal office hearing to arrange voluntary settlement of minor criminal disputes.

√ A six-month continuance of a minor case to allow the defendant to demonstrate his good behavior and receive a dismissal of charges is unofficially termed "DA's probation".

√ A civil compromise is possible for misdemeanor cases where the victim informs the court of satisfaction and the defendant agrees to pay court costs.

√ Some charged defendants may have their cases dismissed under a grant of immunity to testify for the prosecution, subject to penalties for contempt and perjury.

√ Defendants suffering serious mental impairment may be adjudged incompetent or dangerous, and committed to treatment facilities for involuntary care. W&I 5150 is used to obtain a 72-hour detention for evaluation of dangerous persons.

√ When two or more cases are pending against the same defendant, the less serious case may trail behind the more serious case for ease of disposition.

√ Deportation of aliens is sometimes an effective alternative to criminal prosecution.

√ The court can order a dismissal of a pending case in the interests of justice, for reasons stated, on either the court's or prosecutor's motion.

√ A dismissal can properly be conditioned on the defendant's execution of a stipulation and release of involved officials for civil liability purposes.

ISSUES FOR DISCUSSION

1. Is it surprising to you that more than three-quarters of criminal defendants plead guilty? Does this necessarily suggest that the remaining defendants who choose to go to trial are more likely to be innocent? Why, or why not?

2. How could plea bargaining be eliminated altogether? Should it be? Does it serve a legitimate purpose in weeding out marginal cases, or simply provide an excuse for lazy or indifferent officials to dispose of cases with minimal effort?

3. Is the expansion of diversion programs an indication that the criminal justice system is incapable of handling present crime problems? Or is diversion a socially-responsible way of dealing with the underlying causes of certain types of criminal behavior? Does it work better than punishment?

4. Should victims and their families have a say in whether or not charges should be dismissed? How could this be accommodated?

5. Is it fair to require a defendant to sign a probable cause stipulation and liability release before dismissing charges against him? What if he has a legitimate grievance against police? What might happen if police could not be assured of this protection? Would they be less likely to do their jobs, or more likely to do them more carefully?

CHAPTER 9

PREPARATION FOR TRIAL

Learning Goals: After studying this chapter, you will be able to correctly answer the following questions:

√   What is "forum shopping"? Why is it done? How?

√   Can a witness in a criminal case give his testimony in a deposition? What is "conditional exam?" When can it be used?

√   Who can issue a subpena for a witness? Are there any restrictions? How is it served?

√   Are there special provisions for serving a subpena on a peace officer? Why? What are they?

√   What is a *subpena duces tecum*? What is required to make it valid? How is it complied with?

√   What are the guidelines on visiting the crime scene before trial?

√   When should presentation aids be prepared for a case? What are their advantages?

√   How are exhibits identified and recorded?

IMPORTANCE OF PREPARATION

A trial is an adversary contest. It is a competition between the parties, in which each attorney has a duty to zealously represent his client's position, within the bounds of the law. As in any adversarial endeavor, preparation is half of the battle.

If the prosecutor is unprepared for trial, continuances may have to be sought, thereby "aging" the case at the risk of losing witnesses or impairing their recollection; or if the matter proceeds to trial in an inadequate state of readiness, there may be interruptions and delays during presentation of the case as the prosecutor "scrambles" to secure witnesses, demonstrative evidence, or other aids that should have been arranged before trial. Lack of preparation as to legal issues that are likely to arise at trial may leave the prosecutor suffering adverse rulings by the court affecting evidence admissibility, examination of witnesses and scope of argument to the jury. In short, for want of preparation, the case may be lost.

Most of the same observations hold true for the defense attorney (except that "aging" of the case normally works to the defendant's advantage). In addition, an unprepared defense attorney who is appointed by the court can be removed from the case, subjected to disciplinary sanctions, and blamed for "ineffective assistance of counsel" problems that could result in mistrial and retrial.

Thus, both sides have substantial incentives to prepare adequately for trial. This means gathering "intelligence" about the adversary attorney, the judge, the witnesses and the jury. It also means learning as much as possible about the facts of the case, researching legal and procedural matters, assembling their proof, and preparing trial aids for presentation of the case to the jury.

EVALUATING THE ATTORNEY

Although the basic approach to a trial will be predetermined by the facts of the crime, the particular trial strategy will be determined by the respective attorneys. This strategy may be affected by many variable factors, but will largely be a reflection of each attorney's personal style. An important step in planning the tactics, then, is assessing the style of the opposing attorney, to blunt his or her strengths and exploit any weaknesses.

Just as a military commander assesses the intelligence on his counterpart in the opposing force, or an athletic team reviews scouting reports and other data on the coaches and players of the opposing team, the conscientious trial attorney develops a tactical profile on his courtroom opponent. This may be done on the basis of past experience with the same attorney in previous trials, contact with other attorneys for their insights, probing during the pretrial negotiations and motions, published information in attorney directories, and review of transcripts from the attorney's prior trials of similar cases. Most attorneys also maintain their own files on news stories and professional publications written by or about practicing attorneys in their area.

The size-up of the opposing attorney continues throughout the pretrial proceedings and early phases of the trial, to permit constant reevaluation of tactical choices. The trial lawyer who has "done his homework" on his opponent should have a fairly accurate notion by the opening of trial as to whether he is facing an adversary who is skilled or sloppy, smooth or gruff, quiet or vocal, emotional or logical, sneaky or straightforward, aggressive or accommodating, honest or dishonest, etc. The more an attorney knows about his adversary's style and abilities, the better prepared he will be to make strategical choices that serve his client's interests.

FORUM SHOPPING

The judge assigned to preside over a trial can exercise broad discretion, deciding whether to admit contested evidence, sustain or overrule objections, allow particular arguments, or permit particular conduct by the attorneys. If there is a conviction, the trial judge will usually also be the sentencing judge, choosing between probation or incarceration, and setting the amount of fines and, subject to some limits, determining the length of imprisonment or jail.

Both attorneys would normally prefer to try their case before a judge who is sympathetic to their side of the case. Sometimes, but by no means always, the prosecutor prefers a judge with former prosecutorial experience, while the defense attorney prefers a judge who was previously a defense lawyer herself. If the outcome of the case is expected to turn on resolution of technical points of law, the parties may wish to have a scholarly judge; where credibility of opposing witnesses is the crucial issue, a common-sense judge might be preferred. If the trial will be lengthy, good health and patience would be important; with certain kinds of hostile witnesses or obstructionist attorneys, a judge with a reputation for firm control may be needed.

The right judge to insure fairness in a trial will depend on the facts, issues and personalities involved in the case. To the extent they may be able to influence judicial assignment, both attorneys will seek the best available jurist for the case, from their point of view. This again requires information about the reputation of judges, which may be gathered in many of the same ways as attorney intelligence is collected. In addition, the legal newspapers often feature judicial "profiles," which may be saved by attorneys for reference.

As discussed in Chapter 7, each side is entitled to exercise one peremptory challenge to a judge assigned to handle a case. An unacceptable judge viewed by either attorney as too likely to favor the other side unfairly may be eliminated from the case by this procedure. And, as discussed, any judge can be disqualified on the basis of a justifiable challenge for cause.

Other techniques can be used to avoid an undesirable forum. The simplest is a delay. When it appears that a case will be assigned to an unpreferred judge, an attorney in a master calendar court (from which all cases may be assigned out to trial courts) can stall assignment of the case by asking to trail, by moving for continuance, or by intimating that further discussions with counsel might produce a disposition of the case. The attorney could also informally request that the matter not be assigned to a particular court, or suggest that assignment to another judge might be more likely to result in settlement without trial. Motion for change of venue could be used where the entire judicial panel of a particular court was unacceptable. Other tactics may be used by creative counsel to influence forum selection.

The process of scheduling a number of successive pretrial settings is sometimes used by an attorney to gauge reaction from a variety of judges to the general tenor of the case. If the attorney receives indicated sentences from several different judges, he can then attempt to maneuver the case before the one who gave the most favorable indication. The practice of taking the case from court to court to find the most amenable judge is known as *forum shopping*. Once the attorney feels he has identified the best court in which to enter a guilty plea or proceed to trial, he begins to demand speedy trial, and to oppose the other attorney's efforts to wrest the case from the assigned court.

In some cases, the attorneys have agreed after a trial that the choice of forum made all the difference between conviction and acquittal. Although such a situation is facially inconsistent with the precept of equal protection of the law and with the notion that justice should not depend on the predilections of the particular judge, the practical fact is that it sometimes does.

WITNESS EVALUATION AND PREPARATION

A significant part of the trial lawyer's strategy is the decision of which witnesses to call at trial, which facts to elicit from them, and the most strategic order in which to present them for most logical or dramatic effect on the jury. The first step in planning the presentation and use of witnesses is determining who they are and what they know.

The police investigation will usually have identified most or all of the potential prosecution witnesses, and perhaps some of the defense witnesses. The attorneys will thus begin by reading the reports and contacting these known witnesses for interviews. Witness interviews may be conducted directly by the lawyer, or by an investigator. They will usually be tape recorded, or documented in the investigator's notes, for comparison with earlier statements attributed to them in the police reports, or with subsequent testimony in court.

If a particular witness's testimony is crucial to the case, the attorney whose side stands to suffer from this testimony may make pointed efforts to develop inconsistent stories or statements during pretrial interviews. Any such inconsistencies may be useful at trial to impeach (undermine) the witness's testimony. It has been held to constitute inadequate legal representation for a defense attorney to fail to attempt to interview potential witnesses for trial. *In re Hall* (1981) 30 C3d 408. At the same time, it is improper for either attorney to interfere with opposing counsel's efforts to interview any witness (other than the defendant) who wishes to discuss the case. *Walter v. Superior Court* (1957) 155 CA2d 134.

Once potential witnesses have been identified and interviewed (if possible), the attorney evaluates their testimony for its helpful or damaging effect on his client's case. This enables him to determine whether he will call the witness on his side of the case, or prepare to attack the witness when called by the adversary. The lawyer will look for evidence of the witness's vulnerability, including prior criminal record, bias or motive to fabricate, inability to perceive (such as poor vision), inability to recollect details, and inability to express himself or herself, including English language difficulties.

To prepare to meet the testimony of prosecution witnesses, the defense is entitled to the "rap sheet" (criminal record) of convictions suffered by the witnesses involving "moral turpitude" (dishonesty, or readiness to do evil). Preventing access to such potential impeachment material, including juvenile court convictions, may violate a defendant's Sixth Amendment right to confront the witnesses against him. *Davis v. Alaska* (1974) 415 US 308. Also, a prosecutor who intends to use a jailhouse informant as a witness must disclose specified information about the informant's arrangement. Penal Code §§ 1127a, 1191.25, 4001.1.

Per Evidence Code § 720 and Penal Code § 1127b, some persons may qualify to render opinions as *expert witnesses*. These might be such specialists as physicians, criminalists, scientists, engineers, specially-trained police officers, or others with concentrated knowledge on a subject. An indigent defendant may apply to the court for appointment of necessary expert witnesses to help prepare or present his case. Evidence Code § 730. Although juries tend to distrust some experts, such as psychiatrists and psychologists, many experts can be helpful in explaining complicated or technical matters.

After an attorney has determined which witnesses she will call to present her case, she prepares the witnesses for their roles. This includes briefing them as to date, time and place to appear, restrictions on access to the courtroom while proceedings are under way, precautions about discussing the case openly around the courthouse, appropriate dress and demeanor, use of court interpreters, physical layout of the courtroom, guidelines for testifying, and the subject matter to be covered. (See full discussion in Chapter 11.)

CONDITIONAL EXAMINATION OF WITNESSES

Witnesses who are familiar with *civil* procedure often balk at testifying in a criminal case, asking instead that they be allowed to submit to a pretrial *deposition* (recorded examination of their testimony outside court). However, because of hearsay problems and a criminal defendant's confrontation rights, this procedure is not generally available in criminal cases.

The statutes do provide a procedure called *conditional examination* for the out-of-court taking or a witness's testimony in extraordinary cases. This procedure is rarely used. It is authorized only in cases of manifest jeopardy of the life of a witness in a serious felony case, or when the witness is seriously ill and may not survive until trial, or when the witness is leaving the state. Penal Code §§ 882, 1335, 1336. The party calling the witness must submit an application containing specified information and obtain a court order for the conditional exam of his witness. Penal Code §§ 1337-1339. The recorded examination of the witness is then sealed for trial, to be read into the record at trial if otherwise admissible. Penal Code §§ 1343-1345.

THE SUBPOENA PROCESS *under penalty*

Many people willingly become trial witnesses because they have a personal interest in the outcome of the case, or because it is their duty to do so, or merely because it is an act of good citizenship. But the witness's role is not always easy: there may be risks to personal safety in some cases, there will be inconvenience and disruption of the normal life-style, there may be loss of wages, and there could be stress associated with courtroom appearance and scrutiny.

Because of these potential drawbacks, some persons are reluctant to be called as witnesses, even though they may have relevant information that might tend to establish the defendant's guilt or innocence. To secure their mandatory appearance in court, the law gives both parties the right to issue, or have issued, written, enforceable commands called *subpoenas* ("under penalty"). US Constitution, amendment 6; California Constitution, Article I, § 15; Government Code § 204; Penal Code § 1326.

A properly issued, properly served subpena requires the witness's appearance in court as specified, subject to punishment for contempt for failure to obey. Penal Code § 1331. Witness fees of $12 to $18 per day may be authorized, in the court's discretion. Penal Code § 1329.

A subpena in a criminal case can be issued by a judge, court clerk, defense attorney, or district attorney or public defender and their investigators. Penal Code § 1326. Such a subpena is only effective up to 150 miles from the place of trial; to subpena witnesses beyond that radius requires an affidavit of materiality and necessity, and an endorsement by a judge. Penal Code § 1330.

Subpoenas may be personally served by any person (except the defendant) by delivery to the subpoenaed witness (and to the parent of a witness under 12), or by mail or messenger. Penal Code § 1328, 1328d. To protect the confidentiality of the addresses of peace officers, the law allows service of peace officers by delivery of two copies of the subpena to a superior; the superior officer may refuse to accept service if it is not reasonably certain that the subpena can be delivered to the officer before any court date set less than five working days away. Penal Code § 1328.

SUPERIOR COURT OF THE STATE OF CALIFORNIA
FOR THE COUNTY OF ORANGE

SUBPOENA CRIMINAL

CASE NUMBER

THE PEOPLE OF THE STATE OF CALIFORNIA,   PLAINTIFF

VS.

DEFENDANT(S)

THE PEOPLE OF THE STATE OF CALIFORNIA, TO:

Please see Witness Information on the reverse side of
this subpoena.

PHONE NO. (BUS.)
(RES.)

Tony Rackauckas, District Attorney
County of Orange, State of California

YOU ARE COMMANDED TO APPEAR IN THE ABOVE COURT TO TESTIFY
AS A WITNESS AGAINST THE NAMED DEFENDANT(S) AT THE FOLLOWING
TIME AND PLACE.

Court Room:
DATE:
TIME:

CERTIFICATE OF SERVICE

hereby certify that on _____, 19 ____, I served the within subpoena on the person(s) named hereafter by
personally delivering a true copy thereof to said witness.

Not Served (name and reason) _____

declare under penalty of perjury that the foregoing is true and correct.

Executed at _____, California, on _____, 19 ___.

By: _____

F0232-0472 (12/98)   SEE REVERSE   ORIGINAL

Both parties have the power to compel attendance of witnesses by subpoena.

For the convenience of witnesses, the party causing issuance of a subpena can agree with the witness to an "on-call" arrangement, under which the witness remains at home or at work, accessible by telephone. When it becomes reasonably certain that the witness will be needed in court, she can be called on appropriate notice to appear. Failure to comply with an on-call agreement is also punishable as a contempt. Penal Code §1335.

SUBPOENA DUCES TECUM *+documents*

A witness might have not only relevant *knowledge*, but also relevant *documents* or other tangible things of evidentiary value in a case. To compel the witness to attend the trial *and to bring specified documents or other evidence to court*, a party uses a *subpena duces tecum* ("under penalty, bring with you"). This form of subpena must be supported by an affidavit containing the matters specified in Code of Civil Procedure § 1985; it must do the following:

1. Show *good cause* for production of the items sought.

2. Specify the *exact things* to be produced.

3. Set forth the *materiality* of the evidence.

4. Allege that the witness has *possession or control* of the items.

An SDT is not valid unless supported by such affidavit, *a copy of which must accompany service*. Code of Civil Procedure §1987.5.

If an SDT is served on a custodian of *business records* for the production of records only, a special mail-in procedure for compliance may be used, as detailed in Evidence Code §§ 1560, 1561. Compliance with any other SDT is accomplished by the witness *appearing in court*, as commanded, *with the required evidence*. Although police departments, crime labs, property custodians and others served with SDTs often mistakenly believe they are required to turn over the evidence to the attorney requesting it, this is not the proper procedure.

An SDT is not a discovery order authorizing attorney access to the evidence:

> The issuance of a *subpoena duces tecum* is purely a ministerial act and does not constitute legal process in the sense that it entitles the person on whose behalf it is issued to obtain access to the records described therein until a judicial determination has been made that the person is legally entitled to receive them.
>
> *People v. Blair* (1979) 25 C3d 640, 651

If a witness believes he has been improperly or unnecessarily subpoenaed to appear, he can bring a *motion to quash* (vacate) the subpena. If the motion is granted, no compliance is necessary. *Civiletti v. Municipal Court* (1981) 116 CA3d 105.

(The public and media frequently confuse and misuse the terms "subpena" and "summons." As just discussed, a *subpena* compels the attendance of a *witness*; a *summons* is a notice to a *party* against whom complaint has been made, directing him to appear and answer. See Penal Code § 813, and discussion in Chapter 6.)

JURY BOOK

Another aspect of preparing the case for trial is obtaining any available information about the probable performance of potential jurors. Some jury panels are called for a single trial, and then excused; others are called for service for a minimum period of time, such as 30 days or 90 days. During this time, individual members may serve on a number of cases. As they do so, their performance is logged by prosecutors and public defenders to show whether they convicted, acquitted or failed to reach verdicts, and in what kinds of cases. This information, together with opinions and positions they reveal during jury selection, will often be incorporated into a *jury book*, to be circulated and shared with other members of the legal staff.

Also, the district attorney may assemble investigative reports and criminal records on members of the jury panel, to determine which of them have themselves been criminal defendants, and in what kinds of cases. A court has discretion to order disclosure of such information to defense counsel to prevent unfair advantage. *People v. Murtishaw* (1981) 29 C3d 733. Although juror privacy is generally protected (Code of Civil Procedure § 237), identifying information can sometimes be obtained by an attorney seeking information for a client's motion for new trial. Code of Civil Procedure § 206. Commercial jury polling and evaluation services are also available to the parties, supplying computerized data on demographics, community standards and attitudes, and other research data.

CRIME SCENE INSPECTION

Circumstances permitting, and depending on the facts and issues of the case, attorneys should try to visit the crime scene as soon as possible, before the layout is disturbed. Each witness's statement should be reviewed from the perspective of his or her vantage point at the scene; measurements should be made as necessary; and any diagrams or photographs should be completed. If the appropriate time of day and lighting conditions can be approximated, the scene should be examined this way. An investigator must be used for any evidentiary activity, so that he can testify at trial and the attorney can avoid becoming a witness.

PRESENTATION AIDS

In most kinds of cases, the majority of the trial presentation on both sides will consist of oral testimony from witnesses. This manner of proof sometimes lacks clarity and frequently engenders boredom in the jury. To add spice, dramatic effect, and audiovisual impact, the polished attorney tries to find appropriate ways to illustrate information with charts, diagrams, models, enlarged photos, video, slides, transparencies, sound recordings, reenactments and demonstrations. Not only do such aids tend to stimulate the jury's interest and attention, they also help the jury to visualize oral evidence and to understand technical matters. Tactically used, they may have a disproportionate influence on the jury's ultimate decision.

Selection and construction of appropriate aids in presentation of the case is an important preparatory step to give the attorney confidence in her image before the jury. When used in a trial against an attorney who has made no corresponding effort, graphic aids can be particularly effective to help put across the case.

EXHIBITS AND EXHIBIT SHEETS

Any physical evidence that is to be offered at trial will have to be appropriately described and marked for identification. If the attorney plans to introduce only a few such exhibits, they can be marked during the course of trial. If there will be a large number, however, it is best to obtain identification tags from the court clerk in advance, write in a brief description, and number them in the order of planned introduction. (The people's exhibits are *numbered*; defense exhibits are *lettered*: "People's 1." "Defense A.")

To keep track of the exhibits offered by both sides and to record whether or not they have been admitted in evidence by the court, the attorney may prepare and use an *exhibit sheet*. This is simply a handy checklist to facilitate reference to the exhibits during witness examination and argument. A simple exhibit sheet format might consist of a column of numbers with spaces to write a brief description of people's exhibits, a separate column of letters for defense exhibits, and a space for a check mark to indicate that the exhibit was received in evidence. In a case with many exhibits, failure to keep track may not only cause verbal fumbling during examination and argument, but might also cause the inadvertent failure to move critical exhibits into evidence for jury consideration.

Firearms, explosives, and other weapons and dangerous instrumentalities must be packaged or rendered inoperable for safety and security before being brought into the courtroom. Trigger locks are usually available from the clerk or bailiff. The bailiff should be allowed to inspect any such devices before trial to assure courtroom security, and counsel should keep them away from and out of reach of the defendant throughout proceedings.

RESEARCH

The attorney's preparation of the case and his experience during the pretrial motions will generally identify the probable legal issues that will arise at trial. To be prepared to respond, the attorney must thoroughly research and document the law on the elements of all crimes charged in the pleadings and all procedural and evidentiary issues that may foreseeably arise.

Particularly crucial or obscure legal issues should be briefed, with a memorandum of points and authorities to be submitted to the trial judge if needed. Once the trial gets under way, there is usually little opportunity to make up for neglected preparation in this area.

TRIAL NOTEBOOK

The volume of police reports, witness statements, transcripts, jury sheets, documentary evidence, pleadings, pretrial orders, research materials and other documents collected in preparation for trial can easily become unmanageable. Since quick access will be important at trial, it is necessary to organize the materials. Some attorneys prefer a file system, some use lap-top computers, and some put together an indexed trial notebook. The choice is somewhat dictated by the nature of the case, and partly by the personal preference of the attorney.

All that is important is that the system be useful to the trial attorney in presenting a logical, thorough and compelling case. Putting together a notebook or other organizer forces the lawyer to be prepared, and gives her an air of confidence and efficiency that can go a long way toward starting the trial off on a strong note.

SUMMARY

√ Preparation for trial includes "sizing-up the opposition," beginning with the adversary attorney.

√ Pretrial maneuvering to obtain the most favorable available judge is known as forum shopping.

√ Witness interview and evaluation helps determine order of proof and grounds for impeachment.

√ An expert witness is one who can offer an opinion about a matter on which he has a specialized knowledge.

√ Civil deposition procedure is not used in criminal cases, although there are provisions for the conditional exam of witnesses in rare cases.

√ A subpena issued by an attorney is valid up to 150 miles. Witnesses beyond that distance must be subpoenaed by a judge's order.

√ A peace officer's superior can accept service of a subpena, but may decline for hearings less than five working days away without reasonable opportunity for service.

√ A subpoenaed witness can be placed on call to reduce inconvenience.

√ An order to appear and bring evidence is a *subpena duces tecum*. It requires a supporting, accompanying affidavit.

√ Persons served with a SDT should not turn over evidence to the issuing attorney, but should take the evidence to court.

√ A jury book is a lawyer's list of jurors and information on their prior activity.

√ Crime scene inspection should be made promptly, with an investigator, under conditions comparable to those attending the crime.

√ Presentation aids enliven and enlighten the testimonial evidence, and demonstrate preparation by the attorney.

√ Evidentiary exhibits must be described, marked for identification, and logged on an exhibit sheet for easy reference. Weapons require special precautions.

√   Advance legal research, especially into pivotal issues and un-
    common points of law, is a necessary step in trial preparation.

√   A trial notebook or equivalent organizer facilitates a smooth,
    professional presentation of the case.

ISSUES FOR DISCUSSION

1. Is forum shopping a legitimate tactic? Should the courts discourage
    it? How? Does forum shopping impede justice?

2. Should lawyers be allowed to attack the credibility of witnesses by
    exposing their criminal records and prior inconsistent statements?
    Is there a public perception that civic-minded witnesses may be
    treated as if they were on trial? Does this discourage witnesses
    from becoming involved? How could this be improved?

3. Do lawyers run a risk of turning criminal trials into multimedia
    shows if they rely too heavily on technical and graphic aids? Are
    today's jurors too accustomed to being entertained to be able to
    concentrate responsibly on a testimonial trial?

TRIAL PROCEDURE

Learning Goals: After studying this chapter, you will be able to correctly answer the following questions:

√ What are the legal sources of trial procedure?

√ How are juries chosen? What is *voir dire*? What is a "Wheeler motion?" When should it be granted?

√ What is the purpose of the opening statement?

√ What are the various stages of the evidentiary phase of the trial? What sequence do they follow?

√ What is the difference between objections and motions to strike? When is each used?

√ What is an "1118 motion"? When is it made?

√ What are the three stages of argument? What is a "Griffin error"? A "Doyle error"? What is their effect?

√ How is the jury instructed?

√ What are the rights of public and press access to trial?

RULES OF PROCEDURE

The order of trial and rules of procedure are derived from several sources. These include the Fifth, Sixth and Fourteenth Amendments to the US Constitution; Article I, §§14-30, of the California Constitution; various provisions of the Penal Code (especially, §§1041-1168); applicable provisions of the Code of Civil Procedure (see Penal Code § 1102); the Evidence Code, and implementing provisions of various other codes. In addition, the courts sometimes supply "judicially-declared rules of procedure," under their inherent powers of supervision. *People v. Aranda* (1965) 63 C3d 518. Local and statewide Rules of Court supplement procedural laws.

The judge and the attorneys for the parties must be familiar with all of the applicable procedural rules, and must remain abreast of changes. Failure to follow proper procedure may result in miscarriage of justice, as well as disciplinary sanctions against the errant attorney or judge. The typical trial sequence is set forth below, with a brief summary of each step in the trial process, and selected highlights.

WAIVER OF JURY TRIAL

If the prosecution and defense have both agreed to a *court trial* (trial by judge, without jury), each must waive the right to jury trial, since both sides have such right. California Constitution, Article I, § 16; *People v. Peace* (1980) 107 CA3d 996. The prosecutor's waiver of jury can be inferred from his silent acquiescence in a defense request for court trial. *People v. Evanson* (1968) 265 CA2d 698. However, the defendant's waiver of jury trial must be expressly given in open court. *People v. Holmes* (1960) 54 C2d 442. If both parties waive, the judge must allow a court trial, and has no power to insist that a jury be used. *People v. Terry* (1970) 2 C3d 362.

Reasons for the prosecutor to waive jury and submit to court trial might include the saving of time and money (court trials typically take a fraction of the time of jury trials), and the reduced risk of retrial (juries often "hang" at numerical splits of 10-2 or 11-1 for conviction, necessitating costly retrial simply because of one or two recalcitrant jurors, whereas a judge will reach a final decision on guilt or innocence). A court trial might also be preferable where the case turns on technical legal issues, or on the credibility of witnesses (judges have extensive experience at observing the demeanor of witnesses and recognizing fabricated defenses, whereas jurors may be seen as naive, undiscerning and unwilling to accept that witnesses readily perjure themselves to thwart justice).

From the defense viewpoint, a court trial may be a way to simply put the prosecution to its proof where there is no genuine issue of guilt, but the prosecution case is shaky (uncooperative witnesses may not appear or testify, or other proof problems are known to exist). The defendant might also use a court trial to preserve legal issues on appeal where his defense is technical. Sometimes, the nature of the charge is too embarrassing or humiliating for a defendant to air to a jury, though not to a judge. Economics may also be a factor for the defendant who is paying a retained attorney and plans to offer a defense that is no less likely to be accepted by a judge than by a jury.

The overwhelming majority of trials are tried to juries, however. The jury is considered to be an important protection against abuses by governmental officers, and a reliable barometer of community attitudes that may range from outrage to compassion. From the prosecutor's standpoint, the jury is a representative sample of the client he serves—the public; he can hardly argue with their judgment.

From the defendant's standpoint, the jury is a citizen-intermediary between him and the power of the state to accuse and punish. The requirement of a unanimous verdict (all jurors must agree in order to convict or acquit) is a very considerable guardian against the risk of unjust conviction.

JURY SELECTION

From the *venire*, or pool of jurors summoned by the jury commissioner or other officer of the court, a *panel* of potential jurors (usually 30) will be called for selection of the actual trial *jury* which will hear the case. In felony cases, the jury must consist of 12 members; misdemeanor juries may consist of any number from 6 to 12, by agreement of the parties (less than 12 is rare). Code of Civil Procedure § 220; *Ballew v. Georgia* (1978) 435 US 223; *People v. Trejo* (1990) 207 CA3d 1026.

In order to select the 12 jurors who will decide the case, the process of *jury selection* is used. The court clerk will draw the first 12 names from the panel at random, and these 12 jurors will be seated. Code of Civil Procedure § 232. From this point through conclusion of the trial, the judge bears responsibility for control of the proceedings:

> It shall be the duty of the judge to control all proceedings during the trial, and to limit the introduction of evidence and the argument of counsel to relevant and material matters, with a view to the expeditious and effective ascertainment of the truth regarding the matters involved.
>
> *Penal Code* § 1044

The court's exercise of control and discretion begins with the questioning of jurors, or *voir dire*. This double-infinitive French expression means literally, "to see, to tell," though it is frequently translated as "to speak the truth." (Correct pronunciation is *vwa deer*, but *vore dyre* and *vore deer* are often heard.) The voir dire examination of prospective jurors consists of questioning by the court and, as permitted, by the attorneys, to determine whether or not there may be cause for challenging their qualifications to sit in judgment of the case.

A challenge may be made either against the *entire panel* (as, for example, where the defendant feels that the manner of drawing the venire has deprived him of a representative cross-section of the community), or against an *individual juror*. The latter category of challenge, which is the most common kind, may be of two varieties— a challenge *for cause*, or a *peremptory challenge*. Code of Civil Procedure § 225.

A challenge for cause must be based on specifically-stated grounds. Examples might be prior knowledge and opinions about the case, kinship to the parties or attorneys, personal interest in the outcome of the case, or conscientious scruples against the death penalty (in such a case). Code of Civil Procedure § 229. A juror's physical incapacity may also be asserted as grounds for disqualification. Code of Civil Procedure § 228. The judge holds a hearing on any challenge for cause and allows or disallows the challenge. Code of Civil Procedure § 230. If the juror is excused, another name is drawn in replacement. There is no numerical limit to the number of challenges for cause.

The more common challenge, a peremptory, need not be based on any particular grounds or relate to any alleged disqualification. It is the means by which both the prosecutor and defendant may remove any otherwise-qualified juror that they simply do not feel comfortable with, based on body language, attitude, demeanor, or any other subjective factor. *People v. Johnson* (1989) 47 C3d 1194. In most cases, each side is entitled to 10 peremptory challenges (20 each in capital cases, 6 each in 90-day misdemeanors, and 5 more for each additional codefendant). Code of Civil Procedure § 231.

The first peremptory challenge is made by the prosecutor, the next by the defense. After each challenge, a replacement juror is seated and examined. When both the prosecutor and defense consecutively pass on peremptory challenges, the jury is then sworn. In the judge's discretion or on stipulation (agreement) of the parties, one or more alternate jurors may then be selected as potential replacements for regular jurors who might become unable to complete service. (Selection procedure is the same, with one peremptory per side, per alternate.) Code of Civil Procedure § 234.

Although a party need not give any reason for exercising peremptory challenges, the Equal Protection Clause of the Fourteenth Amendment forbids the use of peremptories to exclude members of a particular race, gender or religion because of group bias. *Batson v. Kentucky* (1986) 476 US 79; *People v. Wheeler* (1978) 22 C3d 258. If either side believes that the other is using his peremptory challenges in this manner, he may make a *Wheeler motion* to quash the entire panel and repeat jury selection. The court must then hear evidence, make findings, and grant or deny the motion. *People v. Turner* (1986) 42 C3d 711.

ATTACHMENT OF JEOPARDY

Because of the prohibition of twice putting the same person in jeopardy for the same case, it is necessary to fix the point at which jeopardy attaches: any errors occurring before jeopardy need not doom the case, while prejudicial errors occurring after attachment of jeopardy may end the prosecution. If jury has been waived and the case is to be decided by *court trial*, jeopardy attaches when the *first witness is sworn*, or when the court accepts an agreement for a slow plea. *Bunnell v. Superior Court* (1975) 13 C3d 592. In a *jury trial*, jeopardy attaches when the *jury is sworn* to hear the case. *Larios v. Superior Court* (1979) 24 C3d 324.

Once the jury is impaneled and sworn in a felony jury trial, the clerk or judge reads the information to the jury'and announces the defendant's plea. At the judge's discretion, this formality may be omitted in a misdemeanor trial. Penal Code § 1093(a).

OPENING STATEMENT

The first step in presentation of the case is the prosecutor's *opening statement*. Penal Code § 1093(b). This is a summary outline of the evidence, without argument, to provide the jury with an overview of the case so they can follow it more easily. The opening statement need not detail all of the evidence the prosecutor plans to produce, and should not include reference to evidence of questionable relevance or availability. *People v. Barajas* (1983) 145 CA3d 804.

After the prosecution's opening statement, the defense attorney may make an opening statement outlining the defense, or may defer until after the prosecution rests, or may waive opening statement. (An opening statement is usually not necessary, and so not usually made, in court trials, except in complex or unusual cases.)

A prosecution opening statement in a rape case, for example, might begin as follows:

> On Friday evening, March 26, 1999, Marilyn Alexander, an unmarried woman of twenty-three, retired to bed at about 11:00 p.m. She was alone in her apartment on Palm Street, in Park Viejo, with the doors and windows locked. Sometime later, she was awakened when she felt someone's hand on her throat, and a man's voice said, "Don't make a sound!"

FACTUAL STIPULATIONS

Once the defense has made or waived opening statement, the prosecutor has the burden of going forward with the evidence in support of the charges. Penal Code § 1093(c). If the parties have agreed to stipulate to any facts so that evidence need not be offered to prove them, the stipulations may be stated or read at the beginning of the case, or at a later, more appropriate time. (Tactical considerations will also control the timing of invocation of judicial notice or statutory presumptions.) An example of a situation where both sides might agree to a stipulation would be a vehicular manslaughter trial, in which identity of the deceased could be established by stipulation. This could save the next-of-kin prosecution witness a painful ordeal, while eliminating a sympathy factor objectionable to the defense.

CASE-IN-CHIEF

Since the defendant is presumed innocent "until the contrary is proved beyond a reasonable doubt," the burden of proving guilt is on the prosecution. Penal Code § 1096. To meet this burden, the prosecutor presents to the jury the testimony of any witnesses, the relevant and admissible physical evidence in the case, and any admissible inculpatory statements previously obtained from the accused. The examination of witnesses is governed by various provisions of the Evidence Code. Important features include the following:

- The court is responsible for insuring that witnesses are examined without waste of time or "undue harassment or embarrassment." Section 765(a).

- Witnesses must give "responsive" answers. Any non-responsive answer can be attacked by a "motion to strike." Section 766.

- (Contrast the *motion to strike* an improper *answer* with the *objection* to an improper *question*: if the opposing attorney feels a *question* is improper or calls for inadmissible information, she *objects*; if either attorney feels an *answer* is non-responsive or otherwise improper, she makes a *motion to strike* the answer, and to admonish the jury to disregard it. Thus, it is technically incorrect — though often heard in court—for an attorney to say, "Object, your honor, that's non-responsive.")

- A *leading question* is one that suggests the answer the examining attorney wants the witness to give. (Note: A question is not necessarily leading simply because it may call for a "yes" or "no" answer.) Leading questions may not generally be used by an attorney to examine the witness he calls, but may be used to cross-examine the other party's witnesses.

- (Leading questions are generally permissible, also, to establish preliminary matters not in dispute, to examine "hostile" witnesses and children, to identify exhibits, to impeach or refresh a witness's recollection, and to examine expert witnesses.) Sections 721, 764, 767, 776; *People v. Orona* (1947) 79 CA2d 820, 827; *People v. Campbell* (1965) 233 CA2d 38, 44.

- A witness may use notes or a report or other writing to refresh his recollection during testimony, but this material must be shown to the adverse party. Section 771.

- A witness's testimony may not be the result of hypnosis. Only events remembered and related by the witness before undergoing hypnosis may be recounted in court. Section 795; *People v. Shirley* (1982) 31 C3d 18.

- All other witnesses (except the defendant) may be excluded from the courtroom during the testimony of any witness, to avoid cross-influence. A designated investigating officer may be permitted to remain. *People v. Boyden* (1953) 116 CA2d 278, 283; section 777.

- Anyone can testify as a witness, unless incapable of expression or unable to understand the duty to tell the truth. Sections 700, 701. Unless testifying as an expert, a witness's testimony must be based on her personal knowledge. Section 702.

- Every witness must take an oath or affirm or declare that he will tell the truth. Section 710.

- Every witness must be examined in the presence of both parties. Section 711. The defendant has the *right to confront* all witnesses. US Constitution amendment VI; Penal Code section 686. The defendant may waive or forfeit this right by his voluntary absence or disruptive conduct in court. Penal Code § 1043; *Illinois v. Allen* (1970) 397 US 337.

- A disruptive defendant can only be removed, gagged or shackled on an actual showing of necessity. *People v. Duran* (1976) 16 C3d 282. The defendant has a right to change from jail clothes to street clothes for trial. *Estelle v. Williams* (1976) 425 US 501; *People v. Taylor* (1982) 31 C3d 488.

- The first examination of a witness is the *direct examination* by the party that called him. After the direct exam, the opposing party may conduct *cross-examination*. If additional information is then required, there may be *redirect* and *recross*. Sections 760-763, 772(a).

- Evidence is not admissible unless it is *relevant*. Section 350. "Relevant evidence" is any evidence that tends to prove or disprove a fact in issue. Section 210. Unless otherwise excluded by law, all relevant evidence is admissible. Section 351.

- Neither party may elicit from any witness any inadmissible *hearsay evidence* of an out-of-court statement offered for the truth of its content. Section 1200. A statement is not hearsay if it is repeated in court for some purpose other than to prove the truth of what was said (e.g., threats, bribes, solicitations, obscenities, or words used to show knowledge or supply probable cause). *People v. Smith* (1970) 13 CA3d 897, 910; *People v. Tahl* (1967) 65 C2d 719.

- The hearsay exclusion does not apply to the defendant's prior statement, conspirator statements, statements against interest, dying declarations, business and official records, prior inconsistent statements, spontaneous exclamations, and other categories of statements made under circumstances that strongly indicate trustworthiness. See sections 1220-1350.

- A witness cannot be required to testify to matters that are subject to legal privilege, such as confidential communications between the defendant and his spouse, physician, attorney or clergyman. See sections 930-1060.

During the course of the prosecution case-in-chief, the prosecutor may call any number of witnesses he deems necessary to establish the court's jurisdiction of the offense, all elements of the crime, and the identity of the defendant as the perpetrator. The court retains discretion to limit witnesses whose testimony is cumulative (needlessly repetitive). Sections 352, 723. Tactics and the nature of the case will normally dictate the order of witnesses. Most attorneys prefer to use witnesses with dramatic testimony as their first and last witnesses, inserting weaker and less interesting witnesses into the middle of the presentation. If it can be done, attorneys also like to end on a strong point just before the noon recess and the daily adjournment.

If it should become necessary during a joint trial, the prosecutor may move to discharge one or more codefendants to make them available to testify against other defendants. Penal Code § 1099.

Where it is important for the jury to view the crime scene to understand the testimony or to judge the facts, the court may order the bailiff to arrange such a viewing. Penal Code § 1119. Otherwise, it is improper for jurors to visit the scene during trial or deliberations. *People v. Tedesco* (1934) 1 C2d 211.

Before concluding her case-in-chief, the prosecutor moves into evidence any exhibits that were introduced, and when she has no further evidence to offer on the charges, announces, "The people rest."

DEFENSE

Whether the case is proceeding by court trial or jury trial, the first act of the defense upon the prosecution resting its case is normally to make an "eleven-eighteen motion." Penal Code §§ 1118, 1118.1. This is a motion for dismissal for insufficiency of the evidence. In essence, the defendant is claiming that the prosecution failed to present adequate proof to sustain a finding of guilt, and that therefore the defendant should not have to be put to a defense. *People v. Veitch* (1982) 128 CA3d 460. Both the motion and any hearing on the motion are conducted outside the presence of the jury. If the court grants the motion as to any counts, they are dismissed and may not be reinstated. The prosecution has no right of appeal from the granting of the motion, because of the double jeopardy bar. *People v. Gottman* (1976) 64 CA3d 775.

As to all charges remaining after the motion to dismiss, the defendant is entitled to put on any defense evidence, or to stand on the case as it rests, arguing to the jury that the prosecution has not met its burden of proof. If a defense is to be presented, it follows a similar order as the prosecutor's case-in-chief, beginning with opening statement (if not previously made), and then presentation of witnesses and evidence. Penal Code § 1093(b),(c).

To defend against a criminal charge, a defendant may employ one or more of three categories of defenses: (1) insufficiency of the evidence, (2) mistaken ID, or (3) affirmative defense.

1. "The crime wasn't committed." When the defendant challenges the crime itself, he is asserting that the acts constituting the offense were not committed. To amount to a defense, there need only be a reasonable doubt by the jury as to the proof of a single necessary element of the offense. Thus, in addition to any attack that may have been made on the prosecution case via cross-examination, the defendant may choose to offer evidence that contradicts the prosecution's proof on one or more elements.

For example, the defense may consist of offering evidence to negate specific intent, guilty knowledge, lack of consent, dominion and control, or any other crime element. If his evidence raises a reasonable doubt in the minds of the jury, he is entitled to acquittal. Penal Code § 1096; *People v. Mayberry* (1975) 15 C3d 143.

When there is strong evidence to indicate the defendant's complicity in the acts charged but not fully to support his conviction, the defendant may decide to defend on the basis that he is guilty of a lesser offense, and not guilty of the greater offense charged in the pleading. He can do this by admitting to, or conceding, the commission of a *lesser included offense* (e.g., simple assault, rather than assault with a deadly weapon; manslaughter, rather than murder). Penal Code § 1159. A lesser included offense is one that must necessarily have been committed if the greater offense occurred (all of the elements of the lesser are part of the elements of the greater).

2. **"If the crime was committed, I didn't do it."** A second option for a defendant is to challenge his identity as the perpetrator. This is usually done during cross-examination of the prosecution witnesses by attacking the reliability of pretrial identifications (showups, photo ID, lineups) and any in-court ID. On the defense case, an expert may be called as a witness to impeach the reliability of eyewitness identifications in general. *People v. McDonald* (1984) 37 C3d 351.

Another way to dispute ID is by presenting a defense of *alibi*. Although this term is frequently misused as a synonym for any defense whatsoever, an alibi simply means, "I can prove I was someplace else when the crime happened." If the defendant was someplace else, he could not be the criminal.

Alibi is generally offered through the testimony of the defendant himself and friends and relatives, or others who claim to know his whereabouts at the time of the crime. If defendant has prior convictions that could be introduced to impeach him, he usually exercises his Fifth Amendment privilege not to testify, and presents his alibi through the testimony of others. This prevents the jury from learning of his criminal past, and keeps him from being subjected to cross-examination that might reveal that his alibi is fabricated. A legitimate alibi is usually easy to confirm; however, because most alibi witnesses are persons with strong biases in favor of the defendant who inexplicably failed to come forward to clear him prior to trial, their testimony is largely discounted by judges and jurors.

3. **"If I committed the crime, I have a legal excuse."** The evidence establishing the commission of the crime and implicating the defendant is sometimes so overwhelming that it would be useless to defend on insufficiency or ID. An option for a defendant in such a case is to offer an *affirmative defense*. This simply means that assuming the truth of the pleading, there is a recognized defense at law that negates the defendant's guilt. Affirmative defenses include the following:

- *Mistake of fact* that disproves criminal intent. Penal Code § 26. *Example*: Defendant has a good-faith but mistaken belief that a consenting, physically mature girl is over 18, to negate guilt of unlawful sexual intercourse. *People v. Hernandez* (1964) 61 C2d 529.

- *Accident or misfortune* without criminal negligence. Penal Code § 26. *Example*: A householder draws a gun when he hears noises, and the gun goes off, wounding another occupant. *People v. Thurmond* (1985) 175 CA3d 865.

- *Duress*. The act was committed under threats of death or great bodily harm. Penal Code § 26. *Example*: A person commits an unlawful sex act under threats of physical harm. *People v. Peterman* (1951) 103 CA2d 322.

- *Necessity.* (Includes self-defense.) Protection, shelter or survival made the act necessary, negating criminal intent. Penal Code § 20. *Example*: Rehabilitation center inmate commits an escape from ordered custody because of the necessity to avoid forcible sex by a lesbian gang. *People v. Lovercamp* (1974) 43 CA3d 823.

- *Insanity.* The defendant committed the act while incapable of realizing what he was doing and distinguishing right from wrong. Penal Code § 25(b). *Example*: Under delusions that the NFL, the networks and the government are conspiring to divert athletes from the Vietnam-era draft, the defendant kills his wife to obtain a public forum. *People v. Stress* (1988) 205 CA3d 1259.

- *Unconsciousness of the act*. Penal Code § 26. *Example*: A person without apparent motive kills a total stranger during a psychomotor epileptic seizure which renders him oblivious to what he is doing. *People v. Williams* (1971) 22 CA3d 34.

- *Entrapment* by law enforcement officials or their agents, by use of techniques that might induce a normally law-abiding person to commit the crime (such as offering exorbitant payment, giving assurances that the conduct is not illegal or will not be detected, or relentless cajoling of the suspect).

Example: Officers employ a personal friend of defendant to repeatedly beg him, out of friendship, to get some drugs to keep the friend out of trouble. *People v. Barraza* (1979) 23 C3d 675.

● **Legal duty, privilege or immunity**. Acts that might otherwise be punishable are sometimes not, if committed in official duty. *Example*: Justifiable homicide by a police officer to prevent escape of a suspected murderer. Penal Code § 196; *Tennessee v. Garner* (1985) 471 US 1, 11. Certain conduct may be privileged. *Examples*: Law enforcement eavesdropping (Penal Code § 633); carrying of concealed firearms by peace officers (Penal Code § 12027); exceeding speed limits by emergency physician (Vehicle Code § 21058); possession of marijuana by research personnel (Health and Safety Code § 11478).

Some individuals enjoy qualified legal immunity from certain prosecutions. *Examples*: Peace officers handling narcotics during investigations (Health and Safety Code § 11367); foreign diplomats and their families and servants, as to any offense they commit (Title 22, United States Code, § 254)

● **Mistake of law**. Although it is generally true that "ignorance of the law is no excuse," failure of the government to give proper notice of obscure legal duties may create a due process defense. *Example*: Convicted forger is unaware of city ordinance requiring registration with local authorities within 5 days of moving into the city. *Lambert v. California* (1957) 355 US 225.

● **Double jeopardy**. Proof of a prior conviction, acquittal, dismissal or discharge bars further proceedings. Penal Code §§ 654, 793, 1023. *Example*: After appellate reversal of manslaughter conviction, defendant cannot be convicted of the greater offense of murder. *People v. Peña* (1984) 151 CA3d 462.

Whereas the defendant's burden of going forward with evidence attacking the crime elements or ID is merely to raise a reasonable doubt, his burden of proof on affirmative defenses is generally to establish their applicability by a preponderance of evidence. *People v. Tewksbury* (1976) 15 C3d 953; Evidence Code §§ 115, 500, 522 550.

Just as a codefendant may be discharged to become a prosecution witness, any codefendant against whom the evidence is insufficient may be discharged before the close of defense evidence to become a witness for any remaining defendant. Penal Code § 1100.

If a surprise defense witness testifies during the defendant's case and the prosecutor could not reasonably have been aware of the witness beforehand, the prosecution is entitled to a reasonable continuance to investigate the testimony and prepare cross-examination. If the defendant himself testifies, this continuance may not exceed one day. Penal Code § 1051.

REBUTTAL

To respond to the defendant's proof, the prosecutor may offer *rebuttal* evidence. Penal Code § 1093(d). This is evidence introduced to contradict the defense. It may or may not be evidence that would have been admissible in the prosecution case-in-chief, but it must be new evidence, and not simply a repeat of evidence that has already been offered. *People v. Graham* (1978) 83 CA3d 736.

Some kinds of evidence are admissible only during the rebuttal stage. For example, evidence that may have been inadmissible in the people's case-in-chief because of police violation of the defendant's rights is admissible for rebuttal or impeachment of the defendant's testimony. This is true whether the evidence was illegally seized [*US v. Havens* (1980) 446 US 620], was taken in violation of *Miranda* [*Harris v. New York* (1970) 401 US 222; *People v. May* (1988) 44 C3d 309], or was obtained in violation of the right to counsel [*Michigan v. Harvey* (1980) 110 S. Ct. 1176]. The jury must be admonished that this evidence is admitted for the limited purpose of impeaching the defendant's testimony. *Richardson v. Marsh* (1987) 481 US 200, 207; *People v. Duncan* (1988) 204 CA3d 613, 621.

The prosecutor may not, however, impeach the defendant's trial testimony with the fact that he remained silent after being given *Miranda* warnings following arrest. *Doyle v. Ohio* (1976) 426 US 610, 619.

SURREBUTTAL

If the prosecutor offers any rebuttal evidence, the defendant may then offer *surrebuttal*, which simply means rebuttal on rebuttal. Penal Code § 1093(d). Again, this must be evidence limited in scope to the matters raised by rebuttal, and may not merely repeat earlier proof. *People v. Remington* (1925) 74 CA 371.

ARGUMENT

Once both sides have concluded their offers of proof, the *argument* phase of the trial occurs. This phase has three parts. The prosecutor first makes *opening argument* (contrast this with the opening *statement* made at the beginning of trial). Next, the defense makes its one and only *argument*. And finally, the prosecutor is allowed to make the *closing argument*. Penal Code § 1093(e).

In opening argument, the prosecutor typically reviews the issues of law and the evidence produced, pointing out the arguments in favor of a guilty verdict (unless no good-faith argument can be made in support of a charge, in which case the prosecutor's duty to seek justice would compel a motion to dismiss). The defense argument both responds to the prosecutor's argument and points out the interpretation of the evidence favoring the defendant's plea. The prosecutor's closing argument is then limited to a reply to the defense.

Neither counsel may argue matters that are not in evidence. *People v. Villa* (1980) 109 CA3d 360. It is also improper for either counsel to express a *personal* belief in the credibility of a witness or in the guilt or innocence of the accused. *People v. Murtishaw* (1981) 29 C3d 733. Rather, the attorneys must argue in support of what the *evidence* establishes. *People v. Green* (1980) 27 C3d 1.

It is misconduct for the prosecutor to comment on the failure of the defendant to take the stand and testify. *Griffin v. California* (1965) 380 US 609. It is permissible, however, to point out that the defendant did not call other logical witnesses or offer other logical evidence. *People v. Szeto* (1981) 29 C3d 20; *People v. Ford* (1988) 45 C3d 431. If *Griffin* error does occur, it may be cured by prompt admonition to the jury to correct the error, and by appropriate instruction for the deliberations. *People v. Johnson* (1989) 47 C3d 1235.

MOTION FOR MISTRIAL

The defendant may move for a mistrial at any point when he believes that a prejudicial error has occurred that cannot be corrected with admonitions or instructions to the jury. *People v. Haskett* (1982) 30 C3d 841. An example of such error might be a police officer's inadvertent mention of highly-damaging evidence that had been ordered suppressed, or a prosecutor's improper argument aimed at inflaming prejudices in the jury.

If the judge grants a mistrial on the defendant's motion, the double jeopardy bar is deemed waived and the matter may be retried before another jury, unless the prosecutor deliberately provoked the mistrial motion. *Oregon v. Kennedy* (1982) 456 US 667. The prosecutor may not move for mistrial, since double jeopardy would bar retrial. *US v. Dinitz* (1976) 424 US 600.

CHARGING THE JURY

Before the jury retires for deliberations, they must be instructed on the law relevant to the charges and any included offense, and on the defenses and other issues raised by the proof. Penal Code § 1093(f). Many "standard" instructions on general principles of law and duties of deliberation are contained in the two-volume California Jury Instructions, Criminal, or CALJIC. These instructions are numbered for reference (circumstantial evidence, 2.00, for example).

In addition to applicable CALJIC instructions, the court must give special instructions submitted by the parties if appropriate to the case, and must instruct *sua sponte* (on its own motion) on principles of law necessary to guide the jury in deciding the case before it. *People v. Wickersham* (1982) 32 C3d 307.

DELIBERATIONS AND VERDICT

After the charge, the jury may reach a decision in court (highly unlikely) or retire to a private place to deliberate. Penal Code § 1128. They may take their notes, the trial exhibits and written instructions into the jury room with them. Penal Code § 1137. If they have any questions on the law during the course of their deliberations, they must be brought back into court for further instruction or clarification by the judge, in the presence of both parties. Penal Code § 1138; *People v. Thoi* (1989) 213 CA3d 689.

Only in a rare case is a jury sequestered (kept in a controlled setting, such as a hotel) during deliberations.

In most cases where deliberations are not completed in one day, the jury is admonished by the court prior to adjournment that they are not to discuss the case or form an opinion while separated. Penal Code § 1122. Jurors are not permitted to conduct their own crime scene investigations, nor to consult any outside source of information (such as friends, attorneys, newspapers, dictionaries, law books, etc.). *People v. Ladd* (1982) 129 CA3d 257; *People v. Sutter* (1982) 134 CA3d 806.

If the jury is unable to agree unanimously on a verdict after a reasonable time, the court may declare a mistrial and set the case for retrial before a new jury. Penal Code § 1140. Although the court can encourage the jury to reconsider opposing viewpoints and see whether a verdict can be reached, no pressure can be applied to the minority members to change their votes to conform to the majority. *People v. Gainer* (1977) 19 C3d 835.

Once the jury has reached a verdict, they are returned to the court to announce their verdict in the presence of the parties. Penal Code §§ 1148, 1149. The verdict may find the defendant "guilty" or "not guilty" as to any charge (there is no verdict of "innocent"). Penal Code § 1151. The jury must fix the degree of crime, if appropriate, and make special findings on such issues as sanity, truth of prior convictions, and truth of special sentence enhancement circumstances. See Penal Code §§ 25, 190.4, 1152-1158, 12021.5-12022.9, for examples. Either party may request that the jury be *polled* (asked individually if they agree with the verdict). Penal Code § 1163. Once the verdict is received, the jury is discharged. Penal Code § 1164.

If the defendant is acquitted of the charges, he must be discharged; if convicted, he may be taken into custody or permitted to remain on bail on OR release pending sentencing, in the court's discretion. Penal Code §§ 1165, 1166.

ACCESS TO TRIAL

The inevitable tension between a defendant's right to a fair trial and the public's right to free speech and press is the subject of continual litigation. The conflict has been addressed by the US Supreme Court many times:

> The principle that justice cannot survive behind walls of silence has long been reflected in the Anglo-American distrust for secret trials.... A responsible press has always been regarded as the handmaiden of effective judicial administration, especially in the crimi-

nal field.... This Court has, therefore, been unwilling to place any direct limitations on the freedom traditionally exercised by the news media, for what transpires in the court room is public property.

But the Court has also pointed out that legal trials are not like elections, to be won through the use of the meeting-hall, the radio, and the newspaper. Freedom of discussion should be given the widest range compatible with the essential requirement of the fair and orderly administration of justice. But it must not be allowed to divert the trial from the very purpose of a court system....

...[T]he presence of the press at judicial proceedings must be limited when it is apparent that the accused might otherwise be prejudiced or disadvantaged.

*Sheppard v. Maxwell (*1966) 384 US 333

To balance the conflicting rights of fair trial and free speech, the courts have essentially established a presumption that court proceedings must remain open to the public, including the press, unless a judge specifically finds that limited restrictions on access are necessary because of a reasonable likelihood of substantial prejudice to the accused. *Press Enterprise v. Superior Court* (1984) 464 US 501.

While a court cannot generally order the media not to cover a case or report what it learns, the proceedings can be closed or moved if necessary, and all officers of the court can be ordered not to comment on the case to the media ("gag order"). *Nebraska Press v. Stuart* (1976) 427 US 539.

SUMMARY

√   Both the prosecution and defense have a right to a jury trial. They may waive this right and submit to a court trial, by judge alone.

√   Jury selection involves the questioning process called voir dire, in which prospective jurors are examined to assess their qualifications to sit. Unacceptable jurors may be challenged for cause or, if no legal cause appears, by peremptory challenge for any reason except group bias.

√   In a court trial, jeopardy attaches when the first witness is sworn; in a jury trial, jeopardy attaches when the jury is sworn.

√   The opening statement is a non-argumentative outline of the case to be presented.

√   During the testimony of witnesses, opposing counsel makes an objection when a question is deemed improper, and a motion to strike when an answer is thought improper.

√   Direct exam is the first examination of a witness by the party that called him; cross-exam is conducted by opposing counsel. With some exceptions, leading questions may be used on cross-exam, but not on direct.

√   At the close of the prosecution case-in-chief, the defense routinely makes a motion for dismissal under Penal Code § 1118.1 for insufficiency of evidence.

√   If the defendant chooses to offer a defense, it may challenge sufficiency of the evidence on one or more elements, allege inaccuracy of the ID, or assert an affirmative defense. Alibi is an attack on ID, claiming defendant was someplace else.

√   The entrapment defense focuses on whether police methods were so compelling as to induce an otherwise law-abiding person to commit the offense.

√   During rebuttal of the defendant's testimony, some illegally obtained evidence may be introduced for impeachment. Defendant's *Miranda*-induced silence is generally inadmissible.

√   Sequence of argument is prosecutor's opening argument, defense argument, and then prosecutor's closing argument.

It must focus on the evidence, and not on personal beliefs or the defendant's failure to testify.

√   Because of double jeopardy, only the defendant may move for mistrial based on prejudicial error.

√   Jury instructions submitted by the judge include standard CALJICs, special instructions from the parties, and sua sponte instructions necessarily given on the court's own motion.

√   Jury deliberations must be private and may not be influenced by improper "juror investigation."

√   The public/press right of access to trials must be balanced against, and if necessary must yield to, the defendant's right to fair trial.

ISSUES FOR DISCUSSION

1. Is a jury of working-class, law-abiding citizens really a jury of "peers" for the typical criminal? Can they understand and appreciate his situation? Do they need to?

2. How reliable is the jury system at determining guilt or innocence? What are its drawbacks? What are its benefits? What might work better? Should we change?

3. It is constitutional error for the prosecutor to draw the jury's attention to the fact that the defendant did not testify in his defense. Is this so-called Griffin error really a necessary protection of self-incrimination rights, or a meaningless technicality? Doesn't the jury already notice when a defendant fails to take the stand and deny the charges? What is the logical, inescapable conclusion to be drawn?

4. Which should take precedence — the defendant's rights to due process, or the right of free speech and press? In the long view, which is more important? Why do they conflict?

CHAPTER 11

TESTIMONIAL PROCEDURE

Learning Goals: After studying this chapter, you will be able to correctly answer the following questions.

√   What steps should a subpoenaed witness take in preparation for testifying in court?

√   What is an expert resumé? When should it be developed? What should it contain?

√   What are the most significant features of a winning court room demeanor? Why is demeanor so important?

√   When testifying on direct exam, what guidelines should a witness follow? How should objections be handled?

√   How does cross-examination differ? Should the witness make adjustments? Are there special guidelines for handling cross-examination?

√   How can the witness best cope with leading questions from the adverse attorney?

231

Sooner or later, most people find themselves called to testify in a criminal case, whether as victim, witness, or investigating officer. Although it may be an unfamiliar activity, it need not be particularly uncomfortable. The witness who understands the value of preparation and proper demeanor, and who observes a few basic "do's and don'ts" while on the witness stand, can give a confident, convincing presentation of testimonial evidence.

PREPARATION

As with most activities, testifying in court requires a certain amount of groundwork. Because of the probing nature of the adversarial questioning that marks a court hearing or jury trial, any misinformation or lack of information is likely to be exposed. It is the job of the attorneys to develop important details from the witnesses, to draw fine distinctions, to seek precision in answers, and to identify inconsistencies, misrecollections, misperceptions and other human imperfections that may affect the overall credibility of the testifying witness. Knowing this, every witness who receives a subpena to testify is in effect being given a warning: "Get ready."

If relatively little time has passed between the event in issue and the court date, preparation may not need to be too extensive. Unfortunately, in most cases the delay from crime to trial will be a period of months, and sometimes years. In this interim, memories fade, details become blurred with other events, and the chances of testimonial error increase. In these cases, greater preparation is absolutely essential to effective testimony. Depending on whether the witness under subpena is a civilian or a peace officer, some or all of the following steps may apply:

Talk to the attorney. Although this may not always be possible, a call to the attorney who issued the subpena may disclose why the witness is being called, what he may expect to be questioned about, and where he should concentrate his preparation. The attorney would also be able to suggest areas of likely cross-examination the witness should be prepared to meet. As long as testimony is not "rehearsed" and the witness is advised to tell the truth in every answer he gives, there is nothing improper about discussing the case beforehand with the attorney, and this may be readily acknowledged in court if the opposing attorney inquires.

Review reports. Any written reports or tape recorded statements previously made by or available to the witness should be carefully reread, checked for accuracy, marked for quick reference, and taken to court to refresh recollection, if necessary. Such details as dates, times, days of the week, and physical descriptions and sequences of events should be especially noted.

Visit the scene. The day before court, the witness might need to revisit the crime scene to review physical configuration, lighting sources, lines of sight, obstacles, relative sizes of objects, and relative distances between them. Again, there is nothing wrong with either doing this, or acknowledging it in court.

Review the evidence. If it is available, any physical evidence collected in the case should be examined so that it can be accurately described and identified in court. The location of initials or other identifying markings should be noted, and attached evidence tags should be reviewed for chain of custody and analysis annotations. The property custodian or investigating officer should check with the subpoenaing attorney as to any physical evidence needed in court, to be sure it is present on time. As discussed in Chapter 9, physical evidence described in a *subpena duces tecum* is to be brought to court by the witness, and should not be turned over to the attorney.

Prepare exhibits. If enlarged photos, detailed diagrams, models or other presentation aids are necessary to make the oral testimony more understandable to the jury, they should be prepared in advance, in consultation with the subpoenaing attorney.

Maintain a resume of expertise. Both civilians and police witnesses may be called on to give expert opinions in court. To qualify as an expert, the witness must be prepared to detail his or her specialized training and experience in the particular area of expertise. This can best be done by reference in court to a prepared *expert witness resumé*.

A resumé should include a complete history of all training and experience relevant to the topic, such as *schools attended*: academies, seminars, conferences; *professional readings*: books, periodicals, journals, articles, training bulletins, video programs; *practical experience*: studies, research, experiments, observing others, making evaluations; and *previous qualification* as an expert: number of times in justice, municipal, superior and federal court. Each additional qualification should be added, to keep the resumé constantly updated. A copy can be provided to the examining attorney before trial to assist her in establishing the foundation.

Get intelligence. If possible, it is nice to know the habits, tactics and idiosyncrasies of attorneys and judges before entering the courtroom. Such intelligence may be available from other attorneys, police officers, lab personnel and others with prior experience with the attorneys and judge assigned to the case. (Other witnesses who have already testified in the pending matter should not be consulted if they are under instructions from the court not to discuss their testimony with prospective witnesses.) Also, courtroom personnel, such as the bailiff, may be able to pass along information on both the judge and adverse attorney that could help the witness avoid problems on the stand.

DEMEANOR

The witness's impact on the jury is based partly on the content of his verbal testimony and partly on the influence of his nonverbal "testimony." When the judge instructs the jury on the law pertaining to evaluating the credibility of witnesses, she reads CALJIC 2.20, which states in part,

In determining the believability of a witness you may consider anything that has a tendency in reason to prove or disprove the truthfulness of his or her testimony, including...the *character and quality* of the testimony, the *demeanor* of the witness while testifying and the manner in which he or she testifies, and the witness's *attitude* toward the action in which he or she testifies or toward the giving of testimony. (Emphases added.)

In the words of the cliché, "It's not just what you say but how you say it." Credibility of any witness can be either damaged or enhanced by the demeanor displayed around the courthouse, both on and off the witness stand. Guidelines on appropriate conduct include the following:

Be dressed for impact. The civilian witness who comes to court in sloppy, dirty or suggestive clothing, or the officer who arrives in a crumpled uniform or inappropriate civilian attire, seriously undermines the positive first impression that each witness needs to make.

Be on good behavior. Jurors sometimes wear visible "juror" badges, and sometime they do not. Since it is not always possible to tell who is a juror and who is not, the waiting witness must be careful not to engage in objectionable behavior outside of court (such as telling offensive jokes, criticizing the court or the "system," discussing controversial public-interest issues, or commenting on the case). Hallway horseplay hurts.

Be on guard. It is also not always possible to identify the parties, their attorneys, their witnesses, their investigators and their friends. Careless discussions about the case, the other participants, or the prospect of testifying, may come back to haunt a witness in court. ("Officer, earlier today in the cafeteria, didn't you say that you hoped they didn't ask you too many idiot questions, because you really didn't remember this case at all?")

Be courteous. It can be a discomforting experience for a witness to be called into the courtroom to be sworn and recognize the judge or a juror as the person he challenged earlier for a parking space, or squeezed ahead of into a crowded courthouse elevator, or gave a sarcastic response to a request for directions to court, etc. Common courtesy may be sufficiently uncommon to make a highly favorable impression.

Be prompt. There is probably nothing more irritating to a sitting judge, an impaneled jury and a courtroom of waiting staff than to be staring at a clock and wondering what kind of witness thinks they are all so unimportant that he can keep them waiting past the time when he was scheduled to appear. A witness who will be unavoidably delayed should call the court as soon as possible to let them know why, and when he will arrive.

Be serious, but be human. If the jury is going to take the trial seriously, they have to see that everyone else does, too. Judges, lawyers and witnesses who are in court on a regular basis can forget that this may be a dramatic event for the jurors, who have forsaken homes, families and jobs to come to court and perform their civic duties. The witness should approach the case and her testimony in a serious and dignified manner, without a show of lighthearted joking.

At the same time, a witness should not appear to be completely humorless, stiff or stuffy. A good witness does not try to impress the jury with his own self importance. The most convincing witnesses are those that the jury perceives as "real people," who are simply behaving in a normal, businesslike way.

This means avoiding technical or occupational jargon with which the jury may not be familiar. Dispense with any effort to impress the court with a "power" vocabulary. Plain English and plain talk work best.

Be sharp. The witness's "body language" is not lost on the jury. From entry into the courtroom to exit, good deportment counts. The witness should enter with a bearing of confidence, and stand alertly while taking the oath. One should sit tall in the witness chair, listen attentively to questions, speak up clearly and firmly when answering, and comply respectfully with directions from the judge. Carefully avoid any distracting nervous habits (such as tapping fingers on the witness box, covering the mouth with the hands while talking, repeating the question before answering it, or beginning every answer with a throat-clearing noise and a drawn-out "uh.."). Finally, treat both counsel with equal courtesy and responsiveness, and leave the courtroom directly after being excused (unless required to remain).

TESTIFYING ON DIRECT

The attorney calling a witness is usually doing so (except with "hostile" witnesses) because the witness is expected to cooperate freely in giving favorable testimony for that side of the case. This makes testifying on direct examination relatively easy, since the attorney who offers the witness is not attacking his credibility.

However, this is not to say that the witness should "coast" through direct exam, agreeing with every suggestion the attorney seems to be making. The more careless a witness is on direct, the more incredible his testimony will appear after an effective cross-examination. During his testimony on direct, the witness should have two objectives in mind: (1) to tell the truth in such a way as to convince the trier of fact, and (2) to tell the truth in such a way as to create no ground of attack:

Staying in bounds. It is fairly likely in any criminal case that some evidence has been ordered suppressed during the pretrial and *in limine* (preliminary) motions. Before taking the stand, the witness should consult counsel to determine what evidence, if any, is out of bounds.

An inadvertent reference to a defendant's prior arrests or to crucial evidence that was excluded by 1538.5 or 352 motion could cause a mistrial. Exception: If the adverse party "opens the door" by pointedly asking about suppressed evidence, a truthful answer may be given.

Answering the right question. Sometimes the answer does not fit the question. This can be anything from comical to misleading to disastrous. A witness may give an incorrect response either because she did not *hear* the question (and so she guesses at it), or because she did not *understand* the question (and so she guesses), or because she did not *believe* the particular question was the one the attorney really meant to ask (and she guesses).

Guesswork is cross-examination ammunition. The careful witness says either "I didn't hear the question," or "I didn't understand the question." When the question is repeated, she answers the question that was actually asked, not the one she would rather answer. No guessing.

Being disciplined. Because of the unstructured style of most ordinary, everyday conversations, the controlled process of witness examination comes as an unnatural experience. In most of our intercourse, spontaneous interjections and interruptions are common, and anticipatory answers are freely volunteered.

In the courtroom, however, where every utterance must be correctly heard by the jury and transcribed by the reporter, and where the question-and-answer science is tightly restricted by the Evidence Code and highly refined by years of litigation, listening and talking must be done with discipline. Otherwise, answers will be stricken as "nonresponsive," the witness will be admonished by the judge to "just answer the question," confusion will set in, and credibility will suffer. Do not volunteer uncalled-for information.

Knowing, not knowing, and approximating. Every witness will *know* the answers to some of the questions he is asked. He should be *precise and positive* in giving this testimony. Every witness will be asked some questions that he has no basis for answering. He should have no hesitation in saying, "*I don't know*." With those questions falling in between—those calling for information that the witness thinks he knows but is not certain of—the answer should be appropriately qualified:

"I think it was a Mazda."

"As I recall, it was dark blue."

"He was approximately 25-30 years old."

"We were about 10-12 feet apart."

"He looked about 160-170 lbs."

"I believe it was his left hand."

"As I remember, it was just getting dark."

"It could have been a .357 or a .38."

Using chalkboards and diagrams. A witness who is asked to step down from the witness stand to draw something on a chalkboard or chart paper should remember a few simple points. There will no longer be a microphone, so he may need to raise his voice. The jury needs to see whatever he is drawing (or the judge, in a court trial), so he should not block their view, and he should draw objects as large as the available space and proportion will allow. As he testifies, he should have his face, not his back, turned toward the trier of fact.

Points of reference on the diagram should be indicated by prominent letters of the alphabet, beginning with "A," not "X." When using an exhibit during testimony, it should be held up to the jury's view, and features should be clearly pointed out.

Using flip-charts and chalkboards for diagrams.

Making eye contact. As he takes his seat in the witness chair, the witness should look at the jury with a slight, polite smile, make eye contact with them, and give a small nod of wordless acknowledgment in their direction. He should then face the examining attorney, and should do so while testifying as to matters requiring only brief response.

Whenever the examiner asks, "Would you please tell the jury...," he should face the jury with his answer. And whenever he is using an exhibit or diagram, or giving a lengthy or technical explanation, his testimony again should be addressed to the jury.

When both sides have completed examination and he is excused, the witness should again acknowledge the jury with a polite nod, and step down. If he is required to remain in the area after testifying, he should avoid any contact with jurors during recesses, beyond a courteous greeting, to prevent the appearance of any impropriety.

Reacting to objections. During direct examination, the adverse party will object to any question that he deems improper *and* damaging (inexperienced and obstructionist attorneys may object to questions, even though the answer would *not* be damaging to their case).

When any objection is made to a pending question, the witness should stop talking and wait for the judge's ruling. If the objection is *overruled*, the answer may be given; if the objection is *sustained*, the witness must wait for the next question.

TESTIFYING ON CROSS

All of the guidelines on testifying on direct exam are equally applicable to cross. However, because the attorney conducting cross-examination will generally have a purpose of discrediting the witness, additional guidelines also apply:

Being objective. It is possible, luckily, for a witness to favor one side or the other in a case and still be an objective witness. Such a witness will receive a high credibility rating in the eyes of the jury. It is also possible, of course, for a witness to favor one particular side and demonstrate such a lack of objectivity as to render his testimony virtually useless.

This latter sort of witness is easily recognized in trial: while on direct exam by the party who called him, he is eager to answer questions, responds respectfully to the attorney, and has a matter-of-fact tone to his voice; when turning to cross exam, however, he visibly shifts and braces himself, gets an antagonistic scowl on his face, tries to evade answering the adverse attorney's questions, reveals obvious hostility toward the adverse party, and tinges his voice with unmistakable bias.

The objective witness, on the other hand, exhibits evenhanded candor and courtesy to both counsel, without apparent efforts to help or hurt either prosecution or defense. This is the sort of witness the adverse attorney dreads, because such a witness stands in good stead with the jury, and open attacks on him may alienate the attorney from the jury. Thus, this objective kind of witness is the kind every witness should strive to be.

Handling leading questions. Since leading questions may be used on cross-examination and not on direct, a noticeable difference on cross will be the constant attempts of the attorney to put words in the witness's mouth by use of leading questions. In fact, the skilled examiner may be so polished at framing questions that seem so reasonable and so harmless that the unwary witness may be lulled into agreeing with suggestions he does not really mean to embrace.

The starting point for dealing with leading questions is realizing that it is *not necessary to agree* with everything (or anything) that the attorney casually suggests. *Every question* the attorney asks has some purpose—and often that purpose is hidden, and may not be revealed until the case is being argued to the jury. Then, the attorney reminds the jury of what the witness said on direct, and how he changed his answer just slightly to a slightly different question on cross, and how he changed still again when essentially the same question was repeated in another context.

This is a proven tactic for undermining a witness's credibility. It only works with a complacent witness who does not insist on complete accuracy, but allows an attorney to lead him into seemingly-meaningless, but eventually devastating, agreeable inaccuracies. The form of some questions may be a tip-off that the attorney is looking for concessions:

"Isn't it possible...?"
"Wouldn't you say...?"
"Isn't it fair to say...?"
"Couldn't it just as likely be...?"
"But you would agree, wouldn't you, that...?"

When a witness on cross-examination hears a question begin with such leading phrases, the attorney wants "yes" for an answer. And though it's possible that "yes" may occasionally be the right answer, the odds are substantial that some part of the question is not quite right. The witness should cautiously consider his answer, and if he spots the concealed discrepancy, he should answer accordingly:

"I couldn't say."
"Not exactly."
"I would only be guessing."
"Not necessarily."
"Yes, and no."

Correcting mistakes. Human beings being human, a witness may make a mistake. Mistakes are more likely to become apparent under the scrutiny of cross-examination. When a witness realizes, at any point, that he has made a mistake in his testimony, he should set the record straight immediately: "Your honor, I'd like to correct something I said earlier." "Counsel, I believe you're right. I should have said...."

Staying level. During calm, cool, reflective discussions fewer mistakes are made. During excited, heated, reactive debate, more mistakes are made. Realizing this, many attorneys attempt on cross-examination to put the witness on a roller-coaster.

By alternately raising and lowering the voice, using rapid fire questions, insinuating that the witness is lying, interrupting answers with another question, or even engaging in unprofessional histrionics, the attorney may attempt to get the witness emotionally agitated. If he succeeds, errors in testimony may result, and even if they do not, the witness will lose his stock with the jury.

The correct way to deal with the offered roller-coaster ride is to decline it, by maintaining a level tone of voice, a patient and measured response, and a conviction not to be tricked into surrendering emotional control to the lawyer. Once he takes control, the witness is his.

SUMMARY

√ Preparation for court should include discussing the case with the attorney who issued the subpena, reviewing reports, visiting the crime scene, reviewing the evidence and preparing testimonial aids.

√ Any witness who wishes to qualify to give expert testimony should compose and update a resumé of all training and experience related to the area of expertise.

√ Demeanor in and around the court can make or break the witness's credibility. A witness should dress appropriately, be reserved and courteous around others, get to court on time, and present a positive, confident image in court.

√ On direct exam, the witness should observe evidentiary restrictions, resist guessing at questions or answers, refrain from volunteering extra information, know when to approximate, and keep the jury in mind when using exhibits and diagrams.

√ At any objection, the witness should cease talking until the judge has ruled, answering only if the judge overrules the objection.

√ It is critical that a witness shifting from direct to cross-exam maintain the same objectivity he displayed while on direct.

√   Leading questions are used by the adverse attorney on cross to try to get the witness to agree to the attorney's altered version of his testimony, or to prompt the witness to speculate. Confronting a leading question, a witness should be careful not to accept any inaccuracy, no matter how trivial.

√   Mistakes made while testifying should be candidly acknowledged and promptly corrected.

√   Effectively handling cross-examination requires maintaining an even disposition, especially when the attorney uses irritating techniques to provoke an emotional reaction.

ISSUES FOR DISCUSSION

1.   What do you think is the rationale for permitting leading questions on cross-exam, but not on direct? Does this tend to promote truth-seeking, or confusion and distortion?

2.   Are most witnesses really at the mercy of an attorney who specializes in the skillful use of language and logic? How could the average person be better trained or educated to speak with greater care and precision? Is there something in common between trial attorneys and advertising copy writers?

3.   Does the criminal justice system demand too much perfection of witnesses who are human beings, and not video cameras or computers? Do juries? Does this advance the pursuit of justice, or impede it?

CHAPTER 12

SENTENCING PROCEDURE

Learning Goals: After studying this chapter, you will be able to correctly answer the following questions:

√   What are the primary goals of sentencing in California?

√   How does the prohibition of cruel and unusual punishment affect the sentencing choice?

√   How soon after verdict is judgment pronounced in misdemeanor cases? In felony cases?

√   What are the sentencing ranges for infractions? Misdemeanors? Felonies?

√   What are concurrent and consecutive sentences?

√   What is the difference between formal probation and conditional sentence?

SENTENCING OBJECTIVES

After the defendant has been convicted, it becomes the duty of the court to determine the proper punishment, and to impose it. Penal Code § 12; *People v. Eberhardt* (1986) 186 CA3d 1112. In choosing among the available alternatives, the court may consider the varying objectives of sentencing. These include punishment, protection of the public, deterrence, restitution to victims, and rehabilitation of the offender. Although an "enlightened" approach to penology prevalent in the 1960s and early 1970s stressed rehabilitation as the primary consideration, the disastrous consequences (mushrooming crime statistics) forced a change in priorities: "The Legislature finds and declares that the purpose of imprisonment for crime is punishment." Penal Code § 1170(a)(1). And in deciding whether to grant probation in lieu of imprisonment, "The safety of the public shall be a primary goal...." Penal Code § 1202.7.

By constitutional amendment, the electorate made its priorities known in 1982:

> The People of the State of California find and declare that the enactment of comprehensive provisions and laws ensuring a bill of rights for victims of crime, including safeguards in the criminal justice system to fully protect those rights, is a matter of grave statewide concern.
>
> The rights of victims pervade the criminal justice system, encompassing not only the right to restitution from the wrongdoers for financial losses suffered as a result of criminal acts, but also the more basic expectation that persons who commit felonious acts causing injury to innocent victims will be appropriately detained in custody, tried by the courts, and sufficiently punished so that the public safety is protected and encouraged as a goal of highest importance.
>
> Cal. Const. Art. I, § 28(a)
> ["Proposition 8" preamble]

Thus a court considering sentencing choices is expected to be less concerned with the criminal's individual plight than with society's demand for just punishment and public safety. There was a widespread perception that some justices of the state's highest court were more concerned with protecting criminals than with protecting the public. It is one of the explanations usually given for the unprecedented vote, in 1986, not to retain Chief Justice Rose Bird and Associate Justices Cruz Reynoso and Joseph Grodin.

SENTENCING CONCEPTS

Arriving at a lawful, fair and effective sentence is one of the most complicated procedures in the entire criminal process in California. (A single sentence-computation section, such as Penal Code § 1170.1, for example, is virtually incomprehensible, and must be considered in conjunction with many other provisions.) Certain concepts provide general guidelines in determining sentence.

Cruel and Unusual Punishment. Both the Eighth Amendment to the US Constitution and Article I, section 17, of the California Constitution prohibit the imposition of any cruel or unusual punishments. The US Supreme Court has ruled that any punishment that is excessive and disproportionate to the seriousness of the crime is "cruel and unusual" as applied, even though such punishment might not be unlawful in the abstract. *Coker v. Georgia* (1977) 433 US 584 (death penalty excessive for rape); *Enmund v. Florida* (1982) 458 US 782 (death penalty excessive for robbery). Compare *Rummel v. Estelle* (1980) 445 US 263 (life imprisonment for $120.75 fraud under Texas recidivist statute upheld).

Proportionality. In addition to prohibiting a punishment that is excessive for the *crime*, the prohibition of cruel and unusual punishment also precludes a punishment for one defendant that is disproportionate to his individual *culpability*, as compared with codefendants in the case, or as compared with other offenders who were punished less harshly for graver offenses. For example, a seventeen-year-old who shot and killed an armed marijuana grower received a disproportionate sentence of life in prison, while other second-degree murderers received lesser terms; the life term was therefore ordered reduced. *People v. Dillon* (1983) 34 C3d 441.

In *Solem v. Helm* (1983) 463 US 284, the US Supreme Court held that proportionality analysis should consider such factors as gravity of the offense, harshness of punishment, comparisons within the jurisdiction, and comparisons in other jurisdictions. If a court finds that these factors dictate a lower punishment in a particular case than is prescribed by statute, the lesser penalty should be imposed.

Multiple Punishment. Penal Code § 654 prohibits punishing an offender more than once for a single act or omission. When the defendant is charged with and convicted of two or more separate crimes, the court must determine whether punishment for each would be permitted or prohibited by 654. For example, possession of a sawed-off rifle by an ex-felon could not be punished twice, even though at least two statutes (Penal Code §§ 12020 and 12021) had been violated. *People v. Perry* (1974) 42 CA3d 451.

If the sentencing court determines that multiple punishments would violate 654, the usual procedure is to impose punishment on all charges, but to *stay* the execution of punishment as to all but one charge (usually, the most serious). *People v. Quinn* (1964) 61 C2d 551. If the defendant serves his sentence, the stay becomes permanent; if the conviction underlying the executed sentence should be reversed on appeal, the stay could be vacated and the punishment applied. *People v. Malamut* (1971) 16 CA3d 237.

PROBATION SENTENCING REPORT

In felony cases where the defendant is statutorily eligible, and in misdemeanor cases in the court's discretion, the county probation officer must prepare a presentence report for the court. Penal Code §§ 1203(b)(d), 1203.10. This report covers the defendant's background and the circumstances of the offense, and includes a recommendation for or against probation. Before sentence is to be pronounced, copies of the report are furnished to the prosecution and defense, and to the crime victim (or next of kin, if the victim has died). Penal Code § 1203d.

An arresting or investigating officer who wishes to submit information for the sentencing judge's consideration must do so via the probation officer, for inclusion in the report. Penal Code § 1204. It is improper for an officer to visit, telephone or write directly to the judge to express his opinions on a pending sentencing. Such impropriety may be punished as a contempt of court, under Penal Code § 166, subdivision 8. *People v. Shaw* (1989) 210 CA3d 859.

TIME FOR SENTENCING

Again unlike television, convicted defendants do not immediately rise to be sentenced after the jury has delivered a verdict of guilty. To allow the judge an opportunity to reflect on the issue of proper punishment, and to permit the parties and others a chance to prepare information and argument for the court's sentencing consideration, the law requires a delay between verdict (or plea) and sentencing.

In misdemeanor and infraction cases, the court must wait at least six hours, and no longer than five days, to impose sentence. These time limits can be waived, or extended for good cause. Penal Code § 1449. The sentence for one convicted of driving under the influence is to be imposed "in a reasonable time," after receipt of a DMV driving record and any presentence investigation report ordered by the court. Vehicle Code §§ 23205, 23206.

Sentencing on a felony conviction is to be set within 28 days after verdict (or plea), though this limit may be (and frequently is) extended. Penal Code § 1191.

SENTENCING OPTIONS

To make the punishment fit not only the crime but also the criminal, the law provides a wide variety of alternatives the sentencing judge may use, subject to some restrictions imposed by the legislature.

CYA Diagnostic. If the defendant was between the ages of 18 and 21 when arrested, he may be referred to the California Youth Authority for 90 days of observation and diagnosis. Welfare and Institutions Code § 1731.6. The CYA conducts an evaluation to determine whether the defendant is a proper subject for commitment to CYA, or should be returned to court for other sentencing.

A person committed to CYA may be held no longer than the maximum prison term to which he might have been sentenced, and no longer than his 25th birthday. Extensions are possible in cases of extreme danger; and at age 25, the defendant may be transferred to adult prison to serve any remaining balance of time. Welfare and Institutions Code § 1782.

Narcotics Facility Commitment. If the court has reason to believe that the convicted person is addicted, or is in danger of becoming addicted, to narcotics, he must be referred to the Department of Corrections for confinement in a narcotic detention, treatment and rehabilitation facility (formerly called "California Rehabilitation Center," or "CRC"). Specified violent felons are not subject to this commitment. After 16 months (or earlier if rehabilitated), the addict is returned to court for further sentencing, as appropriate, with credit for the time spent in rehabilitation. Welfare and Institutions Code §§ 3050-3201.

Probation and Conditional Sentence. As defined in Penal Code § 1203, "probation" means "the suspension of the imposition or execution of a sentence and the order of conditional and revocable release in the community under the supervision of the probation officer." A grant of probation is what is commonly known as a "suspended sentence" that is, if the defendant obeys the conditions of probation, the court will suspend any sentence that might otherwise have been imposed or carried out. Penal Code § 1203.1.

In cases of infractions and misdemeanors, the defendant may be placed on probation or given a "conditional sentence." Also known as "informal probation," a conditional sentence is ordered by the court without a probation investigation report, and does not involve supervision by the probation officer. Penal Code §§ 1203(d), 1203b. In essence, a conditional sentence is a summary grant of informal probation, under which the defendant is on his own supervision.

Many categories of violent and serious offenders are statutorily ineligible for probation. See, generally, Penal Code §§ 1203(e)-1203.09.

The period of probation in misdemeanor cases is a maximum of three years. Penal Code § 1203a. By statute, exceptions are made for a maximum of five years probation for convictions of being under the influence of certain drugs (Health and Safety Code § 11550), driving under the influence (Vehicle Code § 23206), and contributing to the delinquency of a minor (Penal Code § 272). Also, where a misdemeanant is liable to consecutive sentences exceeding a total of three years, his probation may be extended accordingly. Penal Code § 1203a.

Felony probation is for a period up to five years, or longer if a longer period of imprisonment was possible. Penal Code § 1203.1.

As conditions of probation, the court may order the probationer to serve a specified term in the county jail or on a public work project, and may require payment of fines, restitution and costs of supervision. Additional terms may include community service, drug testing, warrantless search and seizure, counseling or therapy programs, education or training, employment, and restrictions on association with designated persons or on permissible places and activities. As appropriate, the probationer may be required to pay for medical or psychological treatment of his victims, and may be ordered to reimburse public agencies for the costs of emergency response. See Penal Code §§ 1203.11203.11.

A probationer who violates the terms or conditions of his probation can be returned to court for a probation violation ("PV") hearing. If the court finds a violation, probation may be revoked and reinstated with new conditions (such as additional incarceration), or sentence may be imposed. Penal Code §§ 1203.2-1203.3.

House arrest. In lieu of incarceration in a correctional facility, the court may order a defendant to participate in a "home detention program," if available within the county. Penal Code § 1203.016. Under this program, the defendant must remain inside his home as designated by a correctional administrator, must allow inspections to verify his compliance, and must agree to the use of prescribed electronic monitoring devices. He is subject to being returned to custody, without warrant or court order, if his compliance cannot be verified. The house arrest program is only authorized for probationers and minimum security inmates.

Fines. Infractions are not punishable by jail. Penal Code § 19.6. Unless otherwise specified by statute, infractions may be punished by fine of up to $250. Penal Code § 19.8.

Misdemeanor fines, unless expressly provided for particular violations, are set at a maximum of $1000. Penal Code §§ 19, 672. A fine may be imposed as a condition of probation, or as the sentence, or as part of a sentence in conjunction with incarceration or other punishment.

Fines in felony cases, unless otherwise specified, may be up to $10,000. Penal Code § 672. A fine may be imposed in addition to imprisonment, or in lieu of imprisonment, except where a term in prison is mandated for certain offenses. Penal Code § 18.

All fines imposed by the court are also subject to a 70 percent "penalty assessment." Penal Code § 1464. This assessment operates like a surtax, so that a defendant sentenced to a $500 fine actually must pay $850, etc. Penalty assessment monies are distributed to the restitution fund, the peace officers' training fund, corrections training fund, prosecutors and public defenders training fund, victim-witness assistance fund, and other component programs. An additional 20% penalty assessment may be provided by county resolution to fund local programs. Penal Code § 1465. In many counties, therefore, a fine of $500 actually costs the defendant $950, etc.

If a defendant does not immediately pay any fine imposed, the court may stay payment for a specified time to allow payment, or may immediately incarcerate the defendant until the fine is paid. Credit of $30 toward the fine is allowed for each day served in custody. A defendant may not be required to serve a longer term in satisfaction of a fine than the maximum confinement set for the offense. Penal Code §§ 1205, 2900.5. (Thus, no incarceration would be permissible in infraction cases.)

If the defendant's nonpayment of a fine is due solely to inability to pay, the equal protection clause forbids his incarceration. An indigent cannot constitutionally be confined under circumstances where a person of means would avoid confinement. *In re Antazo* (1970) 3 C3d 100.

Jail. Unless otherwise expressly provided, misdemeanors are punishable by incarceration in the county jail for up to six months. Penal code § 19. County jail time is also frequently imposed as a condition of felony probation, in lieu of a prison term. Whether as a sentence, or as a condition of probation, confinement in county jail is subject to a maximum of one year. Penal Code § 19.2. (An exception exists for consecutive sentences totalling more than one year.) Attempts are punishable by one-half the designated term for a completed crime. Penal Code § 664.

Depending on the inmate's length of sentence, the seriousness of his offense, and the escape and safety risks, an inmate may be assigned by the county sheriff to serve his sentence in a cell, in a bay, at a penal farm, on a road camp, or at a work camp. Penal Code §§ 19.2, 4017. Short terms may be served on consecutive weekends, so that the prisoner maintains his employment during the week. In the sheriff's discretion, an inmate may also be permitted to participate in a daily work furlough program, being released from jail each day to report to his job, and returning to jail after work.

Prisoners may earn "work time" credits of one day for every six days served, if they perform satisfactorily in work assignments made by the sheriff. In addition, prisoners are entitled to receive "good time" credits (also one day every six) for good behavior in obeying institutional rules. Penal Code § 4019. By combining "good time-work time" credits, a jail prisoner effectively receives one-third off his sentence, so that a sentence of 90 days in jail usually means 60 days served, etc. If a municipality operates a city jail and agrees with the misdemeanor courts to accept city prisoners, such prisoners may be confined there, subject to the same provisions as apply to the county jail. Penal Code § 4022. A city jail confinement might be used, for example, where the police department wants to keep close watch on a "snitch" (informant) sentenced to incarceration, but possibly at risk in a general jail population.

When the sentencing judge imposes more than one jail sentence on a defendant who suffered multiple convictions, the judge must specify whether the terms are to be *concurrent* or *consecutive*. Penal Code § 669. "Concurrent" terms run at the same time, so that the defendant's period of incarceration is determined by the longest sentence. (Example: Three concurrent terms of 30 days, 45 days and 10 days would, in effect, be a sentence of 45 days.) "Consecutive" terms run sequentially, one after another, and would be added together to determine actual incarceration. (Example: Three consecutive terms of 30 days, 45 days and 10 days would mean a total sentence of 85 days.) A failure by the court to specify that sentences are to run consecutively automatically makes them concurrent. *In re Patton* (1964) 225 CA2d 83.

Prison. The punishment for felonies, except where otherwise provided, is imprisonment in the state prison for 16 months, or two or three years. Penal Code § 18. There are many statutory exceptions to this general rule, imposing sentencing ranges up to life, or death. (Examples: Mayhem: 2-4-8 years; arson with injury: 5-7-9 years; residential burglary: 2-4-6 years; second-degree murder: 15-life; first-degree murder: 25-life, life without parole, or death.)

Although California once used an "indeterminate sentencing" scheme, under which prisoners were sent to prison for indefinite terms to be released when corrections officials so determined, this approach resulted in disproportionate, unequal treatment of prisoners. It was subsequently replaced (in 1977) with the "determinate sentencing law," which was aimed at providing both uniformity and predictability of sentences.

Various provisions of determinate sentencing have been amended virtually every year since enactment. The legislature has repeatedly increased maximum sentences, restricted probation eligibility in more and more categories of crimes, and limited or removed the authority of courts to strike or dismiss allegations that would require stiffer sentences. [See, for instance, the legislative note to Penal Code § 1385(b), specifically abrogating the court decision of *People v. Fritz* (1985) 40 C3d 227.]

Under the determinate sentencing statutes, the court follows a complicated sentence-computation formula, which begins with the selection of a *base term*. This is ordinarily the *middle* term of the three terms within the range; however, if mitigating factors are present, the *lower* term may be chosen, while if mitigation is outweighed by aggravating factors, the *upper* term may be selected.

The court next adds additional terms for any *enhancements*, which generally range from one to five years, for such facts as use of a firearm, prior conviction of serious felonies, infliction of great bodily injury, and many others.

The base term, plus enhancements, as computed for the most serious offense, is known as the *principal term*. To this term are added any consecutive *subordinate terms* for other crimes of which the accused was convicted. The total sentence (principal term plus subordinate terms) is known as the *aggregate term*.

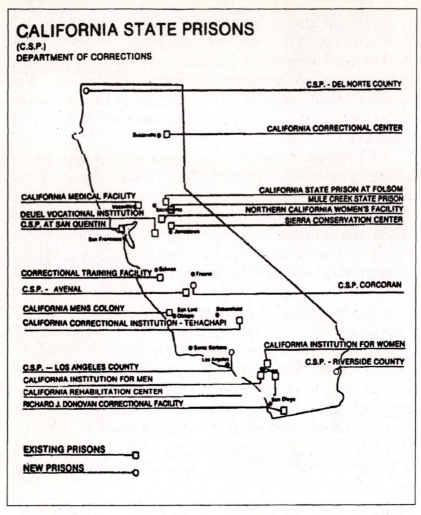

CALIFORNIA STATE PRISONS
(C.S.P.)
DEPARTMENT OF CORRECTIONS

C.S.P. - DEL NORTE COUNTY

CALIFORNIA CORRECTIONAL CENTER

CALIFORNIA MEDICAL FACILITY
DEUEL VOCATIONAL INSTITUTION
C.S.P. AT SAN QUENTIN

CALIFORNIA STATE PRISON AT FOLSOM
MULE CREEK STATE PRISON
NORTHERN CALIFORNIA WOMEN'S FACILITY
SIERRA CONSERVATION CENTER

CORRECTIONAL TRAINING FACILITY
C.S.P. - AVENAL

C.S.P. CORCORAN

CALIFORNIA MENS COLONY
CALIFORNIA CORRECTIONAL INSTITUTION - TEHACHAPI

CALIFORNIA INSTITUTION FOR WOMEN

C.S.P. — LOS ANGELES COUNTY
CALIFORNIA INSTITUTION FOR MEN
CALIFORNIA REHABILITATION CENTER
RICHARD J. DONOVAN CORRECTIONAL FACILITY

C.S.P. - RIVERSIDE COUNTY

EXISTING PRISONS

NEW PRISONS

A felon may be sentenced to any one of the many state prisons in California.

A person convicted of a felony after a previous violent or serious felony conviction (a "strike") is subject to a prison term of twice the normal length; a person with two or more proven "strikes" is punishable by a triple term, or 25-to-life, or the longest term otherwise applicable. Penal Code § 667. For good cause set forth on the record, a sentencing court can "strike a strike" (or more) in order to reduce the total commitment. *People v. Superior Court (Romero)* (1996) 13 C4th 497.

(Judges have devised sentencing worksheets, scripts and computer programs to attempt to cope with the complex intricacies of the determinate sentencing law. Unfortunately, however, the scheme has proven so complicated that a survey has shown one of every three appellate reversals of trial court judgments is due to error in sentence computation.)

As with jail sentences for misdemeanants, multiple prison sentences for felons must be designated by the court as concurrent or consecutive. Penal Code § 669. A prisoner is entitled to presentence credits against his prison term for any time spent in custody on the case before and during trial, and while awaiting judgment. Penal Code § 2900.5. "Good time-work time" credits can be earned in prison at a day-for-day rate, so that a prisoner sentenced to 16 months may by eligible for parole after serving 8 months. Penal Code §§ 2931-2933. Also, up to 12 months of sentence reduction can be granted for heroism in prison or exceptional contribution to safety and security of the institution. Penal Code § 2935. Murderers, some recidivists, and other designated offenders are either precluded from receiving credits or are subject to 15 or 20 percent limits. Penal Code §§ 2933.1-2933.5.

A sentencing judge can, prior to imposing a prison sentence, order the temporary placement of the defendant in a diagnostic facility for 90-day observation and evaluation by the Department of Corrections. The Department then submits a diagnostic report to the court with recommendations as to disposition of the case and placement within the correctional system. Time spent in diagnostic confinement is credited against any subsequent prison commitment. Penal Code § 1203.03.

The court may recall a prisoner, within 120 days of sentence, and modify the sentence (except that it may not be increased). Penal Code § 1170(d).

If a person convicted of a felony was a Vietnam combat veteran with resultant substance abuse or psychological problems, he may be committed to federal facilities (if available), instead of state prison, for the equivalent term. Penal Code § 1170.9.

Execution. In cases of first-degree murder with proven "special circumstances," such as killings during other serious crimes, or directed at specified groups or individuals, the court may impose a sentence of death. Penal Code § 190.2. Where a trial jury has found the defendant guilty of murder and has found any of the charged special circumstances true, a separate penalty phase trial is conducted to fix punishment, either at death, or life imprisonment without possibility of parole. Penal Code § 190.1.

The jury (or judge, if jury was waived) must weigh evidence of mitigation and aggravation, focusing on circumstances of the killing and character and history of the defendant. Penal Code § 190.3. If the jury returns a verdict imposing the death penalty, the judge must review the evidence, and may either modify the penalty to life without parole ("LWOP"), or impose the death penalty. Penal Code § 190.4.

Punishment of death must be inflicted within the walls of a designated state prison, by lethal gas or injection. Penal Code §§ 3603, 3604. Executions must be attended and witnessed by the warden, and may also be witnessed by physicians, ministers, defendant's relatives, peace officers, and at least 12 reputable citizens. Penal Code § 3605.

Other Sentencing Components. Whether the court grants probation or imposes a fine or incarceration or other punishment, additional penalties may be included as appropriate. For example, if a crime committed by any public official involved dereliction of duty, the court may order the officer removed from public office. Penal Code § 661.

Certain sex offenders are required to register with their local sheriff or police chief, and to submit to fingerprinting and photographing. Penal Code § 290. A similar registration requirement is imposed on certain drug offenders. Health and Safety Code § 11590.

Prostitutes and certain sex offenders are subject to court-ordered blood tests for the AIDS antibody. Penal Code §§ 647f, 1202.1.

PRONOUNCEMENT OF JUDGMENT

When the defendant appears for judgment, he is arraigned for sentence. Sometimes called the "allocution," this step requires that the defendant be informed of the charges of which he stands convicted. He is then asked whether there is any legal cause why judgment should not be pronounced against him. Penal Code § 1200.

If the defendant alleges that he is insane, or that he has grounds for a new trial or arrest of judgment, appropriate proceedings are conducted. Penal Code § 1201. Otherwise, judgment must be pronounced against the defendant (i.e., sentence imposed). Penal Code § 1202.

If the defendant's conviction resulted from entry of a guilty plea, he has a right to be sentenced by the same judge who took his plea, if available. *People v. Arbuckle* (1978) 22 C3d 749; *In re Mark L.* (1983) 34 C3d 171.

SUMMARY

√ Of the several legitimate objectives of sentencing, punishment and public safety are the primary goals.

√ To avoid the imposition of cruel and unusual punishment, the sentence must not be excessive for the nature of the crime or disproportionate to the defendant's relative culpability.

√ A single act or course of conduct that violates more than one law can only be punished once.

√ A peace officer who wishes to provide input to a sentencing judge must submit the information to the probation officer, for inclusion in the presentence report.

√ Misdemeanor sentencing is delayed from six hours to five days after verdict, while felony sentencing is postponed up to 28 days.

√ Unless a defendant's crime or background makes him ineligible for probation, he may be granted formal, supervised probation, or informal, unsupervised probation. A probationer's sentence is suspended, on condition that he abide by all terms and serve any incarceration made a condition of probation.

√ Fines may be assessed, up to $250 for infractions, $1000 for misdemeanors, and $10,000 for felonies, unless otherwise specified. A penalty assessment of up to 90% is surcharged. Defendants who fail to pay fines except due to indigency may be incarcerated until the fine is satisfied, at $30 per day.

√ Incarceration for misdemeanors is in the county jail, usually up to six months, and no more than one year. Felonies are punishable by imprisonment in state prison, for one of three specified terms. "Good time-work time" credits may be used to reduce jail terms by one-third, and prison terms by one-half.

√ Multiple sentences may be imposed concurrently (running at the same time), or consecutively (one after the other).

√ First-degree murderers with designated "special circumstances" may be punished by imprisonment for life without parole, or by death.

√ A sentence may include forfeiture of public office, mandatory registration as a sex or drug offender, and mandatory AIDS testing.

√ A defendant must be arraigned for judgment at a proceeding called the "allocution."

ISSUES FOR DISCUSSION

1. When the public views sentences as "too lenient" for serious offenders, who is at fault? Legislators, for setting low punishments? Judges, for imposing light sentences? The public, for refusing to finance prisons?
2. Are concurrent sentences ever justified? Does a concurrent sentence simply amount to a "buy one, get one free" approach to crime? Are concurrent sentences incentives to criminals not to stop at committing a single crime?

3. With both the public and the legislature repeatedly taking steps to limit judicial discretion, is it fair to conclude that judges have been abusing—and so losing—their discretion in failing to deal firmly with convicted criminals? Are judges sufficiently accountable at the polls? What would be better?

CHAPTER 13

POST-CONVICTION ISSUES

Learning Goals: After studying this chapter, you will be able to correctly answer the following questions:

√   What are the legal grounds for a motion for new trial? When is it made?

√   What is a motion in arrest of judgment? A writ of error *coram nobis*?

√   Does the prosecution have any right of appeal? When can a defendant file an appeal?

√   How do the California and federal appellate systems work? How do they interact?

√   What protections exist to insure prisoners' rights?

√   What are the features of the parole system?

√   How do executive and judicial clemency operate?

After a defendant has been convicted, he still has opportunities to challenge his conviction, to contest his sentence, and to obtain reviews and modification of his conditions of confinement.

MOTION FOR NEW TRIAL

Even before sentence is pronounced, the convicted defendant may seek to set aside his conviction by making a motion for new trial. Penal Code §§ 1179-1182. If this motion is granted, the parties are in the same position as before trial, and the case must be completely retried. The specified statutory grounds for the granting of a motion for new trial are as follows:

1. Defendant was unlawfully tried in absentia.

2. The jury obtained evidence from an outside source.

3. The jury separated during deliberations without court approval, or was guilty of unfair misconduct.

4. The jury decided guilt by lottery or other method of chance.

5. The court gave erroneous instructions or made erroneous rulings, or the prosecutor committed prejudicial misconduct.

6. The verdict is contrary to law or the evidence.

7. New evidence is discovered that could not have been obtained for the first trial, and it is material to the defense.

8. No reporter's transcript of the proceedings at trial is available, in a case where such transcript is required (including all felony and juvenile court proceedings).

Like the 1118 motion for dismissal after the prosecution rests its case-in-chief, the 1181 motion for new trial after conviction is automatically, routinely made by most defense counsel, on one or more grounds. If no specific errors or misconduct can be cited, the defendant virtually always asks the court to "re-weigh" the evidence and find the guilty verdict to be contrary to law or against the weight of evidence.

A judge exercising this discretion is sometimes said to be acting as a "thirteenth juror," with the power to nullify the conviction and require a retrial. Although judges occasionally grant a new trial on this basis, such a move cannot be lightly made, for it pits the judge against the intelligence, integrity and conscience of twelve citizens, who would not generally hesitate to express their disapproval in the evening newspaper, and in the voting booth.

If the judge is not prepared to cast the jury's collective judgment aside completely, but believes that the evidence only supports a conviction of a lesser offense, she has the authority to modify the verdict. In doing so, she may reduce the degree of the crime (for example, from first-degree murder to second-degree murder), or may reduce to a lesser included offense (from murder to manslaughter, for example). Penal Code § 1181(6).

MOTION IN ARREST OF JUDGMENT

If no new trial is granted, the defendant may make a motion in arrest of judgment, to prevent the court from imposing sentence. If this motion is granted, the parties return to their pretrial status, and a new trial on new pleadings may be undertaken. Penal Code §s 1187, 1188.

In effect, a motion in arrest of judgment is a post-conviction renewal of demurrer. Any of the grounds for demurring to the pleadings, as specified in Penal Code § 1004, may be asserted in support of the motion in arrest of judgment (unless waived by failure to demur at the appropriate time). Penal Code § 1185. Thus, any defendant whose pre-plea demurrer was overruled would normally renew his attack on the propriety of the pleadings by motion in arrest of judgment.

WRIT OF ERROR CORAM NOBIS

Before filing an appeal of his conviction, a defendant may consider petitioning the trial court for a writ of error coram nobis ("the error before us ourselves"). This essentially asks the trial court to vacate the judgment of conviction itself, due to a factual error, without waiting for appellate reversal. It might be used by a defendant who entered a plea based on an offer by the prosecutor to dismiss another case, when in fact the other case was never dismissed. Or it might be used by the prosecution to seek correction of an error in a grant of probation or in sentence computation, for example. *People v. Wiedersperg* (1975) 44 CA3d 550.

APPEALS

There are limited rights to appeal some judgments and other orders of the trial court. Where appeals are allowed, they must follow strict schedules and procedures set by statutes and by the rules of court.

Prosecution Appeals. The prosecution has very restricted appellate rights, primarily because of the prohibition of double jeopardy. Once jeopardy has attached and the prosecution suffers a dismissal, an acquittal, or other adverse ruling, it would serve no purpose to provide an appeal to the prosecution, since double jeopardy would prevent retrial, even if the prosecutor prevailed on appeal.

The prosecution has a statutory right to obtain pretrial review of an order suppressing evidence on grounds of unreasonable search or seizure. Penal Code § 1538.5(j), (o). While the suppression issue is pending on appeal, the trial is stayed and defendant may be released OR (or on bail). Once the issue is finally decided, the matter is returned to the trial court. If the evidence remains suppressed, the prosecution may proceed to trial on any other evidence (if possible), or the case will be dismissed. Penal Code § 1385. If the suppression order is reversed, the evidence will be admissible (if otherwise admissible), and the trial may proceed.

Other prosecution appeals are provided by Penal Code § 1466 (from justice court and municipal court orders), and § 1238 (from superior court orders). Among the matters that may be appealed by the prosecution are these:

- An order dismissing the charges before the defendant has been placed in jeopardy or where he has waived jeopardy.

- An order setting aside a complaint, indictment or information.

- An order granting a new trial.

- An order arresting judgment.

- An order reducing a conviction to a lesser offense.

- An order dismissing a case under 1385.

- An order imposing an unlawful sentence.

- An order recusing the district attorney.

- A judgment of dismissal based on the granting of a demurrer.

- An order made after judgment affecting the substantial rights of the people. Example: An improper grant of probation to an ineligible defendant. *People v. Belton* (1978) 84 CA3d 23.

Defense Appeals. The defendant's appellate rights are provided by Penal Code § 1466(b) (in misdemeanor cases) and § 1237 (from superior court proceedings). Although the defendant actually has greater appellate rights than the prosecution (since, by waiving double jeopardy, he can obtain a reversal of any prejudicial error and secure a retrial), the procedure is more simply stated.

The defendant appeals from a final judgment, or order made after judgment. Thus, if defendant believes an error has occurred either at the pretrial stage, or during trial, or in his sentence, he makes his objections and waits until after conviction (if any) and judgment, and then appeals.

If the appellate court agrees with the defendant that an error occurred, it must be determined whether the defendant *invited* the error, or *waived* any complaint by failing to object as appropriate. If the defendant is faultless, it must next be determined whether any error was of sufficient *prejudice* as to necessitate reversal or modification of the judgment.

An error that deprived the defendant of a fair trial due to constitutional violation results in automatic reversal. Example: Erroneous introduction of an involuntary confession. *Jackson v. Denno* (1964) 378 US 368. Any lesser error must be weighed by the appellate court to assess whether or not a different result would probably have been reached if the error had not occurred. *People v. Watson* (1956) 46 C2d 818; *Chapman v. California* (1967) 386 US 18.

The California Appellate System. Appeals from justice and municipal courts are heard by a three-judge panel of the superior court. These judges sit in the "appellate department" of the superior court, and in most cases, their decision is final, since there is no statutory right of further appeal in misdemeanor cases. Occasionally, a decision of the superior court appellate department will be considered important enough to be in the official reports. Such opinions are supplemental to published opinions of the court of appeal, and will be designated by the abbreviation "Supp." in the citation. Example: *People v. Powell* (1985) 166 CA3d Supp. 12.

Appeals from superior court are heard in the district court of appeal. California is divided into six appellate *district*s, and these districts may be further divided into *divisions*, consisting of one presiding justice and two or more associate justices. A majority of the justices participating in the decision of a case is sufficient to declare the opinion of the court. The court's decision may be published if it meets criteria of importance and precedent; such decisions are designated "Cal. App.," or simply "CA." Example: *People v. Valdivia* (1986) 180 CA3d 657. Except in death-penalty cases, there is no statutory right of further review, and the opinion of the court of appeal will be final unless discretionary review is granted by the California Supreme

Court, or a federal question is presented in a federal court (see following).

When a judgment of death is imposed at superior court, review by the state supreme court is direct and automatic; the court of appeal is bypassed. Penal Code §§ 190.6, 1239(b). In all other criminal cases, the parties have no absolute right of appeal to the supreme court; however, petition for review of an appellate decision may be made by the losing party, and the supreme court has discretion to grant or deny review.

In deciding whether to review a case on appeal, the court considers the statewide importance of the issue decided, and the lack of uniformity (if applicable) among the opinions of the various district courts of appeal. All of the opinions of the California Supreme Court are published; they are cited as "Cal.," or "C." Example: *People v. May* (1988) 44 C3d 309.

Appellate Procedure. The California Rules of Court specify the timing and format of appellate pleadings. These generally involve limits of 30 and 15 days for most steps, and require a notice of appeal (or petition for rehearing or review), accompanied by an appellate brief. The brief typically summarizes the history of the case, the pertinent facts, the issues presented, and the party's arguments. Oral argument to the court follows, after which the court takes the matter under submission, deliberates, and issues its decision.

The party filing the appeal is referred to as the "appellant," and the opposing party is the "respondent." If a third party's interests will be affected by the outcome of the case, that party may be identified in the action as a "real party in interest."

Once an appellate court has decided a case, it is returned to the trial court for entry of any necessary orders, or for further hearing, retrial or other proceedings mandated by the appellate decision. The written order of the higher court returning the matter to the lower court is known as the "remittitur."

The Federal Appellate System. There are basically two ways that a state court decision can be reviewed by a federal court. Under some circumstances, a final decision of the California Supreme Court can be appealed directly to the US Supreme Court. This is usually done by a procedure called "petition for writ of certiorari." If the Supreme Court "grants cert" (agrees to consider the appeal), the case will be put on the docket for briefing, oral argument and decision. A *federal* statute or constitutional provision must be implicated for the Supreme Court to exercise jurisdiction.

The other common method for removing a state case to the federal system is by the defendant's "petition for writ of *habeas corpus*." After exhausting his remedies in state court, a convicted defendant who is in custody may ask the federal district court to review the legality of his detention, under *federal* law (usually, the Fourth, Fifth, Sixth, Eighth and Fourteenth Amendments). "*Habeas corpus*" literally means "you have the body." As used in criminal procedure, it refers to an order to a custodial official to produce the prisoner in court for inquiry into the lawfulness of his detention. There are provisions for habeas corpus review in both the state and federal courts. See Penal Code §s 1473-1508, and Title 28 United States Code, §s 2241-2254.

A decision of the federal district court can be appealed to the Ninth Circuit Court of Appeals; a decision of the Court of Appeals can be appealed to the US Supreme Court.

Published opinions of the circuit courts of appeals are in the federal reports ("F," or "Fed."), and are identified by the circuit number and an abbreviation for "circuit" (9th Cir.) or "court of appeals" (CA9). Example: *US v. Patterson* (CA9 1987) 812 F2d 1188. All of the opinions of the US Supreme Court are published, in the US reports. Example: *California v. Prysock* (1981) 453 US 355.

PRISONERS' RIGHTS

Once the defendant has exhausted his appeals and habeas remedies, he retains the means to challenge the conditions of his confinement. Again, both state and federal provisions exist for this purpose.

By statute, California has established limited protection for prisoners' civil rights. See Penal Code §§ 2600-2791. The general rule is that prisoners can be deprived of such rights as may be necessary to maintain security of the detention facility and to protect the public safety. Any prisoner who believes his civil rights have been unlawfully infringed can bring an action at law (in addition to filing administrative grievances) for damages and relief. *De Lancie v. Superior Court* (1982) 31 C3d 865.

In addition, where a prisoner feels that the conditions of his incarceration violate the Eighth Amendment or unreasonably deny him other protections of the constitution, he can maintain a civil lawsuit in either state or federal court under Title 42 United States Code § 1983. This section establishes a cause of action against any official who unlawfully deprives a person of federally-protected rights, "under color of authority." *Preiser v. Rodriguez* (1973) 411 US 475.

Even behind the walls of a custodial facility, prisoners retain certain rights and remedies.

PAROLE

A *parole* is a conditional, early release from prison. If the parolee remains on good behavior, he will be discharged and excused from serving the balance of his term; if he does not obey the conditions of his release, his parole will be revoked and he will be returned to prison. (Note the difference between *parole* and *probation*; the public and media often incorrectly interchange the two.)

Most offenders qualify for release on parole after serving one-half of their total sentence. Penal Code §§ 2933, 3000. Although parole terms are initially set for longer periods, parole is actually terminated after one year for most parolees (two years for violent felons, and three years for murderers). Penal Code § 3001. If a prisoner is denied parole when first eligible, he is entitled to a yearly review at a parole hearing. Parole decisions are made by the Board of Prison Terms. Penal Code §§ 3040, 5077.

A parolee who has his parole revoked is returned to confinement. However, he is not committed for the unserved balance of his original term, but only for one additional year. Penal Code § 3057. Thereafter, he is again paroled, for the remainder of his original parole term.

While on parole, the parolee is supervised by a parole officer in the county to which the parolee is released. Usually, this is the same county from which he was sentenced. Penal Code § 3003. Conditions of parole are similar to the standard conditions of probation, including warrantless search and seizure, prohibitions on possession of weapons and drugs, and restrictions on associates, activities and travel.

Whenever a parolee is rearrested by police for a new crime, the parole officer is notified and usually exercises her authority to resume custody of the parolee, by placing a "parole hold" against the prisoner. Penal Code § 3056. When this is done, the prisoner cannot obtain release by simply posting bail on the offense for which he was arrested, since the parole hold will keep him in custody pending a parole revocation hearing.

EXECUTIVE CLEMENCY

Article V, section 8, of the California Constitution empowers the governor to grant reprieves, pardons and commutations to sentenced convicts, "except in case of impeachment." See also Penal Code § 4800.

Reprieve. A reprieve is the withdrawing of a sentence (usually of death) for a temporary interval of time. It is not a permanent stay of the sentence, but only a *postponement* of execution of the sentence to a later time. A reprieve might be granted by the governor to accommodate a family emergency (prisoner's close relative near death requests a chance to communicate, for example), or to permit newly-acquired evidence or information to be evaluated, or for any other reason the governor chooses.

Unless further action were taken to forestall execution of the sentence, however, the reprieve would expire on the date designated by the governor, and sentence would then be carried out. Penal Code § 1227.5.

Commutation. A commutation is simply a *change* of sentence. A judicially-imposed sentence cannot be increased by the governor consistent with due process; therefore, an executive commutation always means a *reduction* in sentence. Examples might be commuting a death sentence to life imprisonment, or commuting a life sentence to a definite term of years, or commuting any sentence to the period of time already served, thereby resulting in immediate discharge.

A statutory scheme for applying for commutation is provided in Penal Code §§ 4803-4852. It essentially requires the prisoner to make application to the governor, who then refers the application to the Board of Prison Terms, the sentencing judge, the prosecutor or the Supreme Court for recommendation.

Pardon. A pardon is a *forgiveness* of the conviction of a felon who has served a period of "rehabilitation" after his release from prison. This period is usually from three to seven years, and requires a certificate that the person has not been rearrested during the rehabilitation period. Penal Code §§ 4852.01-4852.05. The applicant must file a petition in superior court for a declaration of rehabilitation. After hearing on the petition, the court may recommend that the governor grant the pardon. Penal Code §§ 4852.06-4852.13. If the governor does so, the applicant's civil rights are restored, subject to limitations on business licenses and firearms possession. Penal Code §§ 4853, 4854.

Indemnification. If a person who served any part of a prison term is pardoned by the governor because it is determined that he did not in fact commit the crime for which he was imprisoned, he may file a claim against the State Board of Control. The board will then conduct a hearing to determine damages for the person's wrongful conviction and imprisonment, and may recommend that the legislature indemnify him, up to $10,000.

This remedy is not available to a prisoner who pled guilty or otherwise intentionally or negligently contributed to his predicament. Penal Code §§ 4853-4904.

JUDICIAL CLEMENCY

By statute, misdemeanants and persons granted probation can obtain the same kinds of relief extended to imprisoned felons by a governor's pardon. Pursuant to Penal Code § 1203.4a, a person convicted of a misdemeanor and not granted probation can apply to the court for an order setting aside his conviction or guilty plea. If he shows that he has fully served his sentence and is rehabilitated, his judgment of conviction can be set aside and the charges dismissed. The fact of conviction must still be reported on official questionnaires, and the conviction may still be used for DMV licensing purposes and weapons control laws.

Both misdemeanants and felons who successfully complete their probationary period can apply to set aside their convictions and dismiss their cases under the same conditions, per Penal Code § 1203.4. Both of these provisions are utilized most frequently by people who, though normally law-abiding, commit an isolated crime, for example, such as shoplifting, joyriding or soliciting prostitution and wish to clear their records after serving their sentence or probation.

The court also has the statutory power to make a finding of *factual innocence* as to a person who was released after arrest, or who was acquitted upon trial. Penal Code §§ 851.8, 851.85. If the court makes such a finding, it may order the sealing and eventual destruction of all records in the case. The innocent person may thereafter state that he was not arrested, or that he was exonerated by a finding of factual innocence.

SUMMARY

√   After conviction and before sentencing, a defendant can make a motion for new trial, based on prejudicial misconduct or the discovery of new evidence.

√   A judge hearing a motion for new trial may either grant or deny the motion, or modify the verdict to conviction of a lesser included offense.

√   A motion in arrest of judgment is equivalent to a post-conviction renewal of a demurrer.

√   The trial court can correct a factual error in a plea or sentence on a party's petition for writ of error *coram nobis*.

√   Prosecution appeals are limited to orders issued by the court before the attachment of jeopardy, or after jeopardy has been waived by the defendant.

√   Regardless of the stage at which the defendant believes an error occurred, his appellate remedy generally is to appeal from his conviction or sentence.

√ On defendant's appeal, any errors must be weighed by the court to determine their prejudicial impact, unless a constitutional error deprived the defendant of a fair trial, requiring automatic reversal.

√ Appeals from justice and municipal courts are heard in the appellate department of the superior court.

√ Appeals from the superior court are heard in the district court of appeal.

√ Death sentences are automatically appealed directly to the California Supreme Court. Other appeals may be taken to the Supreme Court only if the court grants discretionary review.

√ An adverse decision from the California Supreme Court can be appealed directly to the US Supreme Court if a federal question is involved, and if the court grants a writ of certiorari.

√ Federal issues can be litigated through the district court, the Ninth Circuit Court of Appeals, and the US Supreme Court, by petition for writ of habeas corpus.

√ Prisoners' rights are protected by Penal Code § 2600, the Eighth Amendment, and 1983 civil rights actions.

√ As contrasted with *probation* (supervised release in lieu of sentence), *parole* is a supervised, conditional, early release from prison after one-half of the prison term.

√ Parole usually terminates after one, two of three years. A violator can be returned to prison for one year.

√ Executive clemency includes temporary *reprieve*, reduction of a sentence by *commutation*, and *pardon* of rehabilitated felons.

√ Judicial clemency is available to successful probationers, rehabilitated misdemeanants, and those found to be factually innocent of the charges made against them.

ISSUES FOR DISCUSSION

1. Are there too many ways for a criminal to attack, reverse or set aside his conviction? Are all these procedures necessary, given the protections of the pretrial and trial procedures to insure justice?

2. With as many as three state appeals levels and three federal levels, are there too many layers of appeals courts to review criminal cases? Should convicted persons be limited to one or two appeals?

3. A sentence of 15 years-to-life for conviction of second-degree murder may mean as little as 7½ years in prison before parole. If the murderer receives presentence custody credits of 2½ years for the time he spent waiting for trial and undergoing trial, he has to spend about the same amount of time in prison as many people spend in college. Is this right?

CHAP
T
E
14 R

JUVENILE JUSTICE
PROCEDURE

Learning Goals: After studying this chapter, you will be able to correctly answer the following questions:

√ What are the history and theory of the separate treatment of juvenile offenders?

√ What are the terminology differences evident in the juvenile justice system?

√ Are there any variations in the laws of arrest and investigation of juvenile offenders? If so, what are they?

√ To what do *Dennis H.* and *Manuel L.* refer?

√ Which constitutional rights apply to juvenile hearings? Which do not?

√ What dispositional options are available to the juvenile court to deal with youthful offenders?

PURPOSE AND NATURE
OF JUVENILE PROCEDURE

There is no minimum age at which individuals choose to engage in conduct that violates the criminal laws. There is, however, a minimum age for the prosecution of such individuals under the general law. In California, that age is 18 years, with some exceptions. Welfare and Institutions Code § 602. The philosophy of a separate justice system for youthful offenders has been summarized by the US Supreme Court as follows:

> From the inception of the juvenile court system, wide differences have been tolerated — indeed insisted upon — between the procedural rights accorded to adults and those of juveniles.
>
> * * *
>
> The Juvenile Court movement began in this country at the end of the last century. From the juvenile court statute adopted in Illinois in 1899, the system has spread to every state in the Union, the District of Columbia, and Puerto Rico. The constitutionality of juvenile court laws has been sustained in over 40 jurisdictions against a variety of attacks.
>
> The early reformers were appalled by adult procedures and penalties, and by the fact that children could be given long prison sentences and mixed in jails with hardened criminals. They were profoundly convinced that society's duty to the child could not be confined by the concept of justice alone.
>
> * * *
>
> Accordingly, the highest motives and most enlightened impulses led to a peculiar system for juveniles, unknown to our law in any comparable context.
>
> * * *
>
> The early conception of the Juvenile Court proceeding was one in which a fatherly judge touched the heart and conscience of the erring youth by talking over his problems, by paternal advice and admonition, and in which, in extreme situations, benevolent and

wise institutions of the state provided guidance and help "to save him from a downward career." Then, as now, goodwill and compassion were admirably prevalent. But recent studies have, with surprising unanimity, entered sharp dissent as to the validity of this gentle conception. They suggest that the appearance as well as the actuality of fairness, impartiality and orderliness — in short, the essentials of due process m ay be a more impressive and more therapeutic attitude so far as the juvenile is concerned.

In re Gault (1967) 387 US 1, 14-26

Thus, the juvenile system has become a mixture of both civil and criminal procedure, of both informality and due process, and of both treatment and punishment of the juvenile offender. A separate body of statutory law provides for the special procedures applicable to juvenile adjudication (Division 2 of the Welfare and Institutions Code, §§ 202-1803). At the same time, the substantive criminal laws of the Penal Code and other codified statutes apply to define unlawful behavior (Welfare and Institutions Code § 602; Penal Code § 26). The dual purposes of separate juvenile procedure are legislatively defined as follows:

Minors under the jurisdiction of the juvenile court who are in need of protective services shall receive care, treatment and guidance consistent with their best interest and the best interest of the public. Minors under the jurisdiction of the juvenile court as a consequence of delinquent conduct shall, in conformity with the interests of public safety and protection, receive care, treatment and guidance which is consistent with their best interest, which holds them accountable for their behavior, and which is appropriate for their circumstances. This guidance may include punishment that is consistent with the rehabilitative objectives of this chapter.

* * *

> Juvenile courts and other public agencies charged
> with enforcing, interpreting, and administering the
> juvenile court law shall consider the safety and protec-
> tion of the public and the best interests of the minor in
> all deliberations pursuant to this chapter.
>
> Welfare and Institutions Code § 202(b)(d)

Accommodating the double objectives of rehabilitation and punishment, and attempting to enforce the criminal law through a nominally civil procedure, led to development of a system with many of the characteristics of adult criminal procedure—though frequently employing different terminology. The study of juvenile procedure in California essentially involves two major areas of inquiry: (1) In what ways is juvenile procedure similar to, or different from, adult criminal procedure? (2) What are the differences in terminology between the juvenile system and the adult system?

Both of these inquiries can be considered simultaneously by focusing first on the investigative phase of juvenile justice, then on the adjudicative phase, and finally on the disposition phase. Terminology differences can be noted throughout the process, beginning, for example, with the term used to describe a person coming under juvenile court law. This person will not be referred to as the "accused" or the "defendant," but as the "minor."

INVESTIGATION OF JUVENILE CRIME

Although larger police and sheriff's departments often have a special bureau or detective assigned to juvenile cases, it is obviously not necessarily apparent at the outset that any particular crime was committed by a person under 18. Until such time as a juvenile suspect is identified by police, normal investigative procedures apply. When a juvenile suspect becomes involved, police continue to utilize basic investigative techniques and to observe the same guidelines as in any other case, except where special statutory or constitutional rules permit or require exceptional procedures for juveniles.

Search and Seizure. Where an officer's employing jurisdiction (city or county) has a valid *curfew* ordinance regulating unsupervised minors during late-night hours, an officer may detain a person appearing to be in violation of the curfew. If investigative detention reveals a violation, the officer may deal with the minor under juvenile court law (see "Arrest and Detention," below). *In re Francis W.* (1974) 42 CA3d 892.

A person reasonably appearing to be a minor may be detained for investigation of *truancy*, in violation of the compulsory education law, Education Code § 48264. If it is a school day, during normal school hours, and the person reasonably appears to be of school age, a police check is permissible. *In re James D.* (1987) 43 C3d 903. If the minor is found to be truant, s/he may be returned to school or taken home. Prior to transporting, the officer may frisk the minor, and any evidence thus discovered may be lawfully seized. *In re Demetrius A.* (1989) 208 CA3d 1245.

The US Supreme Court has held that public *school searches* of the student's desk, locker or effects are governed by the Fourth Amendment standard of reasonableness. However, what is "reasonable" in the case of a school student is a warrantless search, without probable cause, based only on reasonable suspicion:

> Under ordinary circumstances, a search of a student by a teacher or other school official will be justified at its inception where there are reasonable grounds for suspecting that the search will turn up evidence that the student has violated or is violating either the law or the rules of the school. Such a search will be permissible in its scope when the measures adopted are reasonably related to the objectives of the search and not excessively intrusive in light of the age and sex of the student and the nature of the infraction.
> *New Jersey v. TLO* (1985) 469 US 325, 343 Accord,
> *In re William G.* (1985) 40 C3d 550

The general rule on *consent* searches is that valid consent can be given by one person to a search of another's property if it reasonably appears that the person giving consent has the authority to do so. *US v. Matlock* (1974) 415 US 164; *People v. Smith* (1966) 63 C2d 779. In the case of a minor's room, this generally means that either parent could consent to a police search of any area and any containers where the parent had the right of access. *People v. Daniels* (1971) 16 CA3d 36. The parent could not authorize a police search of containers or areas set aside for the exclusive, private use of the minor, such as a locked toolbox to which only the minor keeps the key. *In re Scott K.* (1979) 24 C3d 395.

Arrest and Detention. A peace officer's authority to "take a minor into temporary custody" is broader than the authority to arrest an adult. Under Penal Code § 836, an officer may make a warrantless arrest for *misdemeanor* offenses only where committed in his presence; Welfare and Institutions Code § 625 authorizes a minor to be taken into custody on reasonable cause to believe the minor is involved in any criminal activity. This could include a felony, misdemeanor or infraction. *In re Hector R.* (1984) 152 CA3d 1146.

Once a minor is taken into custody, special protections govern his continued detention. Immediately after being taken to a place of confinement, and no later than one hour after having been taken into custody, the minor must be notified and given the right to place two completed phone calls. The officer must immediately notify the minor's parent of his custodial situation. Welfare and Institutions Code § 627.

The peace officer must exercise one of four options for handling the minor once custody is taken. The officer may (1) release the minor; (2) deliver the minor to a treatment facility; (3) issue a citation to the minor and his parents for a court appearance; or (4) deliver the minor to the county probation officer. Welfare and Institutions Code §§ 626, 626.5. The officer must choose the option that is least restrictive on the minor's freedom, subject to the best interests of the minor and the community.

No peace officer may knowingly confine any minor in a jail or lockup together with adult prisoners. Welfare and Institutions Code §

208. If a dangerous minor between 14 and 18 years of age must be secured in a law enforcement facility that contains a lockup for adults pending investigation and processing, strict segregation, supervision and reporting is required, per Welfare and Institutions Code § 207.1(d).

And whether the minor is held in secure custody or is merely detained in an office or other nonsecure area within a police department, the officer "shall exercise one of the dispositional options authorized by section 626 and 626.5 without unnecessary delay and, *in every case, within six hours.*" Welfare and Institutions Code § 207.1(d). (Emphasis added.) This essentially means that once a peace officer takes temporary custody of a minor under 625, he has six hours to release the minor, or lodge him with the probation department.

At the time of delivering a minor to the probation officer, the peace officer must provide a concise written statement of the probable cause and reasons for taking the minor into custody. This statement need not be a full crime and arrest report, but merely a brief listing of the facts warranting the minor's custody. Welfare and Institutions Code §§ 626(d), 626.5(b).

Interrogation. The US Supreme Court has not expressly held that the *Miranda* procedure applies to juveniles. See *Fare v. Michael C.* (1979) 442 US 707, fn. 4. The California courts historically extended *Miranda* to juveniles, *In re Roderick P.* (1972) 7 C3d 801, but state court decisions may no longer expand *Miranda* beyond federally-mandated limits. *People v. May* (1988) 44 C3d 309 (applying the Proposition 8 "Truth-in-Evidence" provision to admissibility of suspects' statements).

Before Proposition 8 (which became law on June 9, 1982), California courts had promulgated some deviant case law on the application of *Miranda* in juvenile cases [see, for example, *In re Patrick W.* (1980) 104 CA3d 615, holding that police had a duty to tell a minor his grandparents were in town; and *People v. Burton* (1971) 6 C3d 375, holding that a minor's request for a parent was an automatic invocation of the right to remain silent]. On their own, some police agencies decided to enlarge the *Miranda* warning to include an admonition to juveniles that they had a right to have a parent present during questioning.

Assuming that *Miranda* applies to juvenile cases (as the Supreme Court did in *Fare v. Michael C.*), the federal rules now applicable in California do not require any deviations in juvenile cases. Recognizing this, state courts have ruled that minors need not be told of any "right" to have parents present during questioning. *In re Jessie L.* (1982) 131 CA3d 202; *In re John S.* (1988) 199 CA3d 441. It has also been acknowledged that under *Fare v. Michael C.*, a minor's request for a parent is not necessarily an invocation of the right to remain silent, but should be clarified with the minor to determine his intentions, since the *Burton* rule is not federally compelled. *People v. Maestas* (1987) 194 CA3d 1499; *In re Ahmad A.* (1989) 215 CA3d 528.

Welfare and Institutions Code § 625(c) specifies that "in any case where a minor is taken into custody" for a criminal offense, the officer must advise the minor of the rights to remain silent and to have counsel. Some police agencies have interpreted this statute as requiring such advice *immediately* upon taking custody of a minor. In fact, no court decision has ever interpreted the phrase "in any case" as meaning "immediately," and the legislature did not use the word anywhere in 625, although express requirements of "immediate" acts are provided in section 627 and 627.5, for example, and in many other statutes. In any event, the US Supreme Court has made clear that suspects need not be "Mirandized" merely upon being taken into *custody*, but only prior to custodial *interrogation*:

> It is clear, therefore, that the special safeguards outlined in *Miranda* are required not where a suspect is simply taken into custody, but rather where a suspect in custody is subjected to interrogation. "Interrogation," as conceptualized in the *Miranda* opinion, must reflect a measure of compulsion above and beyond that inherent in custody itself.

> *Rhode Island v. Innis* (1980) 446 US 291, 300

A peace officer interrogating a minor who was under the age of 14 when he committed a crime should ask questions designed to reveal whether or not the minor was aware of the wrongfulness of his acts. Penal Code section 26, as interpreted, requires clear and convincing evidence that the minor (under 14 years of age) was aware his actions were wrong. *In re Manuel L.* (1994) 7 C4th 229.

ADJUDICATION OF JUVENILE CASES

The probation officer plays a significant role in the juvenile justice system, screening cases for referral to the district attorney, maintaining custody of minors detained for court, investigating and making recommendations to the court, and supervising juveniles who are declared wards of the court, among many responsibilities. The processing of a juvenile case after referral to the probation officer by police or other officials is a modified, streamlined version of general prosecution. The following are the primary features (note terminology; all referenced sections are to the Welfare and Institutions Code):

Application for Petition. The arresting officer who requests that juvenile court proceedings be commenced files an affidavit, applying to the prosecuting attorney (via the probation officer) for a petition to declare the minor a ward of the court. Sections 650(b), 653, 653.5.

Petition. The charging document in juvenile cases is a petition to adjudge the minor a ward of the court, as a person coming under the provisions of section 602. The petition resembles a criminal complaint, but contains additional, specified information about the offense, the minor and his parents. It is filed by the prosecuting attorney, with the clerk of the juvenile court, within 48 hours after the minor was taken into custody (excluding nonjudicial days). Sections 631, 650, 653.5, 656. The petition must specify, as to each count, the code sections alleged to have been violated, and whether they are charged as felonies or misdemeanors. Sections 656, 656.1.

654 Probation. The probation officer screening an application for petition may, except in certain more serious cases, decide not to refer the application to the prosecutor for petition, but to handle the minor informally. The minor can be placed on informal probation for up to six months, with his consent and the consent of his parents. If he fails to comply with this probation, the matter can be referred for petition. Designated serious offenders and repeaters are not eligible for this treatment. Sections 654-654.4. If the applicant officer disagrees with a probation officer's decision to use 654 probation in a case, she may, after 21 court days and before 31 court days, apply directly to the prosecutor for the filing of a petition. Section 655.

Detention Hearing. There is no right to bail in juvenile cases. *In re William M.* (1970) 3 C3d 16. Preventive detention of juveniles is not unconstitutional. *Schall v. Martin* (1984) 467 US 253. To determine whether a juvenile should be released or detained pending proceedings on the petition, the juvenile court must promptly conduct a detention hearing. Unless the minor is an escapee, or at risk to himself or others, or a flight risk, he must be released. Sections 632-636.2.

Dennis H. Hearing. A minor who is ordered detained has a right to a probable cause hearing within 3 judicial days. This hearing is limited to the issue of a prima facie case for having been taken into custody and detained. A prima facie case is usually established by the testimony of the arresting officer and submission of the crime and arrest reports. Section 637; *Dennis H. v. Superior Court* (1977) 72 CA3d 755.

Jurisdiction and Venue. Juvenile court law is within the original jurisdiction of the superior court. The juvenile court judge may appoint referees to hear criminal cases, and traffic hearing officers to hear infractions and certain classes of misdemeanors. Sections 245, 247, 255, 256. Venue in juvenile cases is proper in the county where the crime occurred, or where the minor lives, or where he is found. Section 651. Vehicle Code infractions may sometimes be heard in justice or municipal court, per section 603.5.

Motion to Suppress. Before jeopardy attaches, the minor may move to suppress evidence on grounds of unreasonable search or seizure. If grounds were not apparent prior to hearing on the petition, the motion may be made after attachment of jeopardy. Section 700.1.

Fitness Hearing. A special procedure exists under section 707 to determine the fitness for treatment under the juvenile law of violent offenders aged 16 and 17. If the prosecutor includes 707 allegations in the petition charging one of the specified serious offenses, the probation officer conducts an investigation and makes a written report to the court on the minor's fitness for juvenile court, based on the minor's individual situation and the circumstances of the offense. The court conducts a fitness hearing and determines whether to retain the minor in juvenile court, or to permit the prosecutor to file an accusatory pleading against the minor in adult court for general prosecution. Sections 707, 707.1.

Jurisdictional Hearing. Since juvenile offenses are not technically "crimes," there are no trials. To determine whether a minor comes within the jurisdiction of the court by having committed conduct described in section 602, the court conducts a "jurisdictional hearing," which is the juvenile equivalent of a trial. An arraignment occurs at the beginning of the hearing. Section 700. Jurisdictional hearing must be held within 15 judicial days after filing of the petition where the minor is in custody, or within 30 calendar days otherwise, unless the minor waives the time limit and is granted a continuance. Sections 657, 682.

A minor is not entitled to trial by jury. *McKeiver v. Pennsylvania* (1971) 403 US 528; *Richard M. v. Superior Court* (1971) 4 C3d 370. In the court's discretion, it may impanel an advisory jury. *People v. Superior Court (Carl W.)* (1975) 15 C3d 271.

The statutory and constitutional rules of evidence apply to juvenile hearings. Section 701. The petitioner's burden of proof to establish jurisdictional facts is proof beyond a reasonable doubt. Section 701; *In re Winship* (1970) 397 US 358. Due process and right to counsel also apply to juvenile proceedings, *In re Gault* (1967) 387 US 1;

section 679; as do the rights to confront and cross-examine witnesses, and the privilege against self-incrimination. Section 702.5.

Since the jurisdictional hearing is tantamount to a court trial, jeopardy attaches when the first witness is sworn. *In re Bryan* (1976) 16 C3d 782. A reporter's transcript is required to record all proceedings. Section 677. At the close of the prosecution case, if there is insufficient evidence to sustain the petition, it must be dismissed. Section 701.1. The minor has the right to request issuance and service of subpoenas for his witnesses. Section 664.

Instead of rendering a verdict, the juvenile court "makes findings" as to the truth of the allegations in the petition, and as to whether or not the minor is a person described by section 602. The petition is then dismissed or sustained; if sustained, the minor may be declared to be a ward of the court, or placed on six months' probation without wardship.

Public Access. To protect the privacy of youthful offenders, most proceedings are closed to the press and the public, and only the parties, court staff and a testifying witness may be present. Sections 675, 679, 681. The public may be admitted to proceedings involving specified serious offenses. Section 676. Published opinions in juvenile cases identify the minor by first name and initial of the last name.

Juvenile court is not generally open to the public. Witnesses must remain outside the courtroom except when testifying.

Rehearing and Appeals. Matters heard by referees and traffic hearing officers may be reheard by the judge of the juvenile court, and any prior decision may be vacated or modified. Sections 252-262. Judgments and final orders may be appealed in the same manner as any such rulings. Section 800; Penal Code section 1240.1.

DISPOSITION

To maintain the segregation of juveniles from adult offenders, wards of the juvenile court may not be confined so as to come in contact with adults. Section 208. No person under the age of 16 can be committed to state prison. Section 211. And no person who was under 18 at the time he committed a capital offense may be executed. Penal Code section 190.5.

Given the punishment limitations on juveniles and the treatment objective, alternative dispositions must be utilized. These may include supervised probation, conditional home release ("house arrest"), commitment to juvenile hall, placement in a foster home or group home, commitment to a secure school or training camp, assignment to community work program, transfer to a new county of residence, assessment of a fine, repair or restitution orders, or commitment to the California Youth Authority ("CYA") for structured, institutional correction. See sections 725-740.

To determine the appropriate disposition in each case, the court conducts a *dispositional hearing*. At this hearing, the probation officer submits a social study of the minor and makes recommendations as to disposition. Both the prosecutor and the minor's counsel (and the minor) may also be heard. Sections 706, 725.5. Before ordering the disposition, the court must declare whether it finds the minor's "wobbler" offenses to be misdemeanors or felonies. Section 702. If the court grants probation, it may be on any reasonable terms and conditions. Section 730. Court-ordered physical confinement may not exceed the maximum term to which an adult could have been sentenced. Section 726. There is no "good time/work time" reduction. *In re Ricky H.* (1981) 30 C3d 176.

The juvenile court may dismiss a petition or set aside findings at anytime before the minor reaches age 21, in the interests of justice and the welfare of the minor. Section 782. Any person who was the subject of a juvenile court petition may request a court order sealing his or her arrest and disposition records, after reaching age 18, or five years after jurisdiction has ended. Section 781. The juvenile court loses jurisdiction of a person (and such person must generally be released from any CYA commitment) at age 25. Section 607.

SUMMARY

√ The procedures for handling juvenile offenders (under 18) are set forth in the Welfare and Institutions Code.

√ One of the most noticeable differences between the juvenile system and the adult system is in the terminology applied to the parties and the proceedings.

√ Police authority to conduct reasonable searches and seizures is somewhat greater as to juveniles, particularly in the areas of misdemeanor arrests, curfew stops, truancy stops, and school searches.

√ Once a peace officer has taken a minor into temporary custody, the minor must generally be released or delivered to the probation officer within six hours.

√ After Proposition 8, the application of the *Miranda* rules to juveniles is governed by federal constitutional law, under which no special advice need be given to juveniles; a request for a parent is not a per se invocation of rights; and admonitions need only be given before custodial interrogation—not immediately upon custody.

√ Per Penal Code section 26, and *In re Gladys R.*, the prosecution must prove that a minor under 14 knew the wrongfulness of his act.

√   The charging document in juvenile cases is called a "petition," the trial is a "jurisdictional hearing," and the sentencing hearing is a "dispositional hearing."

√   Juvenile hearings are not as open to the public as adult trials, they have no juries, but they are generally subject to the same rules of evidence and procedural due process as criminal trials.

√   A 707 fitness hearing is held to determine if certain serious offenders, aged 16 or 17, should be tried as adults.

√   Minors may not be executed, and may not be confined with adults. They may be committed to secure facilities for the maximum term applicable to adult offenders, but not to exceed age 25 in the California Youth Authority.

ISSUES FOR DISCUSSION

1.   Given the increasing sophistication of younger criminals and the explosion of youth-gang violence, should consideration be given to lowering the age at which general prosecution could be initiated, without fitness hearings or other juvenile court proceedings? If so, what would a more realistic age limit be?

2.   Is there a legitimate purpose to be served by the noncriminal terminology used in juvenile procedure? Is this just a "word game"? Does it compound the problem of dealing with hard-core juvenile offenders?

3.   If the juvenile justice system is intended to treat and rehabilitate the minor, what message is sent by the suppression of critical evidence on a 700.1 motion? Does this teach the minor that justice is fair, or encourage recidivism?

CHAPTER 15

APPLIED CRIMINAL PROCEDURE

Learning Goals: After studying this chapter, you will be able to correctly answer the following questions:

√ How does a reviewing court set forth the facts and issues in an appellate decision?

√ What kinds of procedural issues are typically raised by defendants on appeal?

√ How does a court dispose of issues on appeal?

INTRODUCTION

One of the most common ways to study criminal law and procedure is by the "casebook" method. A casebook, as the word implies, is a collection of published opinions that illustrate different learning points through the court's application of legal principles to the specific facts of selected cases.

Following is a *substantially-condensed* version of a decision issued by the California Supreme Court in a death-penalty case. (The actual opinion is 74 pages long and addresses many evidentiary and procedural issues in addition to the ones summarized here).

As you read through the opinion, note the various procedural issues raised by the defendant on appeal, and the court's discussion or disposition of them. Note, also, the difference between guilt phase and penalty phase issues.

PEOPLE V. DOUGLAS (1990) 50 C3d 468

Defendant Fred Berre Douglas appeals from a judgment imposing death following his conviction of two counts of first degree murder in connection with the 1982 killings of 19-year-old Beth Jones and 16-year-old Margaret Kreuger.

FACTS AND PROCEDURE

Guilt Phase Evidence. The case against defendant was based substantially on the testimony of his accomplice, Richard Hernandez, who was granted immunity from prosecution in exchange for his testimony. Another witness, Kathy Phillips, also testified for the prosecution pursuant to a promise of immunity. Hernandez and Phillips's statements were substantially corroborated by physical evidence and other witnesses.

Phillips's Testimony. In 1979, Phillips, a heroin addict, wanted money to buy drugs. Her friend, Richard Hernandez, worked next door to defendant's furniture refinishing shop in Santa Ana. Hernandez often supplied Phillips with drugs. He introduced Phillips to defendant, who told her he would pay her if she posed for nude photographs while in bondage. Phillips agreed to pose for defendant and shortly thereafter defendant took her to his shop, where he tied her hands and ankles and gagged her mouth. According to Phillips, defendant showed her photographs of several other women to indicate how he wanted her to pose. He also instructed her to "look scared" but did not harm her during the photo session. Defendant paid Phillips $40 after he had taken pictures of her with a Polaroid camera for about an hour. Phillips eventually left the shop with Hernandez, who then purchased drugs for her.

Two weeks after the above incident, defendant asked Phillips if she would assist him in killing young women in the desert while making sex films that included bondage, sadism and homosexual scenes. Defendant believed that Phillip's presence during the filming would make it easier for the victims to trust him—thus making his crime easier to commit. According to Phillips, defendant told her he would bury the bodies so that no evidence would be discovered and that he would make a lot of money (around $35,000) by selling the films to "people in Las Vegas."

Hernandez's Testimony. Hernandez began working for defendant at his furniture refinishing shop in 1981. After Hernandez had been working for defendant for almost eight months, defendant asked him to have a coworker drive Hernandez to his house in Costa Mesa. When Hernandez arrived, he saw an unconscious naked woman lying on a sofa bed in the living room. Defendant told Hernandez he had drugged the woman. He instructed Hernandez to take off his clothes so he could take pictures of Hernandez with the woman. Hernandez removed his clothing, and posed with the woman. Defendant told Hernandez to insert a baton inside the woman's vagina, but it would not fit. Instead, Hernandez put butter on the object and inserted it inside her rectum. Defendant then told Hernandez to place his penis in the woman's mouth so that defendant could take a picture. When the woman awoke three days later, defendant and Hernandez let her go.

On the day of the murders the two victims met defendant and Hernandez in a 7-Eleven parking lot. The foursome drove, in defendant's car, to the desert south of Indio. During the drive, Hernandez drank beer, and he and Kreuger smoked marijuana. When they arrived at the desert, Kreuger and Hernandez smoked more marijuana, and Hernandez followed defendant's instructions to lay a sheet on the ground and prepare rum and Cokes for the four of them.

After the foursome relaxed for an hour, defendant instructed the victims to remove their clothing. Kreuger asked defendant if she could see the money, and defendant showed her a $100 bill. Defendant then gave Hernandez a rope (which, Hernandez testified, was "a bit thicker than venetian blind cord") and told him to tie up the victims. Hernandez tied their feet at the ankles and then tied their hands behind their backs. When Kreuger asked defendant where he kept the camera, he and Hernandez walked to the car, where defendant retrieved a rifle from the trunk. Hernandez testified that he became scared when he saw the gun. On returning to the victims, defendant put a clip in the rifle and told them, "[h]ere's the camera." He then told the victims to "make love to each other."

He ordered one victim to kiss the other's feet, and then stated he wanted "some tongue on her crotch." When the victims requested a drink, Hernandez gave them each a sip of soda.

Hernandez testified that after he gave the women a drink, defendant cut Kreuger on the neck with a razor blade and sucked on the open wound for about 10 minutes. When defendant stopped sucking the cut, he retrieved a beer from the cooler and told Hernandez that the women "just couldn't go back."

Thereafter, defendant told the victims to suck on his penis, while they remained in a kneeling position. The victims next began to orally copulate Hernandez. When he was unable to sustain an erection, he told defendant that he had to urinate. As he squatted to defecate behind a bush, Hernandez heard one of the victims yell "Leave her alone!" Hernandez stated that as he walked back toward the victims, he saw defendant choking Jones. He also noticed that Kreuger was dead, blood spurting from her mouth. After choking Jones, defendant hit her with the wooden butt of his rifle, killing her.

Hernandez covered the victims with a sheet and hid their bodies behind a bush before the two men went to a bar in Borrego Springs, where they consumed several drinks each.

The next day, Hernandez and defendant were questioned at the Garden Grove Police Department about the disappearances of Kreuger and Jones. Hernandez recited an alibi that defendant had concocted a few days before the murders. That evening, defendant and Hernandez drove north, arriving several days later in Victoria, Canada.

The bodies of Kreuger and Jones were discovered in the Anza-Borrego National Park by a photographer and his wife during the 1983 Easter holidays.

After defendant and Hernandez discovered that the grave site had been disturbed, and that warrants had been issued for their arrest, they traveled to Loreto, Mexico. Defendant left Loreto after spending three weeks hiding from the authorities. Hernandez stayed in the city for approximately 10 months before he was taken into custody by Mexican authorities, who had been told by American police detectives that Hernandez was wanted in the United States. Apparently, as discussed further below, before he spoke to the American officers Hernandez had confessed the murders to the Mexican authorities after they beat him.

Defendant was eventually arrested in North Las Vegas, Nevada, in February 1984. Shortly after his arrest, he signed a waiver of extradition and was returned to California. Both defendant and Hernandez were charged with murder and conspiracy to commit prostitution.

Defense. Defendant presented an alibi defense. Henry Akers, who had known defendant for about 10 years, owned a furniture refinishing shop near defendant's establishment. Akers testified that on the morning of the murders, he spoke to defendant between 5 and 6:30, the same time Hernandez testified that he and defendant were driving to the desert with the murder victims.

Penalty Phase Evidence. The People introduced evidence of three incidents of prior criminal activity. A different woman testified as to each incident, as explained in greater detail below.

GUILT PHASE ISSUES

Lack of Territorial Jurisdiction. At the preliminary hearing and again in superior court, defendant moved to dismiss on the grounds that Orange County lacked jurisdiction. Defendant contends that the Orange County Municipal and Superior Courts lacked territorial jurisdiction over his case because there was no evidence to connect the murders of Kreuger and Jones to Orange County aside from "inconsequential preliminary arrangements" made between defendant and Hernandez prior to the killings.

As both lower courts noted, section 781 resolves the jurisdictional question. That section states: "When a public offense is committed in part in one jurisdictional territory and in part in another, or the acts or effects thereof constituting or requisite to the consummation of the offense occur in two or more jurisdictional territories, the jurisdiction of such offense is in any competent court within either jurisdictional territory."

Improper Venue. Defendant contends the trial court erred in denying his pretrial motion for a change of venue on the ground that he could not receive a fair trial in Orange County because of the combined effect on the jury of publicity surrounding the present trial and his 1977 arrest and subsequent trial for attempted murder.

A change of venue motion must be granted if a defendant can show that absent such relief, there is a reasonable likelihood he will not receive a fair and impartial trial.

The record reveals that none of the jurors selected remembered anything damaging to defendant, none knew about his prior criminal background, and none had formed an opinion concerning his guilt or innocence. Accordingly, we find that under the facts, it is not reasonably likely defendant was denied a fair trial.

Admissibility of Hernandez's Testimony. In March 1984, Hernandez was arrested by Mexican police in Loreto, Mexico. Mexican officials proceeded to question Hernandez. When they were unsuccessful in their initial inquiries, Hernandez claims they resorted to physical violence, subjecting him to a 15-20 minute beating. The officers informed Hernandez that they were going to "take him out to the beach." At this point, fearing for his life, Hernandez gave a full confession.

Defendant asserts Hernandez's trial testimony "was inadmissible as a matter of law because it was obtained by improper and coercive police and prosecution conduct."

Defendant fails to meet his burden here. None of the statements made by Hernandez to the Mexican police was introduced at defendant's trial.

Moreover, defendant lacks standing to object to any perceived violation of *Hernandez's* privilege against self-incrimination. That right is personal, and may not be vicariously asserted by another.

Corroboration Sufficiency of Evidence. Defendant argues that, assuming Hernandez was found by the jury to be an accomplice, the People presented insufficient corroboration of Hernandez's testimony.

Assuming for the purpose of this determination that Hernandez was an accomplice whose testimony required corroboration under section 1111, we are fully convinced that there was sufficient corroborating testimony at trial.

As explained above, in addition to Hernandez's testimony, statements of several other witnesses tended to connect defendant to the murders.

Admissibility of Phillips's Testimony. Defendant asserts the court committed reversible error by allowing Kathy Phillips to testify, over his objection, that in 1979 (three years before the subject murders) she participated in a photo session at defendant's furniture refinishing shop during which defendant photographed her in the nude while she was bound and gagged. The next month, Phillips went for a ride with defendant during which he asked her if she wanted to make more money (Phillips was using heroin at the time). According to Phillips, defendant told her that "he wanted to take some more pictures of other women and take them out in the desert and make what he referred to as a snuff flick or movie...." Phillips stated that defendant told her he wanted to drug the girls in connection with the photography sessions, "have sex with them and be really brutal" and that he "would just make a movie and it would be a lot of bondage and sadistic-type things...." In addition, Phillips testified that she and defendant had discussed burying bodies so that they could not be discovered. Finally, Phillips told the jury defendant had mentioned to her that he would eventually sell the "snuff" movies to the Mafia in the United States and Canada.

Defendant argues that Phillips's testimony should have been excluded under Evidence Code section 1101, subdivision (a), which bars use of character evidence to prove conduct.

Phillips's testimony was relevant not only to prove a disputed fact — that defendant committed the crimes in question — but also to corroborate Hernandez's testimony implicating defendant as the perpetrator of the murders.

Hitch Motion. Defendant claims the trial court erroneously denied his motion to dismiss or, in the alternative, for sanctions under *People v. Hitch* based on the prosecution's failure to preserve and disclose the names of two potential defense witnesses.

Under the *Trombetta* test, we cannot characterize as "exculpatory" or "substantially material" the telephone calls of two people claiming they may have seen the victims after the alleged murders. Moreover, as the People observe, the police here actually preserved the names and phone numbers of the two alleged witnesses.

Defendant's Absence at Reading the Testimony. Defendant asserts he was deprived of his right to be personally present during the reading of some guilt phase testimony.

The day after deliberations began, the jury requested the court to read the testimony of [four witnesses]. Defendant was not present at the reading, although defense counsel was present. After considering the nature of the matter and reviewing the record, we find defendant has failed to demonstrate prejudice.

Counsel Motions. Following the guilt and special circumstance phases of the trial and prior to the penalty phase, defendant filed an *ex parte* motion for substitute counsel pursuant to *People v. Marsden*.

The record shows the court here specifically considered each of defendant's reasons for requesting a new attorney for the penalty phase, and reasonably found that defendant's claims were either unsubstantiated or resulted from a post verdict disagreement with proper tactical decisions made by counsel during the guilt phase of the trial. Accordingly, the *Marsden* motion was properly denied.

PENALTY PHASE ISSUES

Improper *Voir Dire*. Defendant contends the judgment should be reversed because the court gave each juror copies of the proposed "death qualification" voir dire questions prior to individual questioning.

We are not persuaded that the advance notice to the jury of the death qualification questions caused it to become death prone.

Two prospective jurors stated during the sequestered voir dire that they could not vote for the death penalty. Defendant asserts their exclusion resulted in a jury that was unduly death prone.

Our review of the voir dire shows that each of the two challenged jurors expressed views that made it clear that he would feel forced to vote against death regardless of the law or evidence presented. Thus, their exclusion was proper.

Other Criminal Activity. Defendant claims it was error to permit the jury to consider several instances of prior criminal activity.

In 1976, Julie McGettrick worked for defendant at a cocktail lounge called the Villa D'Italia in Orange County. McGettrick testified that defendant approached her with a proposition that she join him in convincing young girls to pose for photographs and then killing and dismembering the unsuspecting victims. To this end, defendant drove McGettrick to Yucca Valley in search of a location to commit his acts. McGettrick testified that defendant told her he wanted the girls "to be cut up, bleeding but still conscious . . . .," and that her role in the act would be simply to appear in the photographs defendant planned on taking once he tortured the girls. Although McGettrick testified that she posed nude for defendant during the trip to the desert, she said she did so out of fear. Defendant had shown her a gun in the car before she removed her clothes and the photos were taken next to the car. McGettrick testified that she followed defendant's instructions to pose for the photos because she feared defendant was going to grab the gun and use it on her.

A few days later, McGettrick approached Vickie Pendleton, another employee at the Villa D'Italia, and asked if she would be interested in posing for defendant.

Pendleton and defendant drove to Yucca Valley. There, Pendleton testified, defendant "got me from behind with a rag and I guess it was ether and he drugged me and I passed out . . . ." When Pendleton regained consciousness, defendant was standing about two feet in front of her with a pistol in his hand.

Pendleton then asked defendant why he was doing this to her. According to Pendleton, defendant "put the gun to my head and said I better urinate on him or he [was] going to kill me." Pendleton stated she was so nervous that she could not urinate. Defendant then forced Pendleton to orally copulate him. Pendleton testified she convinced defendant that she would help him in his plan to torture women and send photos of the activity to Canada, where they allegedly would be bought. Thereafter, defendant gave Pendleton $50 and let her go after she told him she was sick from the ether and she would contact him in a day or two. Pendleton never saw the defendant again.

Defendant argues the trial court committed reversible error by allowing McGettrick and Pendleton to testify about criminal activity.

The prosecutor was entitled to present the testimonial evidence of McGettrick and Pendleton as evidence of prior criminal activity even though defendant was never actually charged with a crime for this conduct.

Defendant's 1977 Arrest for Attempted Murder Testimony of Pamela Sue Williams. Williams testified that she met defendant in July 1977 after he picked her up when she was hitchhiking in Santa Ana. Defendant gave her $50 after they talked for two hours in a bar. She told defendant her name was Debbie Adams.

During their conversation, defendant told Williams that he wanted to make snuff movies, using Williams to find young girls, preferably age 13 to 14 years old, but would settle on a 25-year-old. Defendant wanted Williams to torture the girls while he took the pictures. He promised Williams that she would be paid $1,000 for her effort. Defendant told Williams that the film would be sent to Canada for developing and then distributed in the United States from Mexico.

Williams eventually told the police about her conversation with defendant because she had a 13-year-old daughter, and she "got a feeling this guy was for real." Williams agreed to cooperate with the police in investigating defendant and agreed to wear a tape-recording device and introduce two policewomen (Baucom and Reynolds) to defendant as potential victims. Williams then introduced the policewomen to defendant, who told his potential "victims" that he wanted them to act in a lesbian film he was making in the desert "past Palm Springs." Defendant offered to pay the officers $500 apiece to participate in approximately 120 photographs. Baucom and Reynolds agreed to meet Williams and defendant the next day at the Two Guys parking lot in Garden Grove to implement their plan.

The next morning, defendant and Williams conversed for about 20 minutes in the Two Guys parking lot before the undercover agents arrived. Williams had been wired to record the conversation, which included a gruesome discussion by defendant of his plan to torture and then film his intended victims' agony. During the conversation, defendant also instructed Williams on how to tie the victims, and gave her a pistol to place in her purse. He told her that he also had a rifle in his car.

After the agents arrived, defendant and Williams drove them to an area of San Bernardino county (off State Highway 247) known as "Old Ghost Road." Defendant was subsequently arrested and charged with attempted murder (§ 187), solicitation to commit a crime (§ 653f) and unlawful possession of a firearm (§ 12022) in connection with the incident.

In 1978, after the jury failed to reach a verdict in the above matter, the court declared a mistrial. Defendant pleaded *nolo contendere* to solicitation to commit certain enumerated crimes under section 653f a felony subject to three years' imprisonment. The record reveals defendant understood the *nolo contendere* plea "shall be considered the same as a plea of guilty." Defendant was granted three years' probation with terms including one hundred fifteen days in custody, with credit for all days served.

Thereafter, in 1982, the court denied defendant's motion to reduce the felony to a misdemeanor, but granted his motion, pursuant to section 1203.4, to enter a plea of not guilty and dismiss the information based on his successful completion of probation.

Defendant now asserts the court erred in allowing the jury to consider the evidence. He claims the evidence should have been excluded because: (i) it violated double jeopardy and plea bargain principles, (ii) it was barred under section 1203.4, (iii) it was barred by the statute of limitations, (iv) the reporter's notes from the 1978 trial had been destroyed, (v) irrelevant physical evidence was introduced to corroborate Williams's testimony, and (vi) the 1977 crime did not involve violence or the threat of violence. As we explain, we find that none of defendant's contentions has merit.

Double Jeopardy. First, defendant's contention that double jeopardy principles preclude use of his 1977 crime during his penalty trial is without support. We agree with the People that constitutional guaranties against double jeopardy do not apply to subsequent trials when the prior offense is used as an enhancement, nor do such principles apply when the prior criminal activity is considered by the penalty jury as a proper aggravating factor.

Next, we reject defendant's related argument, that introduction of the charges dismissed pursuant to a plea bargain violated the implicit understanding that he would suffer no adverse sentencing consequences because of the facts underlying the dismissed charge.

Section 1203.4. Defendant's argument that section 1203.4 prohibited the jury from considering the underlying facts surrounding the solicitation is specious. Section 1203.4 merely allows a defendant to withdraw his plea of *nolo contendere* and enter a plea of not guilty once the conditions of his probation have been fulfilled. Contrary to defendant's contention, nothing in that section prohibits the jury in a capital case from considering the facts of the crime that gave rise to the offense.

Statute of Limitations. Defendant also asserts that the prior violent activity was "stale," in the sense that it occurred more than seven years before the 1984 trial, and thus failed to satisfy the Eighth Amendment requirement that the penalty determination be reliable. The evidence was not stale simply because the prior activity occurred seven years before defendant's 1984 trial. Instead, the evidence was relevant and reliable evidence of defendant's prior violent criminality.

Reporter's Lost Notes. Evidence of the 1977 offense was declared inadmissible at the guilt phase as a prior similar act on the grounds that it constituted cumulative evidence and its probative value was outweighed by its prejudicial effect. Another motion was brought to exclude the crime from the penalty phase on the ground that the reporter's notes of the 1978 trial, ending in a hung jury, had been routinely discarded in 1984. Defendant now claims the prosecutor had a duty to preserve the notes.

Defendant's argument is misplaced. Destruction of a court reporter's notes, absent notice to the court indicating defendant wishes the notes preserved, is lawful. We find defendant was not prejudiced by the discarding of the reporter's 1978 trial notes.

Physical Evidence of 1977 Offense. Defendant next asserts that a number of items of physical evidence (a saw, knives, cleaver, rope, tape and women's underwear), found in the desert under a tarp in the sand within a few feet of where defendant apparently took the undercover policewomen, were erroneously admitted at the penalty phase as evidence of defendant's preparation in a plan to commit murder (defendant allegedly placed the items in the sand before returning to the same spot with the intended victims a few hours later).

Permitting the People to rely on physical evidence of a crime ending in a plea of *nolo contendere* or a dismissed charge (here, attempted murder) falls within the scope of aggravating evidence the penalty jury may consider.

Defendant asserts that the court erred in allowing the jury to hear evidence of the prior solicitation because it did not involve force or violence or the threat of violence. We disagree.

Disproportionality of Sentence. Defendant claims that because Hernandez harbored an intent to kill when he acted as an accomplice, defendant's sentence is arbitrary and disproportionate under the Eighth Amendment.

We find these contentions meritless. Defendant was found guilty of the murders of Kreuger and Jones. The evidence indicated that Hernandez was not an active participant in the murders, unlike defendant, who was also the initiator of the acts. In light of the differences in their circumstances and involvement, defendant cannot assert that his punishment was disproportionate to his individual culpability. Nor can defendant show his sentence otherwise violates the *Dillon/Lynch* requirements.

The judgment of death is affirmed.

ISSUES FOR DISCUSSION

1. Note that Douglas's appeal had nothing to do with whether he was guilty or innocent of the two murders of which he was convicted. Nowhere did he make any contention on appeal that he was not guilty, but instead raised 41 different *procedural* attacks (many of them omitted from this excerpt). Is this opinion an example of the misdirected focus of the judicial process on *technicalities*, rather than on the essential question of guilt or innocence? Or is it an example of procedural due process working to insure fairness and reliability of the system?

2. As the facts indicated, the 1977 offense involving the two undercover policewomen had included not only verbal descriptions of his plans to murder them, but also the recovered physical evidence (a saw, knives, cleaver, rope and tape) he had stashed nearby for this purpose. After the jury failed to convict him on any charges arising from this episode, he was allowed to enter a *nolo* plea to one count of felony solicitation, with 115 days already served in jail and three years' probation. Afterward, he was permitted to withdraw his plea and have all charges dismissed. Given the compelling evidence of his intent to commit two brutal and sadistic murders of the undercover officers, where should responsibility be fixed for Douglas's apparent evasion of justice in the 1977 case? Was the jury at fault, for failing to convict an obviously-dangerous, obviously-guilty defendant? Was the prosecutor to blame for agreeing to a lenient plea bargain after the jury deadlock? Should the judge have refused to accept a *nolo* plea in such a violent case? Did the probation department err in certifying Douglas as having "successfully completed probation?" Did the law itself facilitate a "cover-up" by providing for a withdrawal of plea and dismissal?

3. Is it fair to speculate that Douglas's ability to manipulate the system in the 1977 case merely encouraged him to continue his criminal behavior, secure in the assumption that the criminal justice system

was ineffective? Is it fair to theorize that if the judicial process had dealt more seriously with Douglas in 1977, Beth Jones and Margaret Kreuger would be alive today? If Fred Douglas is sitting on death row today because the system gave him "breaks" on his earlier cases, rather than dealing firmly and decisively with him then, did any of the participants in the prior cases really do him any favors?

4. Is Douglas's conviction and death sentence an example of the ultimate success of the system, or of its failure?

CHAPTER 16

CHALLENGE FOR CHANGE

Learning Goals: After studying this chapter, you will be able to correctly answer the following questions:

√ What is the historical background of recent developments in California criminal procedure?

√ What dramatic changes have occurred in recent years? Why?

√ What remains to be done to improve the criminal justice system in California?

Year after year, public opinion polls find that concerns about crime top the people's agenda for governmental action. During every legislative session, the assembly and senate tackle the problems of strengthening law enforcement without impairing the constitutional rights of suspected and accused persons. And from time to time, the electorate demonstrates its impatience with the pace of reform by taking the initiative to amend the state constitution and to enact statutes directly, as in 1982 with Proposition 8, and in 1990 with Proposition 115.

Traditionally, the study and application of law have been divided into matters of *substance*, and matters of *procedure*. During the past several decades, the greatest attention by far has been paid to the procedural aspect of criminal law. Indeed, the vast majority of substantive criminal offenses have been on the books, virtually unchanged, since 1872. Procedural law, on the other hand, is being constantly refined by judicial decision, annually modified by legislative action, and periodically overhauled by popular initiative.

Why is criminal procedure so difficult to stabilize in California? The answer may have dimensions that are political, sociological and cultural, but there are certainly *historical* developments that can be observed.

In 1941, long before the exclusionary excesses of the Sixties, a murder conviction was affirmed by the US Supreme Court in the case of *Lisenba v. California*, 314 US 219, over objections by the defendant that his confession was improperly obtained by police. Even though officials had held Lisenba without access to his attorney, had subjected him to repeated interrogation, and had admitted that an officer slapped Lisenba at one point, the resulting confession was ruled admissible. The State of California was represented in the case by Attorney General Earl Warren.

In the 1950s and early 1960s, Warren's contemporaries included Mathew Tobriner and Roger Traynor, who, as justices of the California Supreme Court, were issuing what were later to be called "catalytic" decisions in the area of defendants' procedural rights. For example, in *People v. Cahan* (1955) 44 C2d 434, an opinion authored by Justice Traynor held for the first time in California that evidence resulting from an unreasonable search or seizure was inadmissible in a criminal prosecution. It was not until *Mapp v. Ohio* (1961) 367 US 643, that the Fourth Amendment exclusionary rule was made applicable to the states by the US Supreme Court's interpretation of the Fourteenth Amendment.

In 1958, another coerced confession case from California made its way to the US Supreme Court. Again, a murder conviction was affirmed, despite police denial of the suspect's request for counsel during interrogation. *Crooker v. California* (1958) 357 US 433. In this 5-4 opinion, however, a strong dissent was registered, on the ground that denial of a suspect's request for counsel during police interrogation was unconstitutional. Among the four justices dissenting in *Crooker* was the court's new Chief Justice, Earl Warren. It could not be ignored that Warren's view, perhaps influenced by his colleagues on the California Supreme Court, now differed from the position he had represented in *Lisenba* and other earlier cases.

The 1965 decision in *People v. Dorado*, 62 C2d 338, authored by Justice Tobriner, held that a suspect's confession resulting from custodial interrogation would be inadmissible in California, unless the suspect had been informed of his rights to silence and to the assistance of counsel. The very next year, in a 5-4 opinion written by Chief Justice Warren, the US Supreme Court made a similar rule applicable to all the states, in *Miranda v. Arizona* (1966) 384 US 436.

What was going on? Were the California exclusionary decisions merely anticipating logical developments in federal interpretations? Were the US Supreme Court justices so impressed with California jurisprudence that they were content to play "follow the leader" behind California? Was California being used as a judicial "proving ground," to test the public's tolerance of the court's experimentation with procedural protections for accused criminals, prior to imposing similar rules on every jurisdiction in the nation via the Fourteenth Amendment? Or was it all just coincidence?

Whatever the explanation, the 1960s and 1970s witnessed a virtual competition between the California and US Supreme Courts to devise and extend new procedural protections for defendants and new restrictions on police and prosecutors. The courts were active, not only in the area of constitutional exclusionary law, but also in cases involving due process issues, speedy trial, discovery, access to evidence, competence of counsel, confrontation of witnesses, lineups and eye-witness identification, jury selection, prosecutorial misconduct at trial, and most of the other procedural issues discussed throughout this text.

As the judicial intervention in procedural law increased, however, so did the crime rates, and the problems associated with them. The jails filled up. The prisons filled up. With 10 percent of the country's population, California was reporting as much as 17 percent of the country's violent crimes, including more than 2000 homicides each year. Drunk drivers became an increasing menace, killing as many as 2600 Californians in some years. Rape, robbery, arson and burglary threatened innocent victims as never before.

The evening news became a daily crime report, bombarding the public with the gruesome details of a seemingly-endless stream of sensational crimes: Robert Sirhan's assassination of Senator Kennedy, the Manson family murders, the Zodiac killer, the Alphabet Bomber, the Skid Row Slasher, the SLA shootout, the Juan Corona case, the Hillside Strangler, the Chowchilla school bus kidnaping, the assassinations of Mayor Moscone and Supervisor Milke, the Zebra killings, the attempted presidential assassinations by Lynette Fromme and Sara Jane Moore, the McDonald's massacre, the Randy Kraft case, the Nightstalker murders, and literally thousands of local killings and other serious crimes associated with the growth of youth gangs and the burgeoning narcotics trade.

By the late 1970s, crime and disposition statistics were confirming what law enforcement professionals had been warning: the pursuit of procedural perfection was choking the judicial system and leaving the general population vulnerable to crime as never before. By some estimates and studies, a criminal's odds of being arrested for any one crime he committed were about 1 in 20; the chances that his case would not be charged by the prosecutor after arrest were 1 in 7; the odds of a reduction in charges or sentence prior to trial were about 95 in 100; the chance of acquittal or mistrial from a jury trial were 1 in 3; the odds of appellate reversal of any conviction were 1 in 6; and the prospect of probation was a 7 in 10 chance. This left the odds of going to prison for any felony committed at less than one-tenth of one percent. With most prisoners receiving parole after serving only half of their original sentences, recidivism rates were ranging from 20 percent for murderers to 65 percent for robbers and rapists and up to 85 percent for burglars and auto thieves. The situation was so uncontrolled by 1978 that the California Legislature found it necessary to enact a special set of laws to deal with "career criminals." (Penal Code sections 13850-13854.)

In the 1980s, the US Supreme Court, under Chief Justice Burger, and later Chief Justice Rehnquist, reflecting its more conservative majority, began to limit, disapprove or overrule some of the procedural decisions of the Warren court thought to have contributed to erosion of public safety. In a series of cases, the High Court consistently reversed opinions of the California Supreme Court on procedural matters of constitutional dimension. For example:

- *California v. Prysock* (1981) 463 US 992, reversing on a *Miranda* issue; confession admissible.

- *California v. Ramos* (1983) 463 US 992, reversing on a death penalty issue; death penalty affirmed.

- *California v. Beheler* (1983) 463 US 1121, reversing on a *Miranda* issue; confession admissible.

- *California v. Trombetta* (1984) 467 US 479, reversing on a due process issue; conviction affirmed.

- *California v. Carney* (1985) 471 US 386, reversing on search issue; vehicle search upheld.

- *California v. Ciraolo* (1986) 476 US 207, reversing on search issue; aerial surveillance upheld.

- *California v. Greenwood* (1988) 486 US 35, reversing on search issue; trash search upheld.

In reaction, the California Supreme Court, staffed primarily with justices in the tradition of Traynor and Tobriner, began to base its decisions on the "independent state grounds" of the California constitution. This technique insulated the California courts from federal review, and allowed the perpetuation and expansion of procedures which benefited criminal defendants at the expense of the prosecution. See, for example, *People v. Ramos* (1984) 37 C3d 136. In its first *Ramos* opinion (30 C3d 553), the California Supreme Court had reversed a death penalty on federal due process grounds. When this decision was subsequently reversed by the US Supreme Court and returned to the state courts, the California Supreme Court again reversed the death penalty, this time ruling that the due process clause of the state constitution, although identical in wording with the federal provision, was to be interpreted differently in California.

The public, however, had had enough of both the California Supreme Court's noble experiments with criminal procedure, and the legislature's seeming unwillingness or inability to take corrective action. In 1982, the electorate passed constitutional amendments (Propositions 4 and 8) that specifically overruled a number of court decisions and provided that state courts could no longer use "independent state grounds" to exclude relevant evidence from criminal trials. California Const. Art I, section 28(d).

In 1986, the electorate took the unprecedented step of removing the chief justice and two associate justices from the state supreme court; Justice Stanley Mosk, an advocate of "independent state grounds" decision making, was barely approved for retention on the court. Subsequently, more conservative justices were appointed, and though the new court drew the line against any further expansion of defendants' rights, its apparent regard for the doctrine of *stare decisis* restrained the court from extensive revision of its own precedents.

Thus, the history of California criminal procedure from the 1950s through the 1970s was characterized by the judicial activism of the California and US Supreme Courts. This was followed by the more restraining influence, in the 1980s, of more conservative court majorities, and by the dramatic assertions of the popular will in the 1980s and 1990 constitutional amendments and judicial elections.

While corrective efforts are being made in the legislature, in the courts and at the ballot box that generally meet with approval by police, prosecutors, victims' rights organizations and the public at large, tremendous challenges remain. The frustrations, criticisms and risks incident to law enforcement work have affected the ability of police agencies to recruit and retain qualified, career officers. Economic pressures have created a similar difficulty as to career prosecutors and trial judges. Federal civil rights lawsuits have resulted in court-ordered conditions of confinement so far in excess of affordable levels that overcrowded correctional facilities are struggling to cope.

The explosion of gang violence and pervasive influence of illegal drugs represent not only law enforcement challenges, but also cultural challenges to the enforceability of the social contract itself. Proliferation of high-tech and environmental crimes adds a new dimension to traditional "cops-and-robbers" law enforcement. And social controversy over such subjects as abortion, censorship, the death penalty and the legalization of drugs will continue to present the justice system with difficult cases.

As California absorbs new citizens with increasingly-diverse political, religious, cultural, racial and ethnic backgrounds, the challenge to accommodate the conflicting guarantees of freedom and security may be substantial. And as progress is made toward reconciling man's natural and developmental inequality with the democratic goals of equal opportunity and equal treatment under the law, continued challenge is inevitable. But just as constant, fortunately, is the commitment to seek justice.

The criminal justice student and practitioner play important roles in meeting the challenges. An appreciation of the orderly, systematic and non-discriminatory administration of justice by means of duly promulgated rules of criminal procedure fosters the approach to determining criminal guilt and imposing just punishment that help to differentiate civilization from anarchy.

California's criminal justice training and education programs, law enforcement officers and public prosecutors are nationally recognized as the most proficient and professional anywhere. With proper preparation and dedication, they will meet the challenge.

ISSUES FOR DISCUSSION

1. What are the most pressing needs for change in the criminal justice system today? Who should take the initiative to change things? How?

2. Should the method of selecting members of the judiciary be changed? Is more public oversight needed? How could the judiciary be made more accountable to the people? Should the judiciary—or any branch of government—be unaccountable?

3. How well does California's initiative process work? How could changes be brought about by the people without this device? Is it overused? Underused?

4. What do you see as the most immediate and challenging social-criminal justice problem on the horizon today? What should be done?

GLOSSARY

ADJUDICATION. Hearing by a court of evidence, and determination of the issue involved.

ADVERSARY SYSTEM. The American system of criminal justice, characterized by a lawsuit between the people as plaintiff and the accused as defendant.

AFFIRMATIVE DEFENSE. One of a number of defenses which admit the conduct of the accused but allege a legal excuse that negates criminal liability.

ALIBI. A defense claiming that the defendant was not present when the crime occurred.

ALLOCUTION. The arraignment for pronouncement of judgment.

ARRAIGNMENT. The initial appearance by the defendant in court to hear the charges against him and to answer them.

BENCH WARRANT. An arrest warrant issued by a judge to secure the appearance of a person who did not appear as required.

BURDEN OF PROOF. The legal duty on one party or the other to prove a disputed fact, to a particular degree of certainty.

CALIFORNIA YOUTH AUTHORITY. ("CYA") Corrections organization for juvenile offenders.

CASE-IN-CHIEF. The party's essential case, setting forth the proof necessary for a favorable verdict.

CIRCUMSTANTIAL EVIDENCE. Evidence which proves a fact indirectly, by logical inference, from two or more proved facts.

CITATION. A written notice issued by an official (such as a traffic ticket, by police), charging an offense, and requiring an appearance to answer.

CIVIL COMPROMISE. Disposition of certain misdemeanor cases by civil satisfaction and payment of court costs.

CLOSING ARGUMENT. The prosecutor's final argument to the trier of fact, after the defense has argued its case.

COLLATERAL ESTOPPEL. "Bar by side action." When an issue in a case was earlier decided between the same parties in some parallel action, its relitigation in another action is stopped, or prevented. The parties are bound by the prior determination.

COMMON LAW. The unwritten body of law inherited from the English tradition on which many California statutes are based.

COMMUTATION. Change; a reduction in sentence.

COMPLAINT. The formal charging document filed in justice or municipal court, either to accuse a defendant of a misdemeanor or to initiate felony preliminary hearing proceedings.

CONCURRENT SENTENCE. Two or more terms of confinement starting at the same time and being served simultaneously.

CONDITIONAL EXAMINATION. Taking the testimony of a witness before trial due to anticipated unavailability.

CONFESSION EVIDENCE. Evidence of the oral statements of the suspect implicating him in the crime. May consist of limited *admissions* to certain facts, or a full *confession*, admitting every material element to establish guilt.

CONFRONTATION. Physical presence of adverse witnesses and evidence for cross-examination and challenge.

CONSECUTIVE SENTENCE. Two or more terms of confinement served in sequence, one after the other.

CONSOLIDATION. The joining together of multiple counts against the defendant for prosecution in a single action.

CORPUS DELICTI. The body of a crime, consisting of the fact of injury, loss or harm, and the existence of a criminal agency as the cause.

COURT TRIAL. The trial of a case by judge alone, without a jury.

CRIME CHARGING. The process of formally accusing a suspected criminal in court via decision made by the prosecuting attorney or the grand jury.

CROSS-EXAMINATION. Questioning of a witness by the party who did not call him.

DELIBERATIONS. The jury's discussion of the case to arrive at a verdict.

DEMEANOR. Conduct; appearance; deportment.

DEMURRER. A defendant's response to the charges, alleging that the charging document is void on its face.

DETERMINATE SENTENCE. A specific term of confinement calculated at time of judgment.

DICTUM. (Plural: *Dicta*) Discussion in a judicial opinion that is not necessary to the result, and is not binding precedent.

DIRECT EVIDENCE. Evidence that directly proves a fact, without requiring that any inferences be drawn or any other facts be proven.

DIRECT EXAMINATION. The first questioning of a witness by the party who called the witness.

DISCOVERY. Obtaining access to evidence known to or held by the opposing party.

DISCRIMINATORY PROSECUTION. Unfair charging by the prosecutor for improper reasons which single the defendant out for exceptional treatment based on race, political activity, or other improper basis.

DISPOSITION. The outcome of a case; its final settlement.

DIVERSION. Removal of a criminal case from the judicial system and referral for treatment by a social service agency.

ENHANCEMENT. An increase to a prison term based on proven allegations of special facts, such as prior record or use of weapons.

EX POST FACTO. "After the fact." Usually refers to a law enacted or charged after conduct has already occurred. The retroactive application of a law that would penalize behavior which was not unlawful when committed is prohibited by both state and federal constitutions.

EXCLUSIONARY RULES. Evidentiary rules promulgated by court decisions to exclude from evidence at trial any matter acquired by the state in violation of a suspect's constitutional rights or court-created protections.

EXCULPATORY. Tending to clear from guilt.

EXEMPLARS. Samples, such as of handwriting, fingerprints or voice characteristics.

EXHIBIT. An item of evidence illustrating or supplementing the testimony of witnesses.

EXPERT WITNESS. A person having specialized knowledge or skill that allows them to give an opinion in court on a set of facts to which their expertise relates.

EXTRADITION. The surrender of an accused or convicted person from one state to another.

FORUM SHOPPING. Moving a case from court to court to locate a favorably-disposed judge.

FOUNDATION. Basic facts that are prerequisite to the admissibility of ultimate facts.

GRAND JURY. A panel of nineteen citizens (twenty-three in Los Angeles County) convened for a one-year term to investigate county government and to charge suspected criminals by indictment.

HEARSAY. Evidence of an out-of-court statement repeated in court to prove that what was stated is true.

HOLDING. The ruling contained in a judicial opinion upon which the result depends.

IMMUNITY. Status of being exempt from prosecution, usually conferred by the prosecutor on a minor offender who becomes a witness against a major offender.

INCULPATORY. Tending to incriminate.

IDENTIFICATION. Establishing the identity of a criminal through evidence. Pretrial identification procedures include the confrontation, field showup, photo display and lineup.

INDEPENDENT STATE GROUNDS. Doctrine by which a state court interprets its own state constitution or laws in such way as to extend greater protections to criminal defendants than the federal constitutional requires.

INDICATED SENTENCE. A suggestion by the court to the defendant as to the sentence likely to be received on a plea of guilty.

INDICTMENT. The formal charge returned by an investigating grand jury against an accused person.

INFORMANT. One who gives information to police about criminal activity or suspects. May be a citizen, an anonymous caller, or a known, confidential informant ("CI") who is also involved in the activity or closely associated with the suspect.

INFORMATION. The formal charging document filed in superior court by the prosecuting attorney accusing a defendant of a felony following preliminary hearing.

JEOPARDY. The danger of conviction and punishment facing a charged defendant.

JUDICIAL NOTICE. Statutory device that allows a judge to accept as true, and direct the jury to do likewise, certain fundamental facts not subject to serious dispute, so that the parties need not offer proof of these facts.

JURISDICTION. The power of a court to render an enforceable judgment, derived from constitutional or statutory provisions creating such power as to particular subject matter, within particular limits as to place and time.

JUSTICE COURT. A local court in sparsely-populated districts with jurisdiction over infractions and misdemeanors.

LAW OF THE CASE. Principle that an issue once decided by writ or appeal in the same case cannot be relitigated in that case, but is settled.

LEADING QUESTION. A question that suggests to the witness the answer desired by the questioner.

LESSER INCLUDED OFFENSE. A less serious charge, the elements of which are necessarily included in a greater charge that has one or more additional elements.

MISTRIAL. An invalid or erroneous trial which cannot stand because of some miscarriage of justice.

MOTION TO STRIKE. A request by a party that the court declare an answer to be removed from the record as having been improperly given.

MUNICIPAL COURT. The trial court with jurisdiction over infractions and misdemeanors. Judges of the municipal court also sit as magistrates for felony preliminary hearings.

NOLLE PROSEQUI. "No further prosecution." Abandonment of a prosecution (abolished in California).

NOLO CONTENDERE. A plea of "no contest," allowing a conviction to be found without trial or admission of guilt.

OBJECTION. An exception taken to a question alleged to be improper as to form, or to call for inadmissible matter.

OPENING ARGUMENT. The prosecutor's first summation of his case to the trier of fact, after all proof has been submitted on both sides.

OPENING STATEMENT. A party's first summary of the case they intend to present to the trier of fact.

OWN RECOGNIZANCE. A release pending further court proceedings without posting bail. The defendant is on his honor to return to court as ordered.

PARDON. A forgiveness of a crime, extended by the governor.

PAROLE. Supervised, conditional release from prison after serving a portion of the sentence.

PEREMPTORY CHALLENGE. A challenge to a judge or juror for which no cause need be shown.

PHYSICAL EVIDENCE. Tangible items that tend to prove same material fact.

PLEA BARGAIN. An agreement by the prosecutor to recommend charge or sentence reduction to the judge in exchange for the defendant's agreement to plead guilty.

PLEADINGS. The formal written statements filed in court by the parties to institute or defend an action, or to frame issues for litigation and court decision.

PRELIMINARY HEARING. A formal hearing before a magistrate in felony cases to ascertain that there is probable cause to believe that a crime occurred and that the accused committed it, so that trial would be proper.

PRESUMPTION. A statutory device to eliminate the need for proof as to certain matters unless contradicted. The law presumes regularity in certain matters, unless disputed.

PRESUMPTION OF INNOCENCE. As assumption the law makes as to accused persons which places on the state the burden of proving guilt.

PRIMA FACIE. "On the face of it; at first sight." A minimal level of proof, sometimes equated with a strong suspicion.

PROBABLE CAUSE. A level of justification for arrest, search or holding a defendant to answer to felony charges after preliminary hearing, equated with a "fair probability" or a "strong suspicion."

PROBATION. Supervised, conditional release in lieu of imposing sentence.

PROPORTIONALITY. Principle of sentencing to "make the punishment fit the crime, and the criminal," based on his individual culpability and relative criminality.

QUASH. To vacate or make void.

RECUSAL. Disqualification and removal of the prosecutor due to an appearance of conflict of interest in a particular case.

RELEVANT EVIDENCE. That which tends to prove or disprove a fact in issue in the case.

REPRIEVE. Temporary postponement of execution of sentence.

RES JUDICATA. "A matter adjudged." Doctrine binding the parties to a final decision; prevents relitigation of the same case.

SEARCH. Governmental infringement of a legitimate expectation of privacy.

SEIZURE. Governmental interference with possessory interests in property; also, intentionally-applied governmental restriction on an individual's liberty.

SEVERANCE. The separation of courts or codefendants from a single, consolidated action into two or more separate actions.

SLOW PLEA. The defendant's agreement to have the court determine his guilt on the basis of reports and records, without contested trial.

SOCIAL CONTRACT. Theory of government under which society agrees to a particular balance of individual freedom and collective security.

STARE DECISIS. "To abide by decided cases." The doctrine compelling courts to honor the prior decisions of courts on the same issue.

STIPULATION. An agreement, concession or statement not to contest some action or state of facts.

SUBPENA. Also spelled "subpoena." An order for a witness to appear in court, "under penalty" of punishment for contempt.

SUBPENA DUCES TECUM. Order to appear in court, and to "bring with you" specified documents or items.

SUMMONS. Written notice to a party to appear in court as specified to respond to a legal action.

SUPERIOR COURT. The trial court of general jurisdiction. It hears appeals from the municipal and justice court, conducts felony trials, and sits as the juvenile court.

SUPPRESS. Exclude from evidence.

SUPREMACY CLAUSE. A provision in Article VI of the US Constitution which makes US Supreme Court decisions binding on state and federal courts as to interpretations of the Constitution.

TESTIMONIAL EVIDENCE. Evidence provided by the oral statements and testimony of witnesses.

TRAIL. Follow behind other cases; remain pending.

TRANSFER EVIDENCE. A category of physical evidence that was deposited at the crime scene by the perpetrator, or was transferred there to him.

TRAVERSE. To deny or controvert a pleading, a warrant, etc.

UNIFORM CRIME CHARGING STANDARDS. Statewide guidelines used by prosecuting attorneys in making the decision to prosecute.

VENIRE. "To come; to appear in court." All persons summoned by the jury commissioner to report for possible jury duty.

VENUE. The place where proceedings are held.

VERDICT. Jury's decision on the matters submitted to it.

VINDICTIVE PROSECUTION. Improperly-increased charging by the prosecutor in reaction to the defendant's exercise of appellate rights.

VOIR DIRE. The oral examination of prospective jurors in a case to determine qualifications and to assist in the exercise of challenges for cause.

WAIVE. Give up; relinquish.

WOBBLER. An offense that may by charged or punished as either a misdemeanor or a felony, depending on the circumstances.

WORK PRODUCT. Material developed by the attorney for a party, reflecting the attorney's subjective analysis and strategy, and not discoverable by the adversary.

WRIT. A written court order.

TABLE OF CASES

US Supreme Court

California Supreme Court

California Court of Appeals

INDEX